❧ Paradise Mislaid ❧

Other Books by Jeffrey Burton Russell:

Dissent and Reform in the Early Middle Ages (1965)

Medieval Civilization (1968)

A History of Medieval Christianity:
Prophecy and Order (1968)

Religious Dissent in the Middle Ages (1971)

Witchcraft in the Middle Ages (1972)

The Devil: Perceptions of Evil from Antiquity
to Primitive Christianity (1977)

A History of Witchcraft: Sorcerers, Heretics, Pagans (1980)

Medieval Heresies: A Bibliography 1960–1979,
with Carl T. Berkhout (1981)

Satan: The Early Christian Tradition (1981)

Lucifer: The Devil in the Middle Ages (1984)

Mephistopheles: The Devil in the Modern World (1986)

The Prince of Darkness: Evil and the
Power of Good in History (1988)

Inventing the Flat Earth: Columbus and the Historians (1991)

Dissent and Order in the Middle Ages:
The Search for Legitimate Authority (1992)

Lives of the Jura Fathers, with K. and T. Vivian (1997)

A History of Heaven: The Singing Silence (1997)

Paradise Mislaid

How We Lost Heaven—
and How We Can Regain It

JEFFREY BURTON RUSSELL

OXFORD
UNIVERSITY PRESS

2006

OXFORD
UNIVERSITY PRESS

Oxford University Press, Inc., publishes works that
further Oxford University's objective of excellence
in research, scholarship, and education.

Oxford New York
Auckland Cape Town Dar es Salaam Hong Kong Karachi
Kuala Lumpur Madrid Melbourne Mexico City Nairobi
New Delhi Shanghai Taipei Toronto

With offices in
Argentina Austria Brazil Chile Czech Republic France Greece
Guatemala Hungary Italy Japan Poland Portugal Singapore
South Korea Switzerland Thailand Turkey Ukraine Vietnam

Copyright © 2006 by Oxford University Press, Inc.

Published by Oxford University Press, Inc., 2006
198 Madison Avenue, New York, NY 10016
www.oup.com

Oxford is a registered trademark of Oxford University Press.

Library of Congress Cataloging-in-Publication Data
Russell, Jeffrey Burton.
Paradise mislaid : how we lost heaven—
and how we can regain it / Jeffrey Burton Russell.
p. cm. Includes bibliographical references and index.
ISBN-13:978-0-19-516006-2 (cloth)
ISBN-10: 0-19-516006-1 (cloth)
1. Heaven—History of doctrines.
I. Title.
BT846.3.R87 2006
236'.2409—dc22
2005032361

1 3 5 7 9 8 6 4 2
Printed in the United States
on acid-free paper

To
Pamela Creighton Russell
Matthew 11:25

Contents

Contents

Preface

Heaven, despite its obituaries, is alive and well. *Paradise Mislaid: How We Lost Heaven—and How We Can Regain It* continues the story of *A History of Heaven: The Singing Silence*, which traced the development of the idea from antiquity to the Middle Ages.

A number of books and articles on heaven have appeared recently. Some approach heaven from what a particular religious group believes is revelation, such as Simon Francis Gaines, O.P., *Will There Be Free Will in Heaven?* (London: T. and T. Clark, 2003), Don Baker, *Heaven* (Portland, Ore.: Multnomah Press, 1983), and Bruce Milne, *The Message of Heaven and Hell: Grace and Destiny* (Downer's Grove, Ill.: Intervarsity Press, 2002). Some approach it from the exterior, with sociological attitudes and categories; of these Colleen McDannell and Bernhard Lang, *Heaven: A History* (New Haven: Yale University Press, 1988) provides encyclopedic details about literary and homiletic views of heaven from the eighteenth to twentieth centuries. Alan F. Segal, *Life after Death: A History of the Afterlife in Western Religion* (New York: Doubleday, 2004) is an exhaustive treatment of the origins and development of various views of life after death to the end of late antiquity, with a vast bibliography. Other books work from interior understanding, and of these the most helpful are William Barrett, *Death of the Soul* (Garden City, N.Y.: Anchor/Doubleday, 1986); A. J. Conyers, *The Eclipse of Heaven: The Loss of Transcendence and Its Effect on Modern Life* (South Bend, Ind.: St. Augustine's Press, 1999); Jean Delumeau, *Que reste-t-il du paradis?* (Paris: Fayard, 2000); Anthony DeStefano, *A Travel Guide to Heaven* (New York: Doubleday, 2003); Ric Machuga, *In Defense of the Soul* (Grand Rapids, Mich.: Brazos, 2002); Alister E. McGrath, *A Brief History of Heaven* (Oxford: Blackwell, 2003); McGrath, *The Twilight of*

Atheism: The Rise and Fall of Disbelief in the Modern World (New York: Doubleday, 2004); R. W. K. Paterson, *Philosophy and the Belief in a Life after Death* (New York: St. Martin's Press, 1995); Jeffrey Burton Russell, *A History of Heaven: The Singing Silence* (Princeton: Princeton University Press, 1997); Peter Stanford, *Heaven: A Traveller's Guide to the Undiscovered Country* (London: HarperCollins, 2002); Jerry L. Walls, *Heaven: The Logic of Eternal Joy* (Oxford: Oxford University Press, 2002); Carol Zaleski, *The Life of the World to Come: Near-Death Experience and Christian Hope* (New York: Oxford University Press, 1996); and Carol and Philip Zaleski, *The Book of Heaven* (Oxford: Oxford University Press, 2001).

To all of these books and to the participants in my National Endowment for the Humanities Summer Seminar on heaven, and especially Cynthia Read, my editor, I owe a considerable debt. I owe special thanks to Joseph Amato, Art Battson, Klaus Fischer, Alan Green, Richard Hecht, Gerhart Hoffmeister, Walter Kaufmann, Leonard Marsak, Michael Osborne, Pamela C. Russell, Jennifer Thomas, Catherine Brown Tkacz, and B. Alan Wallace.

The dates of important figures are to be found in the index, for example "Darwin, Charles (1809–82)," along with the relevant page numbers. Key words that may be unfamiliar also appear in the index, with reference to the place in the text where they are defined. The coining of new words and the invention of new meanings for old words match the development of new ideas. Many such words are explained and dated in this book, and these words are also found in the index with the appropriate references. The sources for these words are the *Oxford English Dictionary* and *The Barnhart Concise Dictionary of Etymology*.

A minor note: I use lower-case "progress" for the word in its general sense, but upper-case "Progress" when it describes a philosophical position (for example, "we are making progress with our remodeling," as opposed to "Jones believed that Progress was inevitable." Upper and lower casing for "criticism" also varies, the upper case being used for specific schools of biblical criticism.

❧ Paradise Mislaid ❦

CHAPTER 1

Shut and Open

Paradise has been mislaid. Heaven has gradually been shut away in a closet by the dominant intellectual trends of the past few centuries. In many milieus today it has simply become uncool to believe in heaven—or God for that matter. It is fashionable to erect a defensive wall of cynicism, arrogance, and irony around oneself. Cleverness trumps conviction and trendiness trumps truth. "Coolness" is a social posture designed to defend the self by disguising it from others and even from ourselves. It is meaningless to ask why something is uncool; it is entirely a matter of fashion. Coolness is not a philosophical position and so cannot be argued against. However, there have been many serious intellectual objections to belief in heaven in the past few centuries, and this book discusses them and shows their limitations. This book invites every one of us who honestly and fearlessly seeks for reality behind our own walls to participate in letting heaven out of the closet. It invites believers of all sorts and those who profess to have no belief. It opens the door, airs out the room, and lets in the light to liberate heaven's colors.

No one can be entirely "objective," and writers claiming to have no point of view are either deluding themselves or concealing their bias in order to manipulate the reader. Authors should write with a mind entirely open to modifying their points of view in the light of evidence. The gap is wide between point of view and bias: the former is inevitable, whereas the latter is point of view made illegitimate by insisting on prejudices and refusing to face evidence. Writers, therefore, should be transparently honest about their views. Heaven in one form or another appears in most world cultures, but (for reasons explained below) it is impossible to write a coherent history of them all. My point of view is that of a lapsed atheist. I want to help unblock degraded, caricatured, or reviled Christian modes of thinking and to uncover the richness of Christian heaven by cleaning away the accumulation of dust and grit that has made heaven difficult to recognize today, let alone accept.[1] I hope to help make heaven more accessible to everyone; I believe that everyone who feels the impulse of gratitude can choose to open to it. All seekers are blessed.

Whether one believes in heaven or not, it has been an important element in the formation of culture for millennia and deserves more attention and respect than it has recently had among academic and media elites. "The history of heaven, touching so directly on a universal experience (death), tells us the history of humankind."[2] Heaven is defined by author and philosopher Jerry Walls as "the community of persons who have entered the fellowship of the Trinity by allowing themselves to be transformed by the perfect love made available to us in the incarnation of the Son of God and outpouring of the Holy Spirit."[3] Heaven is not a place in space and time like Japan or the Roman Empire, and for that reason, no history can be written of heaven in itself. We experience heaven as ineffable, but in order to discuss it we must use human language and human concepts. Even the most inspired writers such as Paul and Dante could go only a little way beyond human limitations (Dante's *trasumanar*: "to pass beyond the human"). This book explains that heaven is best known through metaphor; that metaphor points to reality; and that poetry is one of the best ways of expressing metaphor.

A history of heaven, then, is a history of the human concept of heaven, and that is true whether or not heaven exists in itself. If heaven does not exist in itself and is nothing more than an idea that the mind invented, then it can be studied only in human terms. If on the other hand heaven does exist in itself—in God—it is still revealed to us only in terms that humans can understand. In either case, human concepts of heaven are the key.

"Heaven" can be understood in a number of ways. "Heaven" is an English word (Old English *heofon*), and like every word in every language, it has both a long history and numerous connotations. The word "heaven" has a variety of meanings depending on the context. No word in any other language means exactly the same thing as English *heaven;* terms arising in other language cultures such as Chinese or Hindi do not fit the same template as English "heaven," and even among European languages German *Himmel*, Greek *ouranos,* and French *ciel*—for example—are not completely synonymous. Of course, words can be translated, but all translations are necessarily more or less fuzzy. There are very few complete synonyms in any one language, let alone among the languages of the world.

Even more important is the concept behind the words. In European languages, words about heaven have developed in the context of Christianity and refer to the Christian context of heaven. Although concepts analogous to the Christian concept are found in many cultures throughout the world, they may be translated as "heaven" only with the clear understanding of their fundamental differences as well as of what they have in common. Judaism and Islam (the other two Western, monotheist religions) are closest in their views of heaven to those of Christianity but still remarkably different.[4] Powerful and beautiful insights from more distant religions are gained by considering the inexhaustible other treasures of other religions. Comparisons of different cultural views of heaven are valid and helpful in anthropology, literature, and mythology, but a *history* covering heaven in all religions is not possible because their origins and development are too diverse to treat them as a whole.

Paradise Mislaid is therefore a history of the Christian concept of heaven in particular. Culture has been defined as the ways in which societies create meaning, whether or not the meaning they create is true or adaptive. But equally, meaning (whether it is true or adaptive) creates societies. An external history of heaven is social history assuming that heaven has no meaning in itself and is nothing but a gamut of attitudes created by varying societal conditions and performing various societal functions. An internal history of heaven takes the concept of heaven seriously in itself. This book is an internal history, treating heaven as a serious concept with transcendent meaning. Its meaning is linked with the social but is not based on the social and extends beyond the social. Ideas are real events with real consequences.

What is the Christian concept of heaven? Answers have been offered from the Bible, theology, philosophy, sociology, anthropology, and the arts; physical science has no means of addressing it at all. The best approach is one that is both multifaceted (treating a variety of points of view) and analytical (seeking the best definition). The Christian concept of heaven is *its whole development through time in all its expressions that cohere with its central core.* This book's approach avoids closed dogmatisms on the one hand, and evaporative relativisms on the other. It presents the history of a reasonably coherent concept of heaven over time, including the views of its detractors as well as of its proponents. I define Christian belief, as does Alvin Plantinga, as "what is common to the great creeds of the main branches of the Christian church."[5] Although any definition should always be open to deeper and deeper development of meaning, it must have—if it is to have meaning at all—coherence. The more concrete a term is the less its coherence is in danger; for example, the word "cat" is in much less danger of incoherence than the word "democracy." "Heaven" is at least as coherent as such frequently used concepts as "democracy," "liberty," and "rights." Coherence is expressed in tradition, which is not memory of a dead past but rather the transmission of a living reality that develops through time.[6] I illustrate the development of this reality in literature and the arts as well as in philosophy, for poetry is at least as essential to understanding heaven as logic.

This history invites the reader, whatever his or her beliefs, to take the concept seriously both as a worldview in itself and as one with enormous influence on the world. The argument is that the concept is coherent: it has its origins, its development, and its future. *Paradise Mislaid* describes the basic concept as it was refined in ancient and medieval Christianity, discusses the modifications, criticisms, and defenses of the concept from the sixteenth into the twenty-first century, explains how current views of the subject have developed, and suggests what it means for the present era.

Paradise Mislaid distinguishes between "heaven" and "paradise," although the concepts are often blended. "Paradise" properly refers to the original state of humanity, which God created good; "heaven" refers to the even better state in which humanity can live presently or in the future. The focus of the book is on heaven and touches only tangentially hell, purgatory, angels, and other such related topics. Heaven usually brings to mind the term "afterlife," and although that word did not exist before the twentieth century, the idea of life after death is immemorial.[7] But "after life" is only one of a number of ways to consider heaven. In other views it is not bound by time but is eternal, so that in heaven we are *above* rather than *after* our current life. Whatever death may bring, it transforms each of us radically.

To ignore heaven or to try to explain it away as outdated or superstitious would be foolhardy, for even a quick glance reveals that there are at present over three billion Jews, Christians, and Muslims on the planet in addition to Hindus, Buddhists, and others with beliefs analogous to heaven. Between one-and-a-half and two billion Christians are alive today, and a reasonable number of them presumably believe in some aspects of Christian heaven. Even if they are mistaken in their beliefs (and it would be rash to suppose that they are), they constitute a considerable force in the world. The Christian tradition is powerful, rich, subtle, and worthy of serious consideration. "Heaven is not a mere appendage on the main body of Christian doctrine. Rather, it pervades it through and through."[8]

Statistics are ephemeral, particularly about beliefs in a concept over two millennia for most of which statistics were unreliable or nonexistent, but they seem to indicate that in European countries belief in heaven declined from the mid-twentieth century onwards, whereas in the United States it increased. Some suggest that the decline of European Christianity has been overstated. A Gallup poll of 2004 revealed that 81 percent of Americans believe in heaven, an increase of 9 percent from the previous poll.[9] Figures vary from country to country in the rest of the world, the lowest percentage of those affirming heaven being in the former Communist countries of eastern and central Europe, and the highest percentage in Nigeria. Everywhere the proportion of people saying that they have no opinion on the subject was low. Though individuals' concepts of heaven varied, the characteristics most attributed to heaven were peace and tranquility, union with God, reunion with loved ones, and loving intellectual communion.[10] Of course, statistics and opinions do not bring us any closer to the actuality of whether heaven exists in and of itself. If 100 percent of people believed that heaven was real, that would not prove that it was real, and if 100 percent of people believed that heaven was not real, that would not prove that it was unreal. There is little place for heaven in the conventional worldview currently promoted in academia and the media; it is not clear whether this is worse for heaven or for academia and the media.

The classical Christian concept of heaven—the baseline against which anomalies can be measured—developed over fifteen hundred years and suffused Western thought through the sixteenth century. Before the seventeenth century, the rudiments were much the same in Roman Catholic, Protestant, and Eastern Orthodox Christianity. The heart of the idea is simple: God pours out the cosmos with love and invites it to share his joy in its love for itself and for him.[11]

The use of the pronoun "He" does not imply a sexual limitation or gender preference in God. It has two advantages: because it is common usage, it is better than "She," which presses an extrinsic ideological point, or "They," which connotes polytheism, or "It," which denies personality to God—but substitute whatever pronoun you like. Similarly, the term "Father" referring to God is not a limitation of the Deity to a specific gender but rather an indication of his personal, parental relationship to humans.

What follows in these pages is the classical tradition of heaven as it developed from the beginning through the fourth century, the Middle Ages, the Reformation, and the seventeenth century right into the twenty-first century.

The classical concept is that heaven is where God is, in love and desire. Where there is love and gratitude, there is God. To say that the Christian view of heaven is theocentric—centered on God—is an understatement, for the very definition of heaven places God at its center. Where is heaven? Where is God? Nowhere, in the sense of a place within cosmic space; everywhere, in the sense of being present in every place. When is God? Nowhen, in the sense of occupying a particular moment as opposed to any other moment; everywhen, in the sense that there is no time without him. Further, God is the *point* of the cosmos in the sense of its purpose, its sense, its meaning, its idea, even its substance. Heaven is inseparable from God.

God is eternal. He exists in time and space and also transcends them; therefore so does heaven. It is better to use the word "subsist" rather than "exist" for God and heaven, since in ordinary language we use the term "existence" to refer to physical entities such as matter and energy that are limited by time and space. God does not exist in the same sense that a shirt exists, and a shirt does not exist in the same way that God exists. The verb "subsist" in this sense means that God supports and maintains the entire cosmos. God both transcends the cosmos and is immanent in it: he is both beyond it and present in every moment in it. This view reconciles the apparent contradiction between God as unchanging principle and God as active in human development. Whether God and heaven are *being* or *process* (that is, whether God and heaven are from age to age the same or whether they develop through time) eventually would become subjects of modern theological and philosophical discussions. But these discussions were not part of the classical Christian concept, which assumed the changeless eternity of God and even the changeless eternity of heaven. Although for us prisoners of time on Earth people are born and die and go to heaven, they are all—past, present, and future—always there in God's changeless moment. A chair or a mastodon or a galaxy can exist or not: it was not, is, and will not be, but heaven subsists: it never comes into being or passes away. Heaven exists now. The word "now" can mean either the dimensionless, timeless point forever moving between past and future, or the eternal now that comprises past and future. Of course, the word "now" has many other usages, including the vague indication of a moment in which we happen to be present or in which a society happens to exist, but such "nows" are conveniences and lack precise meaning in physics, philosophy, and even history.

God and heaven are eternal, subsisting "before" time and "outside" space. "Before" and "outside" are metaphorical, since nothing can be before or outside God. Yet for every created thing, for everything in time and space, time has a beginning and will have an end. That is true for individual humans and for humanity as a whole. "Before" creation there is God. Language presents a problem: "is" implies existence at this particular moment (when you are reading this sentence); "was" and "will be" have their own implications. We lack a verb form such as "be's" for something unlimited in time: a shirt is; God "be's." There is no such thing as "before creation." God did not sit around for a while before deciding to create the cosmos. The cosmos is eternal in God. There was never God along with something else, never God and some "thing" we could call "nothing," never God plus an expanse of emptiness. God creates the cosmos from himself, for there is an absence of anything else from which to create it. There is only God.

God is dynamic, not static, and his dynamism is expressed in the mutual movement of Trinity. The Trinity is not three gods or even different aspects of God: it is one God indivisible; it is the dynamic relationship between the Father, the Son, and the Holy Spirit, a dynamic of love that consists of generosity and that spills out in love to the whole cosmos. God the Father generates God the Son as his Idea of Himself: God the Son is not a creature but eternally and equally God. The Father (in Western theology the Father and the Son) generates the Holy Spirit as the Father's Love for the Son and the Son's Love for the Father.

Out of absolutely nothing—and therefore out of nothing other than himself—God creates the world, the cosmos. Throughout this book I use "world" in the classical sense of cosmos or universe, not in the sense of the planet Earth. God's act of creation wells forth through the whole cosmos. God creates for love, a selfless love aimed only at the creation of more good. The Christian tradition holds that the cosmos has divine unity or purpose. This idea is first attributed to the Stoic philosopher Cleanthes in his *Hymn to Zeus*, and the Greek word *kosmos* means exactly that: a divinely ordered universe. No God, no cosmos. Being morally perfect in himself, the only way that God can increase moral goodness is by creating something other-than-himself who can make the free moral choice of the good. The only such creatures we know about at present are angels and humans.

In order to be morally good, one has to have a moral purpose or choice. A chair or a chariot can be "good" in the sense of useful and well made, but it cannot be morally good. God creates beings with freedom of choice—free will. Angels are immaterial beings endowed with intellect and will in order to identify and to choose the good. They make a choice whether to orient themselves toward love of God and neighbor. Some angels choose to love God, others choose self-love; the latter are excluded from heaven, but the former enjoy the immediate presence of God forever.

In addition to angels, God creates humans with intellect and free will. Christian tradition admits the possibility (perhaps even likelihood) of life in places other than Earth; God is able to create (as perhaps he does) an unlimited variety of creatures. Extraterrestrial beings with intelligence or freedom may exist elsewhere in the cosmos too. Curiously, the contemporary popular longing for E.T.s is more akin to the medieval insistence on the existence of angels than to any scientific theory. E.T.s, like angels, are supposed to be powerful creatures who visit Earth with purposes beyond our ken.

The existence of "Adam and Eve" was sometimes assumed to be historical, though terms such as "Old Adam" and "New Adam" (the latter traditionally meaning Christ) indicated the underlying metaphor. It is unimportant to the concept of heaven whether the first humans lived six thousand or two million years ago. The point is that in both humans and angels, intellect implies the ability to distinguish between good and evil, and will implies the freedom to choose between the two: to turn one's character in faith, hope, and love out toward God and toward others—or to turn it inward toward selfishness. Love is not sentimental or mushy; it is the whole point of existence. The fatal choice, or original sin, of humans was choosing their own will over that of God. It is widely but falsely believed that original sin was sexual. Although some Christian authors argued that original sin was *transmitted* sexually (we moderns would say genetically), sex was never thought to be the *cause* of the sin. Biblically, Adam and Eve were punished for their transgression by becoming self-conscious, including sexually self-conscious (the fig leaves), but sexuality was not the transgression itself (however much later preachers—and atheists—portrayed it so). Pride is a more serious fault than lust.

According to the classical concept, humanity, once having chosen selfishness, was bent in that direction. Though free will and predestination have always been in creative tension in Christianity, the classical view embraced both. Our alienation from God is *our* choice, not God's, and therefore God has not the slightest obligation to save us from the consequences of our choice. It is just and right that we bear the consequences of our own action. But God's mercy is greater than his justice, so his eternal plan is to save us from the consequences of our folly—the folly of Adam and Eve, and also the folly of every generation and of each human being. In order to save us from our folly, God the Son becomes human in the person of Jesus. We are all sons and daughters of God, but Jesus Christ is the Son of God in a unique way, eternal with God the Father and the Holy Spirit. God himself becomes fully human, and his manifestation on Earth as human is historical: it takes place at a given time (during the administrations of Herod and Pontius Pilate) in the person of Jesus, called the Christ (*Christos,* the Greek translation of Hebrew *mashiah,* messiah, anointed one, chosen one, or king). Jesus is fully human; his uniqueness is that he is also eternally God. Only God can save us from the consequences of our transgression, and only by suffering all that humanity suffers—including fear and dread—with us and for us; and out of love and mercy he does so.

Through Jesus, God restores the imbalance that humans had created; he brings us back into harmony out of alienation. But he does not negate our free will: humans after Christ as well as before Christ have the freedom to choose selfishness over love—or love over selfishness. God's work, then, continues in the cosmos. As humans needed preparation for Christ's first coming, so they need further preparation for his second coming. When he comes again, at the end of time, those who choose God remain eternally with him while those who reject God remain eternally separated from him. That is the end of human time, when neither individuals nor humanity in general have any more time for choice.

The tradition says that it is not a question of reward and punishment but of one's own choice—one's own character—in life. The idea of universalism—that everyone is in heaven regardless of their character—is an old and persistent one that has been excluded. An unpleasant thread in the tradition is the notion that the saints watch the damned suffering in hell; the tradition as a whole does not support this view, though it does support the idea that the saints are satisfied that justice is eternally done, that the torturer is forever separated from his victim. Justice also means that those who have been persecuted or otherwise deprived of the happiness to which they are entitled on Earth will be restored to their full rights in heaven. Those who choose to love and live in heaven are transformed.

The meaning of "the end of the world" is more ambiguous today than in classical Christianity. Traditional Christian cosmology usually assumed that the end of humanity and of Earth coincided with the end of the entire cosmos. According to modern cosmologists, the end of the cosmos will occur (if ever) after billions of years, long after the demise of Earth and of humanity. Even in the unlikely event that humans should colonize other solar systems or even galaxies, after billions of years the whole universe will run down into higher and higher entropy. Entropy is the innate tendency of systems to disperse into greater chaos; the highest entropy would be the state of the universe at its maximum (and therefore final) state of running down, when no energy is left. The current astrophysical evidence for this eventual Big Whimper of the universe seems strong.

However, there are two considerations. One is that traditional Christians had no idea whatever of the vast physical space of the universe, and for them *cosmos* meant the ordered world as they knew it, or even sometimes human society. The idea of entropy would have fascinated a number of Christian philosophers, but it is irrelevant to the traditional Christian view of humanity. The other consideration is that for Christian tradition the physical termination of the cosmos is completely subordinate to the moral and spiritual end of the cosmos, which will be the transformation of this world into glory. A modern misunderstanding about the Bible and of Jewish-Christian tradition arose from the projection backwards in time of certain current extreme minority views (such as that the Earth is historically and scientifically only a few thousand years old and will end soon). In the view of some, nature is nothing but a huge chest of resources for humans to exploit. But the Bible and the classical tradition are not in opposition to the preservation of the natural environment. The cosmos is full of glory, or God would not have created it, and if it were not for God it would have no meaning. God overflows himself into the cosmos out of his overflowing love and joy, and the glory of heaven is reflected in the glory of the cosmos, the glory in time. It is, as the Jews put it, the *Shekinah,* the presence of God dwelling among humans. In the tenth century, the Christian Saint Simeon wrote:

> O power of the divine fire, O strange energy! You who dwell, Christ my God, in light wholly approachable, how in your essence totally divine do you mingle yourself with—grass? You, in the light, are joined to the grass in a union without confusion, and the grass becomes light; it is transfigured yet unchanged.[12]

Inherent tensions in the concept of heaven actually added to its richness: spirit and body; immortality of soul and resurrection; community and individual; intellectual and sensual; eternity and endlessness; praise and fulfillment; focus on God or focus on the blessed souls. Different Christian thinkers within the bounds of the tradition varied in their emphases. Though heaven has always been "theocentric," it is true that it has always also been "anthropocentric" for most of us, who over the centuries ask "What about me? What happens according to Christian belief when *you yourself* die?" Two considerations in Christian tradition have been much debated. One is the nature of the "soul," the other the place of the soul after death. The word "soul" is English (Old English *sawol*), and confusion about its meaning exists in English as well as Greek and Latin and other languages. Soul has meant the spiritual side of a human being or a human's animating principle. "Soul" and "spirit" often overlapped in meaning, as did Latin *anima* and Greek *pneuma*. Sometimes "soul" meant an entirely nonmaterial part of us, a part that can be separated from the body. That view derives from Greek Platonism more than from the Bible, in which the terms "immortal soul" or "immortal spirit" do not appear other than as attributes of God. Sometimes "soul" meant the essential character of the human individual, in whom spirit and body (immaterial and material) are inseparably connected. In other words, "soul" encompasses "spirit." That is more the biblical view as well as the view of influential theologians such as Thomas Aquinas and Martin Luther. In this view the immortality of the soul means the eternal life of the whole human being in whom body and spirit are not separated. Soul includes personality, character, individuality, and consciousness. Your soul is you—all of you. "Soul" is centered in the free choice "between alternatives which matter."[13]

What happens when we die? According to Christian belief, we are eternally present in heaven with God. Heaven is what we are made for: it is complete fulfillment of all our potential in complete joy. It is also obvious that we leave mortal remains. How to reconcile our presence in heaven with the decomposition of our bodies? The Platonic, less biblical, view proclaims the immortality of the spirit in heaven while the body decays. The more biblical view is that at the end of time we will all be resurrected in the same bodies in which we now live, though perfected and glorified. The resurrection is, of course, a miracle. Yet in time there seems to be a period between the moment of our death and that of the resurrection at the end of time. What happens to our body and spirit while we await resurrection? They are temporarily separated. The body decays. The state of the spirit in the meanwhile is variously assessed. For example, some believed that the spirit ascends immediately to God; others believed that it had to wait in a sort of intermediate sleep until the end of the world. In any case, the spirit is always joyful, and it obtains even more joy when our spirit and body are rejoined.

Our share in God's heaven is eternal. It consists of being in God's presence in a state of complete fulfillment. This state was often called the "Beatific Vision" (Catholic) or the "Vision of God" (Protestant), implying understanding of God—and his creation—in peace and harmony and with dynamic and growing intensity. In the Eastern Church, the term more often used is *theosis*, "participation in the divine life of the Holy Trinity."[14] Although we cannot grasp what heaven is other than being eternally in the presence of God, the tradition is rich in metaphors, a cataract of living waters in theology, art, and literature, from the description in the Book of Revelation (18–22) through Dante's *Paradiso*.[15] Heavenly fulfillment is not static but dynamic: however perfected we are, we become unceasingly more perfect and more fulfilled. Heaven is the opposite of boredom, because the joys always increase. If, of course, we bend ourselves in this life away from heaven toward worldly wealth and power, we may get what we ask for. Although "going to heaven" is a common phrase, we do not "go to" heaven so much as we subsist in heaven, and there is no question of whether God "lets you in." You are there—or not, as you choose.

Christians believe that heaven is just: no one is there who does not wish to be, and everyone is as close to God as they wish to be. Some have greater love than others, and their joy is greater. In that sense heaven is not egalitarian; it is a kingdom—the biblical Kingdom of Heaven. Dante represented the relative closeness of the souls in heaven by imagining that the more perfectly joyful the souls are, the higher in the heavenly spheres they are through the moon, Mercury, Venus, the sun, Mars, Jupiter, and Saturn, up through the fixed stars and the primum mobile to the empyrean—the place of God's eternal light and life. In deeper senses, though, it *is* egalitarian, for each person is continually fulfilled to his or her own greatest potential. The hierarchy in heaven is according to spiritual potential, never on worldly power, as the innumerable traditional representations of popes, kings, and bishops in hell indicate. It is egalitarian too in that the true dwelling place of all the souls is not in the spheres but in the empyrean in the full presence of God.[16]

Heaven is love: God's love for us, our love for God, and our love for one another; it is a love that includes desire, friendship, and devotion yet exceeds all of them. Of faith, hope, and love, all needed in this life, only love remains in heaven, for the others have already been fulfilled. Heaven is joy that includes pleasure and happiness but exceeds them both. The love and joy of heaven are united in their generosity, the complete giving of God to us, us to God and others, and us to ourselves. Heaven is glory: the first words of Dante's *Paradiso* are "*la gloria*." The original strength of the word has to do with splendor, power, love, wonder, awe, and beauty: the essence of the sublime. Glory is what we see when all our eyes are open. In heaven, individuals never cease to be individuals, yet they are also united in a community throughout space and time. This community, traditionally called "the communion of the saints" (meaning all the blessed souls past present and future), is the community of all those throughout time who love God and his creatures. Heaven is fulfillment available to us at any moment, since it is with God and is everywhere and everywhen—except where and when it is blocked by human viciousness and folly. The tradition never shirked the reality of the anti-joy and anti-generosity that is the essence of evil. God as Christ suffers all the pains of the world and in him the world transcends them. Suffering is transformed into joy, and there is kindly laughter in heaven.

The secondary characteristics of heaven, those that are more easily visualized, derive partly from the Book of Revelation, partly from the journey or vision literature that culminated in the *Paradiso*, partly from sermons and folk traditions. Because they are more concrete images, they have become both an easy focus of devotion and an easy target of ridicule. Heaven is "up" above the earth, beyond the planets and the fixed stars, in a realm of pure light beyond the boundaries of the cosmos, the dayspring from on high. Because it is up, people are said to go up to heaven, or heaven is said to come down to earth: "I saw the holy city, the new Jerusalem, coming down out of heaven from God."[17] Heaven is the City of God, Zion, Jerusalem glorified and transcended, a city with walls, gates (to which there are keys) and streets of gold, crystal, and jewels. At the gate of heaven, to which sometimes a ladder leads, Christ (or Saint Peter) sits with the book or register of life. In the city is the court and throne of God, about whom the blessed, wearing crowns, sing and dance in celestial harmony. Heaven is also a lush garden with pure air, trees, fruit, flowers, freshets, or meadows and pastures with rivers. Heaven is an *agapé*, banquet, celebration, holy communion, of all the blessed, who may be dressed in white robes and suffused with light (Dante's *splendori*) that may be represented by an aura or halo. They are at complete leisure that is also intense activity. They are at whatever age they need to be in order to most fully realize all their potentials. These secondary, inessential attributes of heaven are nowadays often reduced to caricatures and cartoons. If one has the idea that what heaven "really is" is clouds, harps, and wings, one is likely to miss the point and therefore assume that it does not exist.

The images "up," "down," "back," "ahead," "in," and "out" were classical and continued to be used up to the present, but from the seventeenth century onward they were increasingly understood as metaphorical rather than as mapping the physical cosmos. "Up" (in the sky) had to be reconciled with the Copernican system; "back" (to a primeval paradise) was adjusted by evolutionary views; "in" (the interior soul) by analytical psychology; "out" (as the kingdom of God on which the human community is modeled) by sociology; "ahead" by the astrophysical theory that the universe will become endlessly more diffuse.

This book describes and analyzes how the classical view was modified, fragmented, denied, and defended. History of concepts is the best method for understanding any human idea because it integrates the development of the concept in areas as diverse as philosophy, psychology, art, religion, mythology, and folklore.[18] It excludes nothing except the fashionable academic delusion that when people in other societies talk about ideas that are real to them, what they "really" mean are things that seem "real" to our own contemporary mode of perceiving reality. In this skewed view, although people might have believed that what they were concerned about was religion, they were really concerned about power. This pervasive intellectual delusion is "chronocentrism," a variety of ethnocentrism quite condescending to its subjects. The purpose of history is more to understand what different people think and feel than to impose our own ideologies and assumptions upon them. People's ideas affect the way they act more profoundly than economic and social structures. We all construct grids in order to understand the world; if we did not filter, classify, learn and unlearn, we would be unable to tell a cat from a clam. The trouble is that we tend gradually to build denser and denser filters until they block, rather than enhance, understanding. The filters often can become so dense that we choose to know nothing other than what we think we already know.

For example, physicalism filters out spiritual reality. "Physicalism" is the belief that any statement must be reducible to a precise statement about matter and energy in order to have meaning or truth. This term, coined in 1931, is preferable to "scientism," "materialism," "naturalism," "reductionism," and "positivism," because these other terms have been used with too many different meanings. "Materialism" is an ancient Greek view associated with Democritus, but the word "materialist" is first attested in 1668 and "materialism" in 1748. The term "scientific materialism" used by the twentieth-century Process philosopher Alfred North Whitehead is misleading, because materialism is philosophical rather than scientific. A mind steeped in physicalism has great difficulty in grasping the meaning of a religious observance in any tradition. An example: A very intelligent, well-educated, and thoroughly physicalist woman, showing us slides of her recent trip to Nepal, pointed out with a mixture of amusement and contempt that Buddhist monks had placed colorful flags along a narrow bridge they had constructed. "They actually think the flags hold the bridge up," she commented. It did not occur to her that the monks were not so ignorant as to imagine that the flags would hold up the bridge by some sort of engineering miracle; she could not see that what the monks intended was for the flags to set the bridge in spiritual harmony with the cosmos. The physicalist view is not stupid, but it is blind in one eye.

Hilary Putnam argues that a "reductive" theory of reference is impossible and that "the notions of being a justified or warranted or reasonable belief are not reducible to physicalistic [*sic*] notions." Putnam also pointed out that concepts are to be understood in terms of "continuity through change" and that "meanings have an identity through time but no essence."[19] This idea is a key to the present book. Putting it in other words, no valid system can be established that assumes that any human concept corresponds exactly to external reality. Thus physicalism fails in its claim for exclusive rights to truth, and there are many other warrants for belief other than physicalism. Continuity through change means that although both words and concepts develop through time, each maintains a thread of identity. The essence of heaven is beyond our powers to understand, and the human idea of heaven develops through time. But to have meaning, it must have a commonality of meaning running through it. To define heaven (to take an absurd example) as a walrus is meaningless. The problem lies in examples that are less absurd, and the less absurd they are—for example, loving your family is heaven—the more the danger of slippage from the core meaning.

One of Putnam's examples is that although the word "plant" conveyed many of the same meanings in 2000 as in 1800, in 2000 it conveyed many different ones as well, because chlorophyll, photosynthesis, and the carbon dioxide-oxygen cycle "are central to our present notion of what a plant is."[20] Since the construction of concepts is more complex than any simple system of referents ("Neptune is a planet"; "the Norman Conquest occurred in 1066"; "Einstein was a genius"), all language is to one degree or another metaphorical. For example, every sixth-grader knows that there are nine planets in the solar system, but that is not necessarily so: some astronomers exclude Pluto and say there are eight, whereas other astronomers number ten or more. It depends on the definition of "planet."[21] A child's mind is incapable of ambiguity: I believe in witches or I don't; I believe in evolution or I don't. Ask first-graders what gravity is and they won't know; ask twelfth-graders and they'll know; ask theoretical physicists and they won't know. Understanding something deeply means understanding the complexities of reality. Does the constellation Scorpius exist? (a) though the stars in the constellation appear to us to be near one another, they are in fact vastly distant from one another; (b) the constellations are differently perceived in China and elsewhere; (c) millions of years from now "Scorpius" will look so different from Earth than its present appearance that the term will be merely historical. Yet it hardly follows that the constellation has no referent. We all know what it looks like. What is the South Pacific? Its configuration at any given nanosecond? Or the islands in it? Or its existence over time in a "vast to disappearing" number of moments? (Modern physicists prefer the phrase "vast to disappearing" to "infinity" in time or space.) Metaphor is a valid way to interpret reality. The "literal" meaning of words—what I call the overt reading—is insufficient for understanding reality because it never exhausts reality.

A metaphor is the use of a word or phrase or depiction to give a fuller understanding of what is referred to; it operates through the tension between identity and difference. "Man is a wolf" shows both the identity (humans are ferocious) and the difference (humans are not quadrupeds).[22] A metaphor cannot be true or else false; but it can be trite or trivial, or else it can express a vibrating connection between the human mind and the cosmos. It can also narrow down our vision rather than opening it up: "Juliet is the sun" retains power even after four centuries, but "the sun is Juliet" never had any power.[23] The greater the variety of meanings, the greater the intellectual stimulation, the greater the emotional depth, the more originality, the more cultural resonance, the more senses it draws upon (for example Dante's "where the sun is silent"), the more archetypal of human experience, the richer the history of the words or phrases, the less worn out by long use—the better the metaphor. Better metaphors are depth-metaphors conveying true meaning and true cognitive content.

Heaven is best understood in terms of representation of reality by depth-metaphors, metaphors that intend to point toward ultimate truth.[24] A metaphor can be brilliant even though trivial, and a metaphor can be stupid even though aimed at depth. When metaphors aim at deeper understanding of humanity, the cosmos, and God, they are depth-metaphors. Metaphors are more profound as they indicate broader and deeper realities, less valid as they confuse or restrict meaning. "Look, how the floor of heaven is thick inlaid with patines of bright gold"[25] gets us farther than "the stars are dandruff on God's black T-shirt." A metaphor is most profound when it is intentional to the ultimate meaning of the cosmos. A current intellectual assumption holds that the cosmos has no ultimate meaning and that therefore it is impossible to consider one metaphor deeper than another. That this is either true or helpful is doubtful; it may simply be that clever intellectuals have limited their imaginations. Metaphors serve a purpose that "standard, discursive language will not and cannot serve."[26]

Depth-metaphors bring us closer to reality, not by narrowing things down but by opening things up. We do not have to choose between understanding by narrowing and understanding by opening. We can adopt a "both/and" attitude to understanding reality rather than an "either/or" mentality. In science it generally helps to reduce to the simplest explanation consonant with the evidence, but in other varieties of thought, such as poetry and religion, it is more helpful to expand our vision. Grasping the world only on a purely overt cognitive level deprives us of a rich hoard of understanding. Religion and poetry cannot be judged by the standards of a different diction—science—any more than science can be judged by the diction of religion or of poetry.

Because the term "literal" is so ambiguous, the term "overt" is preferable. I contrast the "overt" sense of a text to the "symbolic" senses. The simplistic idea that there exists a literal, rational language with a unique relation to truth underlies both biblical and scientific "literalism." For example, the statement that God occupies a throne in heaven, and the statement that Christ sits at the "right hand of the Father" are seldom intended in the overt sense (there is a physical place called heaven where there is a physical elaborate chair, and so on) but rather in the symbolic sense, where God's throne represents his power throughout the cosmos or where the "right hand" expresses closeness and honor. Classical Christian thinkers recognized that metaphor expresses deeper reality than can be obtained through an overt reading.

Multiple levels of understanding the Bible were established in the third and fourth centuries by Origen and Augustine.[27] Their intention was to expand and deepen meaning through depth-metaphor. They read the Bible on at least four levels, the overt, the allegorical, the moral, and the eschatological (referring to the end of the world); all but the first are metaphorical. Since they regarded the Bible as revealed, they regarded everything in it as meaningful. This almost forced the growth of metaphor, since it was clear that everything in the Bible does not have an overt meaning. That the Lord is our shepherd does not mean that we are grazing mammals. It is necessary to avoid hyperliteralism—the interpretation of every word and phrase in the Bible as being free from its cultural setting and therefore correct historically and scientifically. It is also necessary to avoid dismissing the overt level entirely, as some do by classifying the Bible as folk tales or legends. Recognizing the overt meaning has always existed within an overall interpretation of the Bible. The overt has always been *one of the ways* of interpreting the Bible.

Heaven is best understood through metaphors that grow consistently. The fact that heaven does not exist in spacetime does "not raise any linguistic problem different in kind from those of any other metaphors."[28] For the term "heaven" to be meaningful it must be defined in terms of Christian metaphor. This might be thought another retreat, another concession to modernism through symbolist compromise. But that objection is mistaken, because Christian writers and artists traditionally and classically thought in terms of metaphor.

The classical concept of heaven remained basically the same in all branches of the Christian tradition into the sixteenth century. From that time to the present, challenges to tradition, authority, and the Bible implied questions that need to be confronted and penetrated in order to reopen heaven, to find Paradise where it has been mislaid. Those questions must be taken seriously and considered with generosity and charity. Heaven needs not to be shut up any more; it needs to come out of the closet.

CHAPTER 2

Up

In the sixteenth century, people generally still believed that heaven was a place and that it had a specific direction—up in the sky. We still point up to indicate God or roll our eyes to heaven, even though these are simply residual gestures. But five centuries ago, the idea that heaven was quite literally "up" was pervasive. For that reason this chapter is named *Up*, although there were many other such directional ideas in the sixteenth and seventeenth centuries. Christ came *down* from heaven and *ascended* into it after his resurrection. The doxology contains the words "praise him ye creatures here *below*, praise him *above*, ye heavenly host." Dante's description in 1321 of moving *up* from the round Earth through the spheres of the moon, planets, and stars to the empyrean fit the geography and astronomy both of his time and that of two hundred years later. As late as 1600, only a very few people were aware of the heliocentric Copernican model that removed Earth from the center of the solar system. But in the seventeenth century, a dramatic change occurred; by 1700 not many educated people believed in the ancient geocentric cosmology any more.

Early modern Europe was thoroughly Christian despite the exaggerated claims by some twentieth-century scholars about vestigial paganism. Most Europeans in 1600 had a thoroughly Christian worldview. Prevalent ideas of heaven were classical and traditional: it is characterized by light and brightness, glory, and unending joy. On the other hand, there were always undercurrents of dissent throughout the Middle Ages, and a few, such as the dualist Cathars who believed that the cosmos was the stage for an eternal struggle between the good (spirit) and the evil (matter), were radically different from Christian tradition. Dissent grew—though seldom in as radical a form as that

17

of the Cathars—in the sixteenth century and even more rapidly in the seventeenth. The most important change in society was its growing fragmentation in the 1500s, a fragmentation that became rapid in the 1600s. The word "skeptic" in English is first attested in 1587, much in its present usage as "dubious about religion." The word "atheist" dates from 1571 and "bigot" from 1598. Agnostic, atheist, and antitheist are gradations of the general concept "atheist." An agnostic allegedly suspends belief or disbelief in God; an atheist believes that there is no God; an antitheist vigorously promotes disbelief in God. These opinions lie on a practical political spectrum as well: agnosticism is most effective as a ploy for toleration when society is predominantly religious; antitheism when religious beliefs are politically vulnerable.

During the seventeenth century, doubts about heaven as a physical reality grew, and doubts about any sort of heaven at all were expressed by a small but growing number of materialists and pantheists. Doubts had reached such a degree that in 1650 an Act of Parliament found it necessary to prescribe prison for those denying the existence of heaven and hell.[1]

The "decline of heaven" was linked to the decline of hell and of the Devil, and these in turn were closely tied to the fading of the witch-craze that arose in the 1500s and gradually died away by 1700. Hell and the Devil had always been a part of the Christian tradition and in some circles (early monasticism, for example) even prominent, but in the sixteenth century belief in them exerted an especially powerful grip on the populace, led by lawyers, theologians, magistrates, and princes.[2] In Western Europe, especially the northwest, educated and uneducated alike, and Protestants and Catholics alike, believed that the Devil was working on earth to destroy the world and that he was doing so through human agents such as heretics and alleged witches, who had to recant or die. The figures on the prosecution and execution of alleged witches have been fantastically and baselessly exaggerated beginning with Matilda Joslyn Gage, *Woman, Church, and State* (1893); in the mid-twentieth century they were popularized by feminist writers Andrea Dworkin and Mary Daly. Now it seems that no amount of overwhelming and indisputable historical evidence persuades those whose ideologies prefer propaganda to fact. The ideologues promote the fiction that millions of women were executed for witchcraft. It is intolerable that even one person should be executed for an imaginary crime, and the witch-craze was indeed evil. But in the end, the evidence proves that over the centuries a total of about 110,000 persons were tried for witchcraft and between 40,000 to 60,000 were executed; in fact, between a quarter to a third of these victims were men.[3]

By 1600, as charges of witchcraft multiplied wildly owing to gossip, politics, and malicious and avaricious "witch-hunters," no one—even civil and religious leaders—could be secure from accusation, and when that happened, the elites were eventually frightened into curbing and eventually debunking the craze.[4] Once people who had been terrified of a huge conspiracy they imagined was led by the Devil learned that there was no such conspiracy, their belief in the Devil declined, and with decline of belief in the Devil came decline of belief in hell—and then, ironically, decline of belief in hell's opposite: heaven.

Other changes encouraged the decline of heaven. The Catholic Church, which had dominated beliefs in the Middle Ages, was split by the Protestant Reformation into Catholic and Protestant churches, and the Protestants themselves broke into a variety of groups. The dissipation of central religious authority weakened belief in the existing Christian worldview; religious fragmentation was accompanied by political division; the bloody religious wars of the 1500s and 1600s discredited all sides, while learned debates promoted uncertainties that filtered down to pulpits and congregations. The obvious statement that skeptical ideas would not have filtered down had the ideas not been there to begin with among the elite needs reiteration, because so many late-twentieth-century historians discounted the importance of ideas in favor of long-term social and economic changes. Ideas are events, and they shape behavior. The attack on Plato, Aristotle, and medieval scholasticism by writers such as Michel de Montaigne, and the extension of the attack to religion as a whole by Francis Bacon, prepared Europe and the whole Christian world for changes in the ideas of heaven.

The concept of heaven in the Protestant and Catholic Reformations of the sixteenth century remained almost identical with previous beliefs, even in most details. Historians Colleen McDannell and Bernhard Lang's position that heaven became less "theocentric" and more "anthropocentric" is misleading at best, but they do report sixteenth- and seventeenth-century views in copious and useful detail.[5] Leading Protestant Reformers such as the Lutherans and the Calvinists made relatively minor changes in the theology of heaven. Both Luther and Calvin were rooted in medieval thought, and they diverged little from medieval theologians on the subject.

One change was the Protestant removal of Mary the Mother of Christ from the core of heaven. This was mainly a reaction against Latin Catholic practice. It also (though the Reformers did not generally recognize it) went against Eastern Orthodox tradition going back to at least the fourth century. Another change was the Protestant de-emphasis on hierarchy or ranks in heaven. The classical tradition had always affirmed that everyone saved is equally saved, equally fulfilled, but it also asserted that some have greater grace and greater glory. Along with their rejection of most aspects of ecclesiastical hierarchy, the Protestant Reformers emphasized the equality of all before God, although they also agreed that distinctions would remain. In the late seventeenth century, John Bunyan wrote that

the People most laborious for God while [on earth] shall at that day [of Resur-
rection] injoy the greatest portion of God . . . because by doing and acting, the
heart, and every faculty of the Soul is inlarged and more capacitated, whereby
more room is made for glory. Every Vessel of Glory shall at that day be full of it;
but every one will not be capable to contain a like measure.[6]

Luther and Calvin recognized the fact that some people are better endowed
than others and that each person will be fulfilled according to his or her own
potential. Calvin believed that the soul in heaven would be so intent upon the
vision of God that the relationship to others in heaven would have little importance. For him and most other Protestants, the emphasis of early Christianity on community was largely replaced by individualism, and the ancient
belief in the communion of saints, originating in the second century, retreated
into the background.[7]

The broadside attack on purgatory, mounted by the Protestant Reformers
on the accurate observation that purgatory is not found in the Bible, bore
unintended consequences for the unity of humanity in Christ. For example, in
England, Elizabeth I abolished purgatory, along with prayers for the dead, and
that entailed breaking the community between the living and the dead, between the past and the future, between individuals and their ancestors and
their progeny. All was here and now, so that everything and everyone was at
the pleasure and mercy of Her Majesty—or whoever and whatever the Majesty of Authority might be at any moment.

Protestant—especially Calvinist—modes of imagining heaven in plain and
ascetic terms fit the plain decoration of their churches and the literalness of
their language, presenting a spare idea of heaven in which there was room for
little but praise of God. Similar ideas were espoused by the Catholic Reformers as well (particularly the strict and ascetically inclined Jansenists), although
Catholics retained and even increased the role of Mary in the plan of salvation, becoming more like the Eastern Orthodox in devout veneration of the
Theotokos, the Mother of God.

Catholics continued to believe that immediately after death the blessed (the
saved) see God face to face in the "Beatific Vision," a belief modified but not
eliminated by Protestants, who continued to believe that the saved would see
God in heaven. Heaven could be stripped so bare as to dull interest in it, but
tendencies in that direction were usually diverted by the visions reported in
the Book of Revelation and by the unquenchable imagination of mystics, artists, and writers, who exclaimed over the thousands and millions of exquisite
objects and experiences we will encounter in heaven, more exquisite than even
the finest beauties of this Earth.[8]

The society of heaven was notable for what it lacked as well as for what it
contained. Medieval writers and artists had always been careful to illustrate

that the hierarchy of heaven would be spiritual and that it would seldom correspond with the hierarchy of power on Earth: kings, emperors, bishops, and popes were often excluded. By the end of the sixteenth century, certain other states in life were seen as impediments on the way to heaven from Earth:

> From thence to heaven's bribeless hall
> Where no corrupted voices brawl,
> No conscience molten into gold,
> Nor forg'd accusers bought and sold,
> No cause deferd, nor vain spent jorney,
> For there Christ is the King's Attourney:
> Who pleads for all without degrees,
> And he hath Angels, but no fees.[9]

Many Protestants rejected the Platonic and medieval idea of the empyrean heaven—the heaven of pure light—as an unbiblical importation into Christianity from Neoplatonism in the twelfth century.[10] The idea was based on the ancient and medieval view of the universe, with Earth at the center, surrounded by the spheres of Mercury, Venus, the sun, Mars, Jupiter, Saturn, the stars, and at last by the primum mobile, the sphere through which God moves the universe. Further, this empyrean heaven beyond the primum mobile (the outermost "membrane" of the universe) faded in the natural philosophy of the seventeenth century, particularly from the 1650s on under the glare of Copernican and Cartesian ideas. On March 13, 1781, another astonishing astronomical phenomenon, almost as dramatic as Galileo's discoveries, was discovered by William Herschel. That event was the addition of a new planet—Uranus—to the ones known since the origin of humankind, an event that helped to demolish the ancient idea of the planetary spheres.

Nonetheless, the empyrean continued to be part of traditional education well into the eighteenth century. Ignorant educators continued to teach it, and unwittingly undermined belief in heaven by naively postulating the empyrean as something that might even be perceived from physical space. Such a notion was not only false and pointless, it also invited scientific scrutiny of the heavenly realm, which of course found no physical evidence for the empyrean. To both biblical "literalists" and to scientific investigators the empyrean was useless, though for different reasons. Thus heaven was separated from the rest of the cosmos in a way that would have been unthinkable to Aquinas or Luther. Heaven was henceforth seldom regarded as a topic for natural philosophy to consider. "Natural philosophy," though initially congruent with "natural theology," focused increasingly on the physical world. In astronomy, the idea of spheres centered on Earth was superseded by the idea of a continuum from sun and planets through the stars.

Well past the Reformation and through the seventeenth century, even while basic belief in heaven was being undermined, the most fundamental theological ideas of heaven held firm. Heaven is where God is; heaven is centered on God; the blessed (saved) are together in heaven loving and praising God. Theologians also continued to teach the combination of the resurrection of the dead *and* the immortality of the soul. The consolidation of these two originally quite different beliefs had begun in early Christianity.[11] Whether taken together or separately, the doctrines always raised questions of how either the disembodied soul or the resurrected body could be identical with the person we now are. The Fifth Lateran Council of 1513 declared that "the immortality of the soul [is] . . . required Catholic doctrine," and the Catholic Council of Trent (1545–63) also emphasized it.[12] This insistence on immortality of the soul marked the first time in the Western Church that immortality was affirmed as a matter of doctrine, thus reopening the question of the relationship between immortality and resurrection.[13] Resurrection also entailed tensions between beliefs: we will be resurrected in the same bodies we have in this life; those bodies will be glorified so that we will have strength, knowledge, and love beyond what we have now; yet there is an essential continuity between our present bodies and our glorified bodies.

A century after the Fifth Lateran Council, the Presbyterian Westminster Confession of Faith (1647) declared that

> the bodies of men after death return to death, and see corruption; but their souls (which neither die nor sleep), having an immortal subsistence, immediately return to God who made them. . . . The souls of the righteous being then made perfect in holiness are received into the highest heavens where they behold the face of God in light and glory, waiting for the full redemption of their bodies.[14]

Soul-sleep came to be commonplace among some seventeenth-century writers: John Donne wrote in the second "Anniversarie" (1612), "Thinke that they bury thee, and thinke that rite / Laies thee to sleepe but a Saint Lucies night."[15] William Perkins believed that

> Glorification, is the perfect transforming of the Saints into the image of the Sonne of God. . . . The beginning of Glorification, is in death, but it is not accomplished and made perfect before the last day of judgement. The death of the Elect, is but a sleepe in Christ, whereby the bodie and soule is severed. The bodie, that after corruption it may rise to greater glorie. The soule, that it being fully sanctified, may immediately, after departure from the bodie, be transported into the kingdom of heaven. . . . Soules being once in heaven, remaine there [a modern phrasing would be "once in heaven, souls remain there] till the last day of

judgement, where they partly magnifie the Name of God, and partly doe waite, and pray for the consummation of the kingdom of glorie, and full felicitie in body and soul.[16]

Donne's "Resurrection" (1633) linked immortality of the soul with resurrection of the body:

> If in thy little booke my name thou enroule,
> Flesh in that long sleep is not putrefied,
> But made that there, of which, and for which 'twas;
> Nor can by other meanes be glorified.
> May then sinnes sleep, and deaths soone from me passe,
> That wak'd from both, I againe risen may
> *Salute the last, and everlasting day.*[17]

The Protestant Reformation's greatest shift was in the underlying, basic approach to authority. Whereas Roman Catholic and Greek Orthodox tradition granted authority to the ancient church fathers, the bishops, and the theologians as well as to the Bible, the Protestant Reformers vehemently argued for the sole authority of the Bible (*sola scriptura*: Scripture alone). This root change encouraged healthy critical reexamination of traditions. It also often encouraged hyperliteralism—the interpretation of every biblical text in the overt sense, dispensing with the three classical metaphorical meanings wherever possible. The change opened the way to more freedom in interpreting the Scriptures; greater personal attachment to and reverence for the texts of the Bible; permissiveness in various individuals' reading of the text; jettisoning most previous biblical commentaries; indifference to the various multileveled interpretations of the text; the withering of multidimensional depth-metaphor; and the eventual decease of typology.

Typology explicates the parallels between Old and New Testament persons and deeds, for example the journey into Egypt by Moses and the journey into Egypt by Joseph, Mary, and Jesus. Typology is linked to prophecy; certain events, passages, persons, and figures of the Old Testament are taken as precursors of Christ himself, for example Moses or the "suffering servant" in the Book of Isaiah. In other words, there are certain eternal types in the mind of God that he brings to pass in time present, past, or future in order to reveal his eternal plan. Typology by extension deals not only with parallels between the holy people of the Old and New Testaments but also between those people and the saints after Christ. For example, Susanna in the Book of Daniel (sixth century BC?), who was falsely accused and condemned, prefigures Christ; whereas Perpetua (third century AD), who was falsely accused and condemned, *post*figures Christ.[18]

Hyperliteralism tended to limit ideas of heaven to the few biblical texts that treat heaven explicitly. From the Reformation onward, understanding of heaven shifted from focus on what the "authority of the church" said about it to what the "authority of the Bible" said about it. But when philosophers and biblical scholars began to question biblical authority itself, all the perennial questions about eschatology, the soul, heaven, and hell reopened. Benedict de Spinoza was the first major philosopher to maintain that the Bible is a historical document that must be considered in its historical context just like other ancient documents.

In the seventeenth century, perennial Christian disagreements about resurrection continued. For some thinkers, heaven became more ethereal and incorporeal; for others, the reunion with loved ones when we die gained importance, partly as a reaction against the dourness of Calvinist and Jansenist Catholic views. Though most believed in the physical resurrection of human bodies at the end of the world, the timing and meaning of that resurrection varied. Some, such as the Cambridge Platonists (including Henry More), continued the retreat from the resurrection of the present physical body in the direction of a separate eternal soul or a resurrected "body" that was really ethereal. More believed that "personal identity resided not in the body but in the soul" and that the resurrection of the body was only figurative. In 1703 William Assheton defended the immortality of the soul.[19]

For some, heaven was identical (or almost identical) with the kingdom of God as it would be established at the end of the world. In the last days, the physical world would be destroyed and then reconstructed perfect: "We will all be changed, in a moment, in the twinkling of an eye . . . the dead will be raised imperishable" (1 Cor. 15:50–52). Radical millenarian ideas, which had been common in the later Middle Ages but discouraged by both Protestant and Catholic Reformers, flourished anew. The confusion between "heaven" and "a millennial life" on earth was already common and continued to be so.[20] For Gilbert Burnet, for example, the sequence of events at the end times would be: the resurrection of the body; the millennium (a thousand-year reign of God on earth); the final resurrection at the end of the millennium; the last judgment; the translation of the saints into heaven; and the final conflagration of Earth, which would become a star. Such a complex series of events, which could be squeezed from the Bible if one chose, indicates how various and complex speculations about "heaven" could become once they were freed from the restraints of Catholic, Protestant, or Orthodox tradition. Still, Burnet encouragingly suggested that heaven would consist of devotion and contemplation, the entertainments of friendship, and the study of natural philosophy—an ideal not much different from that of Saint Augustine. At the endtime, Earth will "be chang'd into the nature of a Sun, or of a fixt Star:

and shine like them in the Firmament."[21] Heaven is both peace and activity: souls rest in the sense of being free from vexatious labor, but they are not idle, for they are continually learning to love and to know. Love remained the essence of heaven: Thomas Traherne wrote: "By lov alone is GOD Enjoyd By Lov alone Delighted in, by Lov alone approached or Admired. His Nature requires Lov. Thy Nature requires Lov."[22]

Burnet argued that the resurrected body would be ethereal like that of the angels, a curious echo of the medieval idea that the saved will fill up the ranks of heaven decimated by the fall of the evil angels. Donne believed that God eternally wills the immortality of humans and that the souls of the blessed are in heaven immediately after death.[23] Henry More argued in his *Immortality of the Soul* (1659) that the soul preexisted conception and that after the death of the body it would be immortal. For More, personal identity resided not in the body but in the spirit, and heaven is a place where souls engage in spiritual and intellectual conversation. The idea that the soul was a spiritual, eternal, and demonstrable entity separate from the body and consisting of "constantly fleeting particles" would eventually lead to an absurd twentieth-century alleged disproof of the soul on the grounds that one does not find it when dissecting a body. Some sectarians denied resurrection altogether; others claimed that the soul and body both die and must both be resurrected. Milton espoused a view similar to that of ancient traducianism, holding that the soul was transmitted to the unborn child by the parents. Universalism (belief in the salvation of every creature) and pantheism (the identity of God and the cosmos) were not uncommon.[24] Frederik van Leenhof, a minister in the Dutch Reformed (Calvinist) Church, was defrocked for arguing that heaven and hell are states of the human mind and character in this life—a view that would become much more widespread in the twentieth century than in his own.[25]

Heaven continued to be understood primarily as being with God and "seeing" him, secondly the company of the saints (the elect), and thirdly meeting friends and relatives again. This third emphasis is found for example, in the works of Richard Baxter, *Saints Everlasting Rest* (1650) and John Dunton, *An Essay Proving We Shall Know Our Friends in Heaven* (1698). John Donne wrote in "A Valediction: forbidding mourning" (1633):

Our two soules therefore, which are one,
Though I must goe, endure not yet
A breach, but an expansion,
Like gold to airey thinnesse beate.[26]

This emphasis grew more pronounced through the following centuries, and it was recently expressed by Jerry Walls—in heaven "We will know each other truly and completely for the first time."[27]

Without the gift of divine grace, no one could be in heaven.[28] Nathanael Culverwel said that "Grace is *aurora gloriae,* the dawning of the beatifical vision. Grace is glory in the bud, and glory is grace at the full." Culverwel went on to present God as

> a fountain, essence continually bubling forth, from whence the several drops of inferiour beings have their original; and as he is the main spring that sets the wheels of those petty Entities on working: for *in him we live, move, and have our being.* . . . Then when a believing soul returns to God that gave it, it sees him face to face, and fixes its eye upon him to all eternity. As soon as ever the soul is unsheath'd from the Body, it glitters most gloriously; as soon as ever it is unclouded from corruption, it shall beam forth most oriently; as soon as it is let loose from this cage of clay, it sings most melodiously; nothing hinders a Christian from a sight of God face to face, but the interposition of a gross earthly body, it is death's office to break down this wall of separation, that the soul may be admitted into the presence of God."[29]

For John Milton,

> Glorification is either *imperfect* or *perfect. Imperfect glorification* is that state wherein, being *justified and adopted by God the Father, we are filled with a consciousness of present grace and excellency, as well as with an expectation of future glory, insomuch that our blessedness is in a manner already begun.*[30]

Seventeenth-century views of heaven were more coherent than some have recently supposed, but as views of heaven diversified, skepticism about the whole idea increased: in 1685–91 a number of "atheists" were arrested for "denying miracles, Heaven and Hell, and the divinity of Christ, as well as claiming Christ was an 'impostor, . . . men are composed of atoms like animals, and all things are ruled by Nature.'"[31] The historian Jonathan Israel provides other examples of persons in that period denying heaven, the Incarnation, and the inspiration of the Bible.[32] Especially from about 1650 onward religious skepticism increased—as a result of the general disgust with a century of witch-crazes and religious wars, of the growing emphasis upon the physical world by intellectual elites, and of the gradual propagation of secular views from the elites through books, tracts, sermons, and schools. "This world" had doubtless always been foremost in most people's minds, but now intellectuals could openly and even modishly admit that their concern with the "other world" was less important than their business "in this one."

The most original theological thinking in the seventeenth and eighteenth centuries was in the area of natural theology. "Natural theology" had long been defined as the aspect of theology that depends on reason without the need for revelation, whereas "revealed theology" is that aspect that uses reason to explicate revelation. In the seventeenth century, natural theology tended toward secularism in several ways: it became more congruent with natural philosophy; its most influential practitioners were laymen; and it was concerned more with the life of this world than with that of the other world.

Traditional views of heaven continued in literature, especially popular literature and tracts, witness John Bunyan's *Pilgrim's Progress* (1678), which refers to heaven as "Zion" and "The Celestial City." Bunyan, a nonconformist dissenter, declared a vision of heaven in which the angels announce:

> You are going now, said they, to the Paradise of God, wherein you shall see the Tree of Life, and eat of the never-fading fruits thereof; and when you come there, you shall have white Robes given you, and your walk and talk shall be every day with the King. . . . In that place you must wear Crowns of Gold, and enjoy the perpetual sight and vision of the Holy one, *for there you shall see him as he is.* There also you shall serve him continually with praise, with shouting, and thanksgiving. . . . There you shall enjoy your friends again . . . and there you shall with joy receive even every one that follows into the holy place after you. There also shall you be cloathed with Glory and Majesty.[33]

Here the venerable teaching of the communion of saints and the vision of God were set forth by a nonconformist Protestant whose embroidery on Revelation encompassed many of the symbols for heaven often associated in literature and popular thought: glory, kingship, and majesty. The majesty of God, a commonplace originally derived from the position of the Roman emperors, was reinforced in the sixteenth and seventeenth centuries by the growing power of European monarchies and the so-called divine right of kings. William Perkins wrote:

> [In heaven] our bodily eyes shall come to see God, as much as it is possible for any creature to see him; because God shall bee let through the humanity of Christ, as much as it is possible for the divinity to appeare in any corporeall substance, or in any creature.[34]

Milton's view of heaven was peculiar to him and quite different from that of Dante. Milton's majestic *Paradise Lost* (1664) and *Paradise Regained* (1671) offered unforgettable images of heaven:

> The multitude of Angels with a shout
> Loud as from numbers without number, sweet
> As from blest voices, uttering joy, Heav'n rung
> With Jubilee, and loud Hosannas fill'd
> Th'eternal Regions: lowly reverent
> Towards either Throne they bow, and to the ground

With solemn adoration down they cast
Their Crowns inwove with Amarant and Gold. . . .
Then Crown'd again their gold'n Harps they took,
Harps ever tun'd, that glittering by thir side
Like Quivers hung, and with Praeamble sweet
Of charming symphonie they introduce
Their sacred Song, and waken raptures high;
No voice exempt, no voice but well could joine
Melodious part, such concord is in Heav'n.[35]

Henry Vaughn in 1655 wrote of the deceased, "They are all gone into the world of light. . . . If a star were confin'd into a Tomb / Her captive flames must needs burn there; / But when the hand that lockt her up, gives room, / She'll shine through all the sphaere."[36] Donne's "Second Anniverarie" affirmed that "in heaven thou straight know'st all, concerning it, / And what concernes it not, shalt straight forget."[37]

By 1700, religious authority had yielded for intellectuals to the authority of human reason unaided by divine light. This purely human reason was particularly asserted in "natural philosophy," which was just beginning to be called "science." That view constituted an enormous change in thought, displacing the emphases of fifteen hundred years. By the late seventeenth century, more writers were more concerned with demonstrating that Christianity was compatible with philosophy than with arguing that philosophy was compatible with Christianity. Indeed, many writers chose to modify Christianity to *make* it compatible with their views. It came to be thought that Christians should not interfere with natural philosophy, but that natural philosophy should interfere with Christianity. The old idea of the cosmos, where only God is first and right, and where writings were valued as to how well they reflected ultimate truth, gradually metamorphosed into a society where glory was measured not by its reflection of God's light but by earthly fame. The old cosmos, where physics, morality, and theology had a common center, devolved into a cosmos that had no center. Progress, which for Saint Augustine and most of Christian tradition had meant a gradual realization of God's plan for the world, came to mean any motion into the future, or rather a variety of futures with usually undescribed goals. In an increasingly pluralistic world with its erosion of the divine center and an increasing variety of centers, the venerable concept of heaven was called upon to adjust.[38]

Thus the most radical shift in the seventeenth century was what has often been called "the scientific revolution." This revolution has been perceived as a radical break with the past, but in fact it was a rapid development and mutation of trends already in place.[39] The scientific revolution grew out of the medieval desire to understand reality, the medieval belief that nature is a book in which to read reality, and the medieval confidence in the ability of reason to explore reality.[40] An early landmark in the development of science was the distinction made by William of Ockham between the *absolute* power of God and the *ordered* (or *ordained*) power of God.[41] On the one hand, God has the absolute power to do anything he likes, including creating the universe, not creating it, or uncreating it. On the other hand, we observe that God has ordered or ordained the universe such that it follows regularities that we can investigate. Ockham and his fellow "Nominalists" pointed to the impossibility of ever defining ultimate reality, which is beyond human concepts. The Nominalist idea that ultimate knowledge was unattainable pointed in two directions. One encouraged contemplative spirituality and the aim to pierce the darkness with love and will as opposed to theology emphasizing deductive reasoning. The other encouraged an emphasis on what was knowable by reason, namely the way that God actually *wills* to operate in the observable, physical cosmos.

Seventeenth-century natural philosophy or science had political and religious as well as philosophical roots. Though Christian cosmology has been caricatured and lampooned—one common example being the almost universal but absolutely false modern assumption that even educated people in the Middle Ages believed the earth to be flat—traditional authority did draw certain boundaries beyond which discussion was not tolerated.[42] Protestantism gradually permitted challenges that under a central Catholic authority could not have been sustained.

For these and an unbounded number of other reasons, seventeenth-century thought turned in markedly different directions from those of the past. If God's absolute power is unknowable, what *is* knowable is the ordered cosmos that he creates. It then seemed to follow that true knowledge can be only of what is observable, which is matter and motion. Further, it must be knowledge of matter and motion in their regularities, and regularities can be known only by measuring them. Whatever knowledge is not quantifiable is not real knowledge. Or, at best, knowledge of quantities is primary and of qualities secondary.

The ancient hierarchy of quality inherited from Aristotle and Christian tradition was thus gradually inverted. In the thought of Aquinas, for example, what was "real" were the underlying, essential qualities of beings. For example, the essence of a dog was the quality of being a dog, its "dogness." But in the seventeenth century, the meaning of "reality" shifted from the essences of things to external things that can be quantified. The old problem of how cold water (with its essence of cold) could turn into hot water (with its essence of hot) on the stove was elegantly solved by measuring the gradual changes in the temperature of the water. That the change in the water should have been a serious problem for fifteenth-century philosophers seems ridiculous from a modern point of view. But when we find something that appears to be ridiculous in other cultures, we are entitled to laugh, but we need not assume that those cultures are stupid. We can learn a lot by understanding why those cultures think in ways different from the way we do.

This point is crucial in understanding the history of heaven. For two millennia before the seventeenth century, philosophers following the Platonic and Aristotelian traditions believed that everything had an *essence*, a timeless quality that allows us to distinguish one thing from another. For example, windows come in many shapes, sizes, and colors, but they all share the *essence* of window. This way of thinking enabled Christian theologians to argue that in the consecration of the bread and wine at the Eucharistic service, the bread and wine change their *essence* into the Body and Blood of Christ. The once hotly debated question whether the change is "transubstantiation"—the Catholic view—or "consubstantiation," the Lutheran view—is an example of essentialist thinking. The fact that quantitative analysis of any kind shows that the bread and wine are identical before and after consecration was and is irrelevant for people thinking in Aristotelian essentialist terms. In fact, that is precisely what is miraculous in the Eucharistic service. The change in essence at the consecration was amazing to essentialists. A pine tree could not acquire the essence of a rug; bread could not acquire the essence of flesh—unless, of course, by a miracle. For essentialists, such a transformation was, however extremely unlikely, possible. For materialists, it would be impossible. What this meant for heaven is that in a world of essences, there is an *essential* eternal heaven whose physical attributes—or in this case lack of physical attributes—is absolutely irrelevant.

The shift from essential to quantitative thinking is perhaps the most important in the history of thought, far more even than the Copernican shift. That heaven exists is not a disturbing proposition for an essentialist, for whom heaven has an eternal essence. That heaven exists is a problematic proposition for a materialist and an impossible one for a physicalist.

In the increasingly materialist views of the seventeenth-century, "primary" qualities resided in external objects, whereas "secondary" qualities existed only in the mind. For example, that this dog weighs sixty-eight pounds is a primary quality; that this dog is patient with children is a secondary quality. There was no such thing as dogness. The rejection of the essence of being (ontology) entailed a rejection of the ontological argument for God's existence: namely, that he is the greatest possible Being—having the greatest possible quality. That did not work in the new system, because qualities were no longer inherent in substances and were only the epiphenomena (by-products) of measurable components. Carried to its extremes, this doctrine would eventually produce the dogma that if a phenomenon is not measurable it has *no* reality: quality does not exist at all.[43] In this context, the ancient criteria for "reasonableness" were replaced by criteria for physical demonstration.

The only "literal" language acceptable in this view was that of mathematics, and that left no room for the biblical or traditional heaven. Thus in the seventeenth century all the assumptions necessary for dismissing heaven were already in place. Everything had to be counted, measured, and weighed. The Number displaced The Word. Heaven—and God—being immeasurable and unquantifiable by definition—could by definition not be real. This assumption about heaven or any other unquantifiable entity *depends on how one defines reality* to begin with, but the definition of "reality" as material and measurable gradually became the dominant model. "Objective reality" (the phrase dates to 1662–66) came to mean material phenomena outside the human mind.

Accompanying the shift to the quantitative was a similar displacement of traditional ideas of epistemology—how we know anything. The question of how we know anything, first clearly raised and debated by the Greeks, was answered in Christian tradition by the argument that we can know through revelation (the Bible), through nature, through the exercise of the power of reason that God created in us, and through the guidance of the Holy Spirit.

The idea of "reason" took on a variety of other meanings during the seventeenth century.[44] Reason could be metaphysical, political, religious, or what is now called "scientific." (The term "metaphysics" has lately been used too broadly. Throughout this book I use the term in its traditional sense from Aristotle through Kant: the study of what lies beyond, or transcends, physical nature.) What happened in the 1600s was that "rationality" replaced "reasonableness." The longstanding and sophisticated methods of determining degrees of reasonableness by evidence based on carefully weighed judgments as to the degree of credibility of witnesses were set aside for "rationality" (the term first appears about 1626) based on mathematics and empiricism. This "fundamental shift in the art of reasonableness had huge consequences for hard-to-believe testimony and especially the reasonableness of the foundational bases of Christianity, Islam, and Judaism."[45]

Beginning with Descartes, epistemology changed radically. Whereas for Aquinas, the most knowable entity was God; for Descartes it was "clear and distinct ideas." Descartes was the first in modern times to question whether our cognitive facilities are reliable. A "fact," previously meaning a deed or action, came from 1632 to mean "a thing known to be true or to have really happened": "facts" had come to be understood as material realities existing outside our minds. Conversely, ideas are not events because they exist in the mind; therefore knowledge is not based in the mind but rather in external "facts." The word "phenomenon" is first attested in 1625 with the meaning of a physical "occurrence."[46] If everything can be reduced to a complex of matter/energy reactions in space, then there is no need for heaven, God, or even human consciousness, and not much point in such ideas. But there are many gratuitous assumptions in the preceding sentence, especially regarding the meaning of "thing" and "space," let alone "consciousness," "need," "God," and "heaven." If Christians were overly certain that they were right, physicalists too developed their own overconfidence.

Physicalism helped to undermine heaven first among the intellectual elites and then in popular thought. In popular thought, if heaven exists, it has to be somewhere, and if it is not locatable anywhere in the universe, then it cannot exist. Dante had already coped with this objection thoroughly, presenting heaven as being in metaphorical "space" and "time," a truer space and time beyond the spacetime of the universe. His insight, however, was too sophisticated for many to understand.

Literature and art bolstered the change in philosophy. The revival of the classics appeared in artistic and poetic allegories of God in Olympian deities and heaven in the Elysian Fields; the angels, originally awesome in their majesty, were reduced to cupids and *putti*. Literary arguments between "ancients" and "moderns" affected heaven. The "ancients" argued that knowledge and art had been better in ancient times; the "moderns" that knowledge and arts were improving. Both positions were centuries old, but by 1620–40 the tension between them was overt and widely discussed.[47] On the side of the "ancients": the Roman idea of a Golden Age in the past, Christian veneration of biblical revelation and of the church fathers; the medieval sense that contemporaries were only dwarves on the shoulders of giants compared to the minds of classical antiquity; the Renaissance Humanist ideal expressed by Petrarch in the fourteenth century, Erasmus in the sixteenth, and Montaigne in the latter sixteenth that the classics exceeded modern thought; the Protestant desire to return to the pristine church. On the side of the "moderns": Cicero's belief in the advance of Roman civilization; Descartes' effort to build philosophy anew; and the claims of advancing physical science, for example Francis Bacon's *Novum organum* and *The Advancement of Learning*. Tensions between two such points of view are inherent in many societies: Christian theologians believed in the perfection of biblical revelation but also in the ability to explicate it and build upon it; Americans believe in the perfection of the Constitution devised by the founders but also in the continual need for adjusting it to the needs of developing society. The seventeenth and eighteenth centuries were strongly influenced by both ancients and moderns, by both the desire to revive classical Greco-Roman achievements and the confidence that European thought was now breaking new ground. Eventually the long argument between the "ancients" and the "moderns" ended (at least for a long time) in the victory of the "moderns." The victory of the "moderns" entailed less respect for venerable traditions such as heaven.

Above all, it was the shift in astronomy and physics that attenuated the "up" view of heaven. The work of Nicolas Copernicus, though not generally accepted before Galileo Galilei and Johannes Kepler demonstrated its correctness, was more important than all the tracts, poems, and sermons of the sixteenth and seventeenth centuries combined. Though several ancient and medieval writers (beginning with Aristarchus) had argued that the sun was at the center and that Earth moves, no one before Copernicus had argued so convincingly that Earth moves both in orbit around the sun and upon its own axis. Copernicus wrote *De revolutionibus* about 1530, and it was finally published in 1543. He still followed classical assumptions in his belief that planetary orbits are circular; later demonstration by Kepler that they are elliptical seemed to make the universe less consciously designed than Copernicus or his contemporaries (or even Galileo) believed.

It is a longstanding but only partly true idea that the Copernican system dislodged humanity from the center of the cosmos. In fact, pre-Copernican Christians had *not* believed that humans were the center of the cosmos. The center of the cosmos was God in heaven, and Earth was the center of only the physical universe. Dante showed how our vision of Earth at the center of the cosmos is turned inside out when we recognize that the center of the whole cosmos is God.[48] Even on the essential scale of values, humans ranked profoundly below angels, each of whom represented a genus to itself and all of whom were intensely closer to God than humans, though ordered according to the nobility of their genus. Still, the traditional view was that humanity was the *dramatic* center of the cosmos, the theater for the moral struggle between God and the Devil. The "anthropocentric" aspect of the ancient and medieval Christian worldview was that God ennobles humanity by virtue of the Incarnation of God the Son in the human and divine person of Jesus Christ.

It took a while for the new model of the physical universe constructed on the lines of Copernicus, Kepler, and Galileo to take hold, for it did seem to turn the view of the physical universe "upside down," as Giordano Bruno observed.[49] Demonstration that the sun, rather than Earth, was the center of what we now call the solar system was only one of the blows that knocked the traditional worldview loose. The perceived authority of the Bible was deeply shaken, because both Protestant and Catholic Reformers chose to emphasize the overt "literal" meaning of the texts. A hyperliteral approach asserted that the story that God had caused the sun not to set on Joshua's victory at the Battle of Gibeon meant that God *did in historical and scientific senses* stop the course of the sun. That is manifestly impossible even from a geocentric point of view, for stopping Earth's rotation would have wrenched the planet apart. Such a view also meant that when the Bible referred to Earth's immobility, Earth was historically and scientifically immobile. Galileo might have fared better in the twelfth century, when metaphorical understanding was more sensitive, than he did in the early seventeenth.

The whole cosmological system of the spheres, accepted since Aristotle and Ptolemy, which placed Earth at the center surrounded by successively larger spheres until the farthest sphere was bounded only by God, was dislodged. The idea of ascending from Earth into higher and finer spheres, up to the primum mobile, the boundary past which is the empyrean and sheer divinity, was lost. Moreover, since each succeeding sphere had been believed to be more ethereal, it had been believed that as we mount through the spheres we become lighter, more ethereal, more radiant, and more pure. One derivation of that cosmological belief was that a Great Chain of Being stretched down from God through the angels through the spheres through humans through animals through plants to inanimate objects. That belief no longer made physical sense, though it continued to have a powerful spiritual meaning.

Light had been believed to be a quality generated by God in the empyrean and then transferred down through the spheres down to the sphere of Earth. Thus, as one ascended from Earth, one was more and more suffused with light. Dante showed spirits (*splendori*) becoming brighter and lighter as they ascended. There is no root connection between the words "light" (not heavy) and "light" (radiant), although in ascending one could become lighter in both senses. But Giordano Bruno specifically denied that light originates from above and diffuses down, and later Newton would demonstrate that light was emitted by material bodies and could be diffracted. This demonstration would lead to a weakening of the idea that heaven is the source of brightness.

The celestial spheres had been supposed to be immutable. Corruption could occur on Earth but not in the heavens above. But Galileo showed that the moon has craters, that Jupiter has moons, and that Venus has phases. This demonstration that the heavens were not perfect and immutable shook the old system even more than did the proof that Earth was movable. Replacing the biblical and Aristotelian ideas that the heavens are *qualitatively* different from Earth was the idea that Earth and celestial bodies were all part of the same natural system operating with the same natural quantitative regularities. If the stars and Earth are made of the same "stuff," possibly atoms, then the heavens are not "better" than Earth, and the idea that they were moved by angelic intelligences made no physical sense.

The venerable argument that there must be a prime mover was weakened by the hypothesis that the cosmos is itself essentially in motion and needs no mover any more than it needs a prime stopper. If the heavens are not qualitatively different from Earth, and if Earth is a planet rather than the center of the cosmos, then there may be other "earths," other inhabitable planets, and that idea seemed to undermine the view that humans are uniquely important. Combined with the discovery by Herschel in 1773 that the sun moves within a galaxy, and with twentieth-century discoveries that the sun is not the center of the galaxy and that the galaxy is the not the center of the universe, Copernican theory became the basis of the current conventional wisdom that humans are simply the inhabitants of an insignificant planet of an insignificant star in a decent-sized galaxy. But this conventional wisdom is an assumption refuted by relativity and modern cosmology, which places the center of the universe everywhere and nowhere in particular. Nicholas of Cusa had already observed centuries earlier that the universe has its boundaries nowhere and its center everywhere, and Blaise Pascal had a similar point of view. If our planet is no less the center of the cosmos than any other place, Earth is as much the center of the cosmos as anything else—and if it is the only place with intelligent life, its centrality is reaffirmed.

Though most Protestants did not readily accept the Copernican theory, Andreas Osiander, a Lutheran clergyman, wrote the preface to the first published edition of Copernicus' works, *De revolutionibus,* which was then translated into English and ran to several editions over the next thirty years. On the other hand, considerable opposition arose in the Catholic Church. Although popes and councils did not condemn the Copernican system, a number of leading Catholic conservatives, such as Diego de Zuñiga and Carlo Conti, spoke out against it.[50]

By the middle of the seventeenth century, Kepler and Galileo established the Copernican model beyond rational denial. Neither of them was irreligious, and they did not challenge the idea of heaven as such. Basically, they were simply uninterested in it: they were concerned, not with the spiritual *heaven* but with the physical *heavens.* The two great astronomers argued that because transcendental concepts such as heaven are ultimately unknowable by human reason, all that we are able to know is "nature," which has a rational and necessary structure that humans can discover. The word "nature" meaning physical and biological phenomena is attested from 1662. Thus "natural philosophy," the precursor of modern "science," was an invention of the seventeenth century. Reality was to be discovered through rational intuition, demonstration, mathematics, observation, and systematic experiment. Both mathematics and induction had existed for more than two millennia before the seventeenth century, but in that century natural philosophers combined them into what came to be known as science, which remains (whatever its limitations) one of the most impressive structures the human mind has ever produced.

What was "real" for Kepler and Galileo was the *exact opposite* of what had been "real" for Plato and Aquinas. Spiritual entities came to be considered "less real" than the tangible, laying the groundwork for the eighteenth century to go farther and translate "less real" into "unreal." Furthermore, the reduction of quality to quantity disrupted the ancient belief in the great chain of being reaching all the way down from God (the highest and most real) to formless matter, the least real of anything. For traditional thinkers, matter was teetering on the edge of unreality; but for the physicalists, it was spirit that was on the edge of the abyss.

However long it took to percolate down and gain general acceptance, the cosmological system that everyone from children to poets to astronomers had previously taken for granted was evanescing. Kepler realized that a basically quantitative view relegated the qualitative from its traditional place as the essence of being to merely secondary characteristics—an idea still vehemently urged by physicalists five centuries later. Galileo and Kepler shifted from the "why" of things to the "how" of things: the mathematical and empirical. The words "empiric" and "empirical," with the sense of reliance upon observation and experience, are attested in English by the sixteenth century. "Science" in the modern sense of investigation of the physical world through mathematics and empiricism (as opposed to "science" in the sense of general knowledge) is not attested before 1725.

Galileo invented the telescope and discovered the large moons of Jupiter and the transit of Venus; he is also known for his condemnation to house arrest by the Roman Inquisition and the censorship (after the initial celebration) of his works. The history of the dispute is still subject to a wide variety of interpretations, and it is of much less interest for the history of heaven than some of Galileo's basic ideas.[51] Galileo, one of the founders of modern scientific empiricism, believed that *truth* was "absolute, objective, and mathematical," as opposed to the "relative, subjective, fluctuating and sensible," which were "opinion" or "illusion." Causality could be explained "solely in terms of forces revealing themselves in the mathematical expressions of matter itself."[52] Galileo's thought began the separation of theology and science—or, to use less anachronistic terms, of natural theology from natural philosophy. The replacement of the spiritual as real by the physical as real meant the relegation of theology to the subjective and the elevation of science to the objective.

Galileo's conception of the cosmos as consisting of physical bodies moving in space and time according to mathematical rules was the background for the work of Isaac Newton. It also raised a still deeply debated question: the nature of consciousness. Is consciousness merely an epiphenomenon—a by-product of the physical cosmos—or does it transcend the physical? Is it a secondary characteristic of the physical brain, or a primary, qualitative characteristic of its own? The seventeenth-century tendency to explain more and more by the physical led many to speculate that the observable physical world is the sum total of reality and consciousness itself a by-product of the physical. But an external, physical event cannot observe and analyze itself: only a conscious being can analyze it. If consciousness is merely physical, our ideas about nature are also merely physical, including the idea that the world is only physical. It still remains difficult—perhaps impossible—for physicalists to resolve this dilemma. In the eighteenth century, Giambattista Vico offered the alternative that we can know only what we create: theology, science, history, as well as other sorts of knowledge. For Vico, history was the "new science."

The prime mover of seventeenth-century empiricism and secularism was Francis Bacon. Bacon's division of philosophical knowledge into "divine," "natural," and "human," along with his separation of "useful" and "practical" from "speculative," removed God and heaven from the realm of practical, rational discourse. For Bacon, only investigation of the physical and human world produced useful knowledge. Thomas Hobbes, who knew both Galileo and Bacon, developed Bacon's views into thoroughgoing physicalism. Reality for Hobbes consisted of nothing but body and motion, and even the mind "is nothing but the motions of certain parts of an organic body."[53] The soul is itself material, a part of the brain, a motion of the internal substance of the head. Hobbes, like Bacon, was technically a Christian and addressed the question of immortality by mixing oil with water—biblical with materialist views. Heaven, he argued, could not exist no place, and since space and time are all that exist, it must exist someplace in space and time. Souls could not be separated from their bodies, and immortality consisted of the material bodies of good persons being resurrected while the evil would be annihilated.

René Descartes, the greatest philosopher of the century, owed much to his predecessors. In 1619, when Descartes had his great intuition that mathematics could explain all phenomena, Montaigne had been dead for seventeen years, and Bacon was already fifty-eight years old. Descartes, once having convinced himself that knowledge was possible, famously proclaimed that what we can know certainly are "clear and distinct ideas," which are mathematical. Mathematics is the key to nature and therefore to reality: the universe is a mathematically perfect machine in absolute space and time, which God creates and maintains but otherwise leaves his created machine to govern itself. "All that we know . . . is the order and measurement revealed in its phenomena" (physical manifestations).[54] The reason to believe in God, then, is that we sense that there is a reality beyond our purely rational ken. We have an innate desire to have our knowledge perfected but must admit that we cannot ever obtain that in our present life.

These views led Descartes and many other philosophers for the next four hundred years to the famous question of mind and body. "We" can know only mathematical ideas and physical bodies, but who is this "we"? *Cogito ergo sum* to be sure, but what is this "I" who is doing the thinking? There must, Descartes believed, be two realities: external extension and thought. The universe is material, a machine, but matter does not think, so another sort of entity must. This entity Descartes called *ego cogitans*, "the thinking I," or *res cogitans*, "the thinking thing," or *mens*, "mind." This cogitating entity could not be separated from the body, since body and soul are one.

One of Descartes' famous images—derived from Plato—was that the world is a stage and that we humans are the audience. Unlike many philosophers of that and the next century, Descartes was not a physicalist; he did not believe that quality existed only as an epiphenomenon of quantity. In the seventeenth century the question was asked whether humans are separate from nature, observing from outside of it, or whether they are a part of nature along with giraffes and planets. If the latter is true, humans, animals, and stars, as well as looms and mills, are machines. But a machine cannot understand anything (an assumption today under challenge). Attempting to maintain a qualitative distinction between humans and other creatures, seventeenth- and eighteenth-century thinkers had to deal with the question of animal souls. Descartes distinguished between the *life force*, the *power of perception,* and the *power of thought*. He believed that a human being has all three, as opposed to animals, which have only the first two. But within a century after Descartes, physicalists assumed that the difference between a human and a gnat was quantitative rather than qualitative: some machines simply have a higher degree of operational complexity than others; humans allegedly think better than gnats. Why then should the soul be restricted to a Cartesian *cogitans* (thinking entity)? If the soul does not exist, then neither humans nor animals have it; but if it does exist in some quantitative fashion as identical with some life force, then both humans and animals have it in differing degrees. In that alternative, "soul" has a vague, fuzzy meaning almost totally different from that of traditional thought.[55]

Without divine special creation or some other special way that humans have a purpose transcending that of other animals, the good of the planet as a whole might best have been served by never evolving *Homo sapiens*, an ape already capable of destroying most of the existing species on the planet including itself. If humans are specially created, heaven is for them; if humans are nothing more than other animals, then all animals must be in heaven. Without special creation, what distinguishes humans from other animals? Until the eighteenth century, the ability to reason distinguished humans from animals; then anatomy began to emerge as the criterion; and by the twenty-first century, genetics set the criteria. According to genetics, the relationship between humans and other apes, especially chimpanzees, is very close. This means that we must inevitably face the question of what constitutes a human being and what constitutes a human soul.

Several alternatives presented themselves to the traditional Christian view that humans are specially created by God with immortal souls. Either the "soul" is identical with reason, so that animals do not have souls; or whereas humans have immortal souls, animals have mortal ones; or the "soul" is simply another word for the animating force or life principle; or it is just another word for "feelings"; or the "soul" does not exist and the concept is meaningless; or animals do have immortal souls. In the last alternative, animals are in heaven. But since animals do not have free choice or rational discernment, animals cannot attain heaven through faith, hope, charity, or good works. Therefore animals must have a special dispensation or "grace" that places them in heaven. But if every animal is with God in heaven, then not only dogs are to be found there but also fleas. The difficulties of this view were considerable. One option was that the entire cosmos is glorified and transcended; since God pours the cosmos forth in love, he receives it all back to him in love. Another option was that animals pleasing to humans are there, such as sheep, rabbits, dogs, songbirds, as well as fruit, meadows, and fountains, all perfected. Martin Luther is reported to have said that beneficent animals such as cows and sheep would be glorified in the restoration of the cosmos after the Second Coming, but that harmful animals such as toads and snakes (which existed because of original sin) would be eliminated.[56] John Wesley later also affirmed heaven for animals. Belief that animals are in heaven also found expression in revived pantheistic views; it was revived sentimentally for pets in the nineteenth and twentieth centuries. Richard Swinburne recently argued on purely reasonable grounds for animal souls on the basis of their mental life.[57] Saint Paul's assurance was that the "creation itself will be set free from its bondage to decay. . . . We know that the whole creation has been groaning in labor pains until now" (Rom. 8:21–22).

John Locke's *Essay on Human Understanding* (1690) is usually considered the foundation of British empirical philosophy.[58] Locke believed in immortality, bliss, eternal life, resurrection, and heaven and hell—including physical bliss in heaven and physical torment in hell—but on the largely utilitarian ground that belief in external judgment was needed to provide the basis of morality.[59] Locke claimed that the existence of God could be demonstrated by our observation of the natural world. His treatise *The Reasonableness of Christianity* (1695) was designed to defend religion by showing that its truth was demonstrable by the study of physical nature rather than by the Bible and tradition. When Locke decried tradition, he thought of tradition not in terms of a rich and dynamic worldview but rather as believing something without critical thought and by convention. He encouraged the removal of miracles and essential mysteries of Christianity. Further, Locke's subjection of religion to evidential empiricism became one of the bases of modern religious skepticism.

Positing two realities—the empirical (the observable world) and the spiritual (what we hold on faith about God and heaven)—Locke distinguished between faith as a *source of knowledge in general*, and reason as a *source of empirically demonstrable knowledge*. There are no innate ideas, said Locke: everything we know we know from experience. God, having thus been removed from the physical cosmos, is of no interest to the rational process. We could (as Locke did) believe in God, but we should not believe anything about God that would be actually contrary to what we observe and analyze in nature. Locke emphasized the distinction between primary and secondary qualities. What we really know can be divided into primary qualities—the objective extension of quanta (measurable physical phenomena) in space and time—and the secondary, the subjective, such as matters of taste. Knowledge consists of our reflection on the data of sense. The mind, Locke famously thought, is a blank slate: there is no knowledge other than that which is conveyed through the senses. However, Locke was acutely aware of the spectrum of credibility in which human reports must be evaluated. Reports had to be judged according to the number, integrity, skill, and consistency of testifiers. For Locke, powerful testimony for an event such as a miracle can legitimately compel assent, but only so long as the miracle is consistent with a larger, consistent pattern of truth.[60] This latter point epitomizes the gradual shift from "reasonableness" to "rationality," opening the way later for Hume to reject the supernatural entirely. One of the few places that rules of reasonableness still persist somewhat is in common law, which distinguishes "reasonable persons" and "reasonable doubts." If reasonableness—evaluation of witnesses—would again be brought into play along with Lockean rationality, the result would be a more complex, richer, and more nuanced approach to knowledge.[61] And evaluation of testimony about God and heaven would provide a basis for renewed belief.

By distinguishing the objective from the subjective, Locke—whatever his intentions—cut the road for the dominant modern view that theism is a hypothesis rather than basic life conviction, knowledge, and experience. Alvin Plantinga calls the Lockean view "classical evidentialism, . . . the claim that religious belief is rationally acceptable" only if the evidence for it is good.[62] If theism is merely a hypothesis, it is one lacking (people often assume today) sufficient evidence. Plantinga rejects this assumption, arguing that theism is not a hypothesis but a conviction. Furthermore, if other worldviews are subjected to Lockean criticism, they are no more evidential than theism, and that extends to the assumption that physical reality is the only reality.

The greatest figure of the seventeenth century was Isaac Newton, author of *Principia* (1686–87). Newton believed in an absolute God who creates the physical world of time and space. For Newton, deeply religious and far from a reductionist mechanist, God is the cause of the physical universe by creating it and maintaining it. But Newton's copious philosophical and theological ideas had little influence, whereas his scientific work was of lasting importance for religion as well as for science. Newton, an empiricist who employed his mathematical genius in the service of explaining what is observable, replaced ancient and medieval categories such as "substance, accident, and causality, essence and idea, matter and form, potentiality and actuality" by modern "forces, motion, and laws."[63] Newton did believe in the existence of a human soul, but this soul existed as a part of the brain that Newton peculiarly called the *sensorium*.

God, as Newton conceived of him, created an eternal framework of time and space in which nature operates according to uniform laws valid everywhere in the universe. Every moment of time is objective: every moment of time is the same moment in every part of the universe. The universe is matter in motion, and the point of natural philosophy is to study matter in motion so as to understand the forces of nature in order to establish principles that explain physical phenomena. These forces, which we can discover through mathematics and experiment, operate in a uniform manner throughout the cosmos.

In such a universe, where is heaven? If all that exists—other than God—is measurable in discrete entities of space and time—heaven is in no space and in no time. "Heaven" is with God, but it is nothing that philosophy can investigate or describe.

Newton himself was a theist and did not believe that the physical universe of matter in motion was "nothing but" matter in motion. Nonetheless, his natural philosophy advanced physicalism. Efforts made by some thinkers such as Nicholas Malebranche to reconcile Cartesian and other contemporary worldviews with Christianity on the basis of rational philosophy only helped shift the basis of religion from revelation to reason, and to replace the authority of religion by that of natural philosophy. In the view of Malebranche and others, faith is subjective, miracles cannot occur, and God becomes "Nature's God," almost in the sense that the reality of God is subsidiary to that of "Nature," which is accessible primarily by science. This attitude would eventually lead to the belief that Christianity is nothing but an ethical system no more inherently valid than any other.

Physicalist dismissal of heaven had a number of weaknesses: it assumed without philosophical warrant the superior reality of the physical to the spiritual; it subsumed the transcendent under the immanent; it narrowed down rather than opening up; it left no room for the essentials of heaven—love, generosity, gratitude, joy, and delight in life. But by the middle of the next century—the eighteenth—the learned and educated, from elite through the middle class, tended to assume a mechanistic universe, and the physicalist view gradually became "common knowledge," "common sense," and "conventional wisdom."

The great historian of science Thomas Kuhn wrote, understandably if hyperbolically, that "the localization of heaven in the skies and of hell beneath the earth's crust became mere metaphors, dying echoes of a symbolism that had once had concrete geographic significance."[64] If heaven was no longer "up," where is it? Wherever it is, it is both here on earth and not here: there are too many millions of agonies every day on Earth for Earth to be perfect; yet we are daily presented with beauty and love. Here, there, everywhere and everywhen, the door is open back up to gratitude.

CHAPTER 3

Enchantment

U p until the eighteenth century, the cosmos had always seemed "enchanted," spiritually alive. The "Enlightenment" of the eighteenth century, when materialism increasingly displaced spirituality and disenchanted the cosmos, produced even broader challenges to Christian heaven than had the seventeenth.[1] Even the name "Enlightenment," *le siècle des lumières,* betrayed the Copernican shift: light was no longer the living substance radiated down through the cosmos by God but instead a material phenomenon of radiation—the "light" of the eighteenth century was reason and wit. The historian Jonathan Israel observed that the Enlightenment had two "rival wings": one, the emphasis upon reason, including practical compromise; the other, radical revolution and the destruction of old institutions and concepts.[2] The basic axioms were that all knowledge is of natural events and objects; that the supernatural does not exist; that heaven, therefore, does not exist. If God exists, he does so only as an abstract prime mover. This chapter examines the origin of such axioms and how they came, by the end of the century, to command wide philosophical acceptance and the beginnings of popular acquiescence. The widespread atheism and agnosticism of the early twenty-first century are ultimately products of eighteenth-century skepticism, which failed to be sufficiently skeptical of its own skepticism.

At the beginning of the century, in 1700, all the basic assumptions of Christianity were still in play, including teleology (God's directing of the cosmos to its appointed end) and eschatology (God's reappearance at the end of the world to establish the Kingdom of God). But Enlightenment thinkers believed that if Earth comes to an end, it will be brought to an end not by God and God's Messiah but purely by natural causes such as a gradual extinction of the sun.

There could be no resurrection of the body. There would be no kingdom of God on earth, and there is no kingdom of heaven elsewhere. The world is shaped not by divine Providence but by natural forces and by human actions. Immortality is not obtained by God's grace in heaven but rather here on Earth by enjoying the respect of future generations, of posterity. The word "posterity," so popular from the eighteenth through the twentieth century, has fallen, like "legacy," into disuse since the 1960s. (Contemporary society does not like placing itself in a historical continuum.)

Theology, once "queen of the sciences," was demoted in favor of the study of "natural science" and the study of human behavior. Religion was to be studied, not as to its ultimate truth or untruth but as to its influences on human psychology and society. Christianity was a historical phenomenon to be explained in terms of its social context. The gods—including the Christian God—had a "natural history."[3] The holistic metaphors of religion were gradually replaced by mechanical models, and instead of a living, breathing unity pulsing with godness, the world became a vast and intricate machine. The famous analogy was that it was like a clock set in motion by a great clockmaker. This is the foundation of modern physicalism—the view that the only things that can exist are physical objects and forces, and that the only true knowledge we have is drawn from observation of these objects and forces. Even though the mechanistic model of the world was later demolished in twentieth-century physics, that model has persisted in the popular imagination into the twenty-first century.

The gradual triumph of physicalism was punctuated by the repeated attempts by idealist philosophers such as George Berkeley and Giambattista Vico to refute or limit it. One gambit was pantheism, a word first attested in 1705 and meaning the congruency of the cosmos and God. For pantheists, the cosmos is God and God is the cosmos; the cosmos is divine, and there is no divinity beyond the cosmos. Pantheists were able to maintain a generous if fuzzy religious sense while denying classic monotheism. "Panentheism" was a view both ancient and modern. It is quite different from pantheism, however much they have been confused. Panentheism is the view that the cosmos is within God; God is immanent in the cosmos and God *also transcends* the cosmos; the cosmos is divine, but divinity is not bounded by the cosmos. Panentheism is compatible with the spiritual, contemplative tradition in classical Christianity.

With the shift toward a natural psychology, the problem of evil was raised anew: how can the existence of evil be reconciled with the reality of God and heaven? One Enlightenment axiom was that human nature is essentially good, and this axiom bears an unexpected resemblance to the traditional Christian view. For Christianity, human nature is good and was created good by God; humans have denatured their good nature by sin and turned it evil, from which they must be saved by Christ. In the Enlightenment view, human nature is good and was good from the beginning of the human race. Evil has arisen because humans have denatured their own good nature by assenting to evil superstition and tyranny, from which they must be saved by the future. Despite the parallels, however, the differences were profound. For Christians, only God can remove the impediments to our goodness; for the Enlightenment only humans can do so.[4] In this view, evil is generated by tyranny and superstition (the following century would add exploitation and poverty); remove these, and the natural man with his good nature will reemerge. That hope, based on the flimsiest evidence, is a hope whose fallacies continued into the twenty-first century to produce an enormous labyrinth of bureaucratic nostrums whose putative benefits are almost always negated by their by-products. The Germans have a nice word for it: *Schlimmverbesserung*, "making things worse by improving them."

The effort to solve the problem of good and evil anew in the context of a purely natural philosophy weakened confidence in heaven. Voltaire's famous response to the catastrophic Lisbon earthquake and tsunami of 1755—parallel to that in the Indian Ocean in 2004—is emblematic of Enlightenment doubt about God's goodness in a world in which such "acts of God" occur; Voltaire's response, though as always rhetorically acidic, stemmed from real outrage at human suffering. Christianity and all monotheisms have always found difficulty with the poignant question why God creates a world with suffering in it to begin with, but the Christian answer was that God in the person of Jesus Christ suffers along with his creation.[5] Most Enlightenment thinkers put God at the edge of a mechanical universe and abandoned Christian views of salvation altogether. When faced with an impassive and remote deity unconcerned with the pain of the world, many found skepticism or even atheism preferable, but these options did not remove the problem of evil. If evil exists, and if neither God nor Devil is responsible for it, the responsibility must rest with humans. The alternative that evil really does not exist, popular at the end of the twentieth century, is one of the most counterfactual ideas of all time, and to their credit very few Enlightenment thinkers (with the exception of the Marquis de Sade) took it seriously.

The Enlightenment was constrained by its physicalism in how it could address evil. It was also constrained by a belief in "constant and universal principles of human nature," an idea later discredited. From such axioms flowed corollaries: the goal of humanity is a good life on earth, not in heaven; through rationality we can perfect the good life on earth; the necessary "condition of the good life on earth is the freeing of men's minds from the bonds of ignorance and superstition."[6] Montesquieu argued in *L'esprit des lois* (1748) that human nature could be set right by being freed from supernatural religion.

Such views came to be known as "Progress." But if human nature really is constant and universal, history allows us no hope, which may be one reason that history is an unpopular subject.

In Germany the most powerfully brilliant Enlightenment figure was Gottfried Wilhelm Leibniz, who effectively wrote on almost every subject, including science, philosophy, and metaphysics. Leibniz's views were in opposition to the empirical philosophy of Locke, a division still evident in the differences between Continental and Anglo-American philosophy. Whereas the British increasingly relied upon "factual" data derived from observation, Leibniz and his followers insisted on a mutual relationship between "mind" and "matter." "In processing the data of the senses, the mind imposes its own character upon them; and in so doing, displays its autonomy and self-activity." The human soul has "autonomous spontaneity."[7] Though Leibniz never affirmed a traditional view of heaven, his philosophy asserted an independent spiritual nature in human beings beyond that of the physicalities of space and time. Some continental philosophers in the twentieth century would argue that spacetime is essentially not matter in motion but thought in motion.

In empirically oriented Britain and America, the powerful critique of religion by David Hume had enormous influence and still provides a strong foundation for atheism and the denial of heaven. Hume did not dwell much on the question of heaven, although he did address it overtly in "Of a Particular Providence and of a Future State," section eleven of his *Enquiry Concerning Human Understanding*. There Hume denies "a providence and a future state" and a "supreme governor of the world" who "punishes the vicious with infamy and disappointment, and rewards the virtuous with honour and success" beyond what occurs in this world "in the ordinary course of nature."[8] (Indeed, Job had reflected on this problem twenty centuries earlier.) There is no point in imagining that what we experience in this life is a portal to a greater reality, "because we can have no thoughts about a greater reality than those based on the experiences of this life and interpreted through our "conceit and imagination."[9] So much for heaven. But what were Hume's bases for these conclusions?

Hume was foremost a skeptic. To know anything, he thought, we must first of all know *how* we know. In that, of course, he agreed with Descartes, but whereas Descartes went quickly on to assure himself that he was in fact capable of knowledge, Hume was never quite sure himself. The true skeptic, Hume said, "will be diffident of his philosophical doubts, as well as of his philosophical conviction."[10] The first thing we needed to understand was human psychology, since it is only through the human mind that we can grasp anything. Human psychology presents the idea that we can understand and know, but our minds are notoriously fallible. Hume asserted that he did not know and did not even know that he did not know. But no one can stop there, and Hume, following and strengthening the British empiricist tradition, argued that we are entitled to say tentatively that we know by using our imagination and reason to analyze the impressions that our senses convey to us. Philosophy, said Hume, should be strictly rational rather than speculative. Since nothing we can know is based on anything other than what we observe in nature, the supernatural is merely speculative.

Although Hume was skeptical of all knowledge, including scientific knowledge, he believed that because religion has no empirical basis, it was among the least credible forms of knowledge. That all religious and metaphysical systems must be congruent with reason had been grasped for millennia, but Hume, like Locke, now demanded the subjection of religion to reason. Moreover, the authority was not to be "reason in general" or reasonableness: only reason in the shape of eighteenth-century rationalism was acknowledged. Revelation of any kind, Hume argued, is absolutely unknowable, so there is no way to "privilege" (as one would say today) Judaism or Christianity over other religions. All religions must be studied psychologically, historically, linguistically, and sociologically rather than metaphysically or theologically. This was the classic naturalistic interpretation of religion and, since Christianity was the religion that Hume encountered daily, a bold statement of disrespect for Christianity in particular.[11] Revealed religion was simply false because it claimed to know the unknowable. Hume went farther, attacking the bases of natural theology as well as of revealed theology. He demolished to his own satisfaction and to that of his Enlightenment contemporaries four of the traditional monotheist arguments for God's existence: the arguments from Motion, Cause, Contingency, and Necessary Being, leaving only the fifth, Design, as viable, and that only under grave suspicion. Hume's critique undermined the classical arguments dominating discourse from Aristotle, Aquinas, and Calvin. Hume's arguments poured into the swelling stream of religious skepticism.

Only what our senses receive and our mind processes is real, Hume believed. Given that axiom, it almost seems superfluous to argue at length for the obvious corollary that God and heaven do not exist, but Hume did it anyway. He rejected the ontological argument that God is a necessary being. The ontological argument is that since reason indicates that there must be a greatest of all possible beings, and that greatest of all possible beings must exist; otherwise it would not be the greatest of possible beings. Hume pointed out that we do not observe any necessary beings: we observe only beings that also *may not exist*: a table, or a continent, or a star may exist at a given moment, but it has not always existed nor will it always continue to exist. We cannot know anything beyond the bounds of experience, and we have no experience of a noncontingent entity; consequently, we have no reason to infer from reason and experience any being that necessarily exists. "There is no being . . . whose non-existence implies a contradiction."[12] Although we observe things existing, there is no reason to posit existence itself as an absolute; if there should "be" a necessary "being," it would be beyond anything we know about existence. We cannot generalize about a cause with only one event. Since there has been only one Creation/Big Bang, we cannot deduce anything at all about its cause. This seems to stop the first cause argument, yet Hume neglected the idea that God may not at all be the classical prime mover but rather constantly active in and through the cosmos. Hume's arguments were limited by the limitations of the classical arguments he was refuting.

To demonstrate any proposition, we must proceed by experimentation to analyze how many times events seem to appear in a cause-effect relationship. Even though we see a set of events correlated a thousand or a billion times, that does not prove that connection is necessary, and the very next time it is possible we may find them unrelated at all. The roulette wheel could come up black a thousand times in a row, but you have no basis in fact for believing that on the next spin it will instead come up red. About that Hume was quite right, though the practical limitation of the insight is in statistical correlation. After spinning the wheel a thousand times, the number of reds will always approximate the number of blacks. Still, the principle holds that any given spin has an equal chance of turning up either way. Hume's insight was akin to William of Ockham's idea of the "absolute power" of God: we cannot be certain that the next time we put hydrogen and oxygen together we will not get beer instead of water. But in practice we must go forward, and we are entitled to say (with the reservation in the back of our minds) that numerous perceived correlations between a perceived cause and a perceived event constitute a degree of probability that can be called a sufficient proof. Though it cannot be *absolutely* proved that a stone can never turn into cake, it does not do to try to take a bite out of the stone.

Hume's argument on Causation and Motion is much more trenchant against religion—as he meant it to be—than against science. Even supposing that what we call cause and effect do exist in some reality outside our minds, he maintained, we observe no ultimate cause of anything, so we have no right to assume that everything (or anything) has an ultimate cause. Aquinas had argued that the universe must have a first cause, but there is no way to know that; Aquinas reasoned that the existence of motion implies the necessity of a prime mover, but there is no way to know that either. Even if there were a first cause, there is no reason to suppose, as Aquinas did, that the first cause must be immaterial since we never observe any material cause that does not have a cause itself. Hume countered that we certainly do not observe anything immaterial causing something material. This response is one reason why the debate over the reality of human consciousness took center stage in early twenty-first century thought: if you write a sentence with a pen, is the process merely chemical and neurological, or are immaterial consciousness and will involved? Hume argued that a first cause might well be material itself, for we do not observe (Hume thought) any immaterial causes and we do observe material causes. So, he argued, it is more rational to argue for a material first cause than for an immaterial one. As for motion, Hume argued that we have no reason to suppose that the universe is not intrinsically in motion and thus in no need of first cause or prime mover.

Hume did admit that the argument from Design had some strength, for we do observe that some objects, such as animals, are intricately made, and by analogy to our own ability to design intricate objects, animals may have a designer. Some sort of intelligent author of the universe is possible, Hume suggested, because there is no possible explanation of how such a complex being as a monkey, for example, could have emerged from matter by any known means. Although we have never observed a cosmic Designer, we also have no experience of intricate and complex objects that are not designed. Hume's followers were on dubious grounds in insisting that we must know the nature of a designer before accepting a design. As William A. Dembski pointed out, if present-day SETI (Search for Extraterrestrial Intelligence) investigators should ever receive a repeated, orderly transmission of a series of prime numbers from another stellar system, they would justifiably assume that the message was intelligent even without having the least idea of what the beings transmitting the message were like.[13]

Hume also rejected the Christian and Neoplatonist idea of the hierarchy of beings (from stones to humans to God). It is curious how the old idea of hierarchy or "great chain of being" would persist in secular form in evolutionary ideas. None of Hume's arguments indicate that the cosmos is incompatible with purpose and design, but their effect on those who accepted Enlightenment definitions of "rationality" was *to shift the responsibility for proof to the other side.* Only by breaking through the limits imposed on reason by Enlightenment rationality can the balance be restored.

Hume's argument against God on the grounds that the existence of evil is difficult to reconcile with a divine Designer was unoriginal yet telling. Hume granted the possibility that some sort of deity may exist. However, that such an entity would be both omnipotent and benevolent seemed to Hume to be contrary to observation and therefore to rationality. "Is the world considered in general, and as it appears to us in this life, different from what a man or such limited being would, *beforehand*, expect from a very powerful, wise, and benevolent Deity?"[14] The effort to reconcile the existence of God and the existence of evil is known as "theodicy." If an almighty and benevolent God creates the world, how could there be evil? Yet we observe evil in enormous, endless, and often cruel suffering in the world. For Hume, there was no convincing theodicy, and that meant that there was no God; Hume, like most eighteenth-century philosophers, would rightly have considered absurd the twentieth-century relativist assumption that there is no such thing as evil. If a deity designed the cosmos, that deity must, in Hume's view, lack compassion. Hume was willing to consider an analogy between human reason and divine reason but not an analogy between human will, character, or value and divine will, character, or value. Lacking this analogy, he could not suppose that God could love. The Deity, he concluded, must be neither good nor evil. In the materialist world of the Enlightenment, where God, if he existed at all, was remote and uninvolved, Hume's conclusion made sense. It did not make sense in the Christian worldview, where God is deeply involved with his creation, suffers every pain with it, and came as the Son of God in order to suffer the most extreme agonies with us.

Hume was consistent in denying any sort of secular theodicy such as "Progress" as well as any religious one. We have, he believed, no reason to assume or expect that any state in which suffering is abolished will ever exist on Earth any more than in heaven. Experience certainly gives us no reason to believe that reason, good will, or knowledge will ever triumph on Earth. Hume steadfastly refused the theodicy that injustice on earth would be remedied by justice in heaven, or that a person deprived of happiness on earth would be recompensed in another life. At the same time he refused the idea that present suffering would be remedied in a better future in this world. Few other philosophers in his century or future centuries would have the courage to consider, let alone accept, such a powerful consistency. They preferred instead to endorse multiple, illogical, and counterevidential ideas of Progress.

Hume's most devastating attack on Christianity was his essay "On Miracles." Hume correctly observed that Christianity is based on biblical miracles, quite a number of them, but especially on the resurrection of Christ. If there are no grounds for accepting miracles, then there is no reason to accept the truth of the Bible or of Christ:

> Upon the whole, we may conclude, that the CHRISTIAN religion not only was at first attended with miracles, but even at this day cannot be believed by any reasonable person without one. . . . Whoever is moved by *Faith* to assent to it, is conscious of a continued miracle in his own person, which subverts all the principles of his understanding, and gives him a determination to believe what is most contrary to custom and experience.[15]

Not even Voltaire commanded more withering irony than that.

The weight of Hume's dismissal of miracles upon later thought has been enormous, leading a large number of Christians to claim belief in Christianity without miracles, which is a contradiction in terms. A motto of "Progressives" was John Toland's "Christianity Not Mysterious" (1696) or, as Flannery O'Connor in the twentieth century would put it ironically, "The Holy Church of Christ Without Christ."[16] Christianity is in actual fact based on miracles, especially the miracle of the resurrection of Christ, and to remove that basis and to assert Christianity without miracles is a meaningless evasion—it is building castles in the air. Both Alvin Plantinga and Hilary Putnam have repeatedly argued that to subtract crucial elements of a concept either changes the concept into something else or renders it incoherent.[17] It is difficult to make philosophical sense of what people, however generous, honest, sincere, and socially benevolent, mean who say that they are "Christians" while denying the Trinity, the Incarnation, the Resurrection, and miracles.[18] It is legally and morally permissible but philosophically incoherent to call oneself a Christian while denying the core beliefs of Christianity. Admiration of Jesus is not enough. I admire the Buddha, but that does not make me a Buddhist (as my Buddhist friends strongly agree). And the analogy is even stronger than it first appears because Christianity, as opposed to Buddhism, has always been a religion stressing creed over practice.

Hume's attack on miracles was, for self-protection in eighteenth-century Christian Britain, overtly focused on the miracles reported in the Old Testament, although without the Old Testament the New Testament is unbelievable—exactly the point, of course, that Hume wanted to make.

Hume's basic tenet was that all knowledge is based on evidence as discerned by rationalist inquiry. In other words, any claimed knowledge *not based on evidence not fitting Humean rationalism* must be false. This was the basis of his dismissal of God and heaven. Hume, like Augustine, distinguished between wonders (marvels) on the one hand and miracles on the other hand. A marvel or a wonder does not necessarily imply the supernatural; it is an event that does not fit the rules of nature that we have established by reason based on evidence. Hume did not say that such a marvel or wonder *cannot* occur, but that we can never have reliable evidence that it does. I personally know two highly skeptical people who report having observed an object moving through the sky that corresponded to no known object. Their conclusion was consistent with Humean skepticism: they could not have seen what they saw. (Neither they nor I are inclined to believe in UFOs.) Another instance: A distinguished scientist I know could not shake off the conviction (clearly irrational in Hume's terms) that he had to go to a friend's house and place his hand on her head. After struggling against this inexplicable impulse, he finally yielded to it: who knows, he thought, it *may* mean something. With considerable embarrassment he went to her house and told her why he was there. It turned out that she had a shocking migraine. When he laid his hand on her head, the migraine vanished. All the above experiences I report secondhand, but I shall go even farther.

"Seeing" means the processing of light by the mechanism of the eye but more importantly the processing of the resulting images by the mind. If we think it impossible that we are seeing what we are seeing, we can convince ourselves that we are not seeing it. A miracle is a marvel that implies the intervention of God in the cosmos—or perhaps better, God's exercise of his "absolute power" in the midst of the cosmos arranged by his "ordained power." Hume notwithstanding, if you observe some event contrary to the "laws of nature," it does not follow that you have not observed it; it is possible instead that the rules of evidence are imperfect or that they are not universally binding or that they can be transcended. Yet it is naturally difficult to convince others that the event occurred, especially in a hyperskeptical society. The point here is not that such "wonders" cannot have any physical explanation. Rather, the point is that we tend to dismiss them out of hand as impossible. We build walls in front of our eyes and then are unable to see past the walls we create. Or we refuse to do so; probably we could if we dared risking the sacrifice of our pretensions to certainty.

Now to a firsthand experience: I have personally observed a spontaneous healing. My late wife had been experiencing pain from a bony outgrowth (osteophyte) about half a centimeter long on her ankle. She had made an appointment to have it surgically removed. A few evenings before the appointment, she went to a prayer meeting for the healing of a woman with terminal cancer. The woman was not healed. However, when my wife came home she said she was experiencing a burning sensation on her ankle, and when she took off her sock we found absolutely no trace of the outgrowth. We cancelled the appointment with the doctor. I know that this happened. But knowing that by observing that, what do I do with the observation? I have not, and almost certainly cannot, observe a series of rapid disappearance of osteophytes such that I can make any generalization about the rapid disappearance of osteophytes. It does not help that in fact two people observed the event, because it may be surmised that both of us were under an illusion or hallucination. The disappearance of the bony growth is exceeded by many orders of magnitude by the miracles reported with doubt, sympathy, and careful criticism by the secular journalist Randall Sullivan in his book *The Miracle Detective* (New York: Grove, 2004). Those of us willing to look past the walls we construct to defend ourselves against the possibility of miracles will be intrigued, even perhaps convinced, by the book.

The disappearance of the osteophyte is far from meeting the criteria of a miracle; it may not even have been much of a wonder. I know a woman whose osteophyte disappeared after her daughter gave her a massage. The lack of confirmation by the physician in my wife's case of its disappearance is an insuperable obstacle to a claim to a miracle. However, it is possible that it was an unprovable miracle, and I suggest that such unproven miracles may happen frequently but are erased by our Humean skepticism and, especially, our fear of appearing foolish to others. There is not the slightest doubt that the disappearance of the bony outgrowth was a physical event. The physical cells were rearranged; the change could have been measured quantitatively (had there been technical means to do so at the moment). But does this remove the possibility that the event was a miracle? Saint Augustine observed sixteen centuries ago that any physical miracles must be describable in terms of the rearrangement of matter. The event is physical; the question is whether the *cause* is purely physical as well as the *effect*. The power of prayer is now being recognized even by some scientific experimenters, puzzled though they remain about it.

Hume thought that it is always more probable that the observer of an alleged wonder may be deluded than that his or her perception is accurate. This is true, he believed, not only of one or two people reporting such an event, but of three, twenty, or a thousand. Hume remarked that he would rather accept the report of one person that Queen Elizabeth had died than the report that she had risen from the dead even if the latter event had been attested by all her physicians, the whole court, and the parliament.[19] But that remark is unjustified, because we have always weighed (and will always weigh) the credibility of any testimony. We do so in court all the time. Hume and his contemporaries discounted the old process of evaluating testimony, a process that (it is to be hoped) will still prevail in both law and the study of humanity.[20]

Hume agreed that wonders might possibly occur but insisted that we can have no evidence that they do. Moreover, reliable reports are made by reasonable and skeptical persons, and that a thousand people in an unreasonable mob may report a wonder is no reason to believe it. The catch in this argument is that if a reasonable and skeptical person had reported a marvel to Hume, Hume would have stricken that person off his list of reasonable and skeptical people. Not only, Hume argued, is there an insurmountable difficulty with verification, there is an even greater insurmountable difficulty of demonstrating a marvel to anyone else. For example, you may prefer to believe that I am lying about the osteophyte than to believe that a marvel occurred, and you are justified in that preference, because it always is more likely that I am lying (people are frequently known to lie) than that an event inconsistent with natural regularities actually occurred. Even if you know me well enough to have moral confidence that I am not lying, you might justifiably still prefer to judge that I am deluded rather than accepting my account. According to Hume's principles, either the wonder never occurred, or if it did, it must fit into some natural law that we have not yet discovered.

If there is no way of credibly establishing a marvel, it follows that it is even more difficult to establish a miracle. A miracle is a marvel that is caused by God's asserting his power in an unusual fashion in the universe. But since marvels (according to Hume) do not exist, it follows that miracles do not exist. Moreover, we have few grounds to believe that any deity exists, and even less reason to suppose that a deity exists who would intervene in the regularity of the universe it creates. If we observe even the most astonishing thing once, we have no grounds for connecting it with any cause, much less a divine cause.

Miracles, Hume was ready to admit, have been widely attested. But who attests to them? Hume argued that they are reported only from what he called "ignorant and barbarous" societies incapable of rational thought. The reports of miracles in the Old Testament are either lies or folktales believed and handed down by the credulous. There is not one miracle in the Old Testament—and by extension in the New Testament—that either cannot be explained naturally or else dismissed as nonsense. A miracle can be believed only if its probability exceeds its improbability, but the rules of evidence make it always more probable that it did not occur than that it did. It is conceivable that miracles may occur, but we can never have grounds for asserting so. Even the testimony of a number of expert and credible witnesses, such as physicians and judges, could not make a miracle more probable than improbable, much less the testimony of an "ignorant and barbarous" people in the Middle East two or three thousand years ago. Since there can be no evidence for miracles, there is no point in talking about them—other than psychologically or sociologically. We might just as well discuss extraterrestrials building the great pyramids. Indeed, we have more grounds for discussing the alleged extraterrestrial architects, for it can be argued on evidential grounds that they did (however preposterously unlikely) or did not do it, whereas for miracles no evidence of any kind may be asserted. There is a circularity in Hume's view. We cannot observe a miracle because it is impossible for anyone to observe one. Since no one can observe them, no one has reason to believe in them. If such and such a miraculous event is claimed to occur, it really did not occur. Hume viewed Christianity, with its assertion of miracles, as a heavy impediment to human knowledge and welfare.

Hume's arguments create cognitive dissonance. We may observe that an event occurred but are forbidden to believe that it did by rationalist philosophy; and that leaves us with stressful choices: denying our senses; keeping quiet and accepting the dissonance; or challenging the dominant orthodoxy. We tend to trust doctors using modern medical technology, and that is often a good thing for us (as well as for doctors). But it is less good and wise to *place our faith* in doctors. First of all, doctors, like other humans, can fail, sometimes horribly. Furthermore, trust in purely physical medicine ends up in our believing that illness is real and health only transitory. Too many of us baulk at the idea that health is the reality and that healing, like heaven, may transcend human means. The idea is that it is preposterous to believe that God heals. And from *the physicalist point of view,* that is true, and that is the point of view many of us fall back on, because it is the conventional wisdom of dominant elites in academia and the media. But healing, hope, and heaven can be around us all the time. The Christian virtue of hope is not to feel, "I'm afraid that this isn't going to work the way I want it to, but I sure hope it does." The virtue of hope is the sure conviction that God guides things aright, which allows us to go where that hope leads us. Again we tend to automatically ascribe response to prayer back to physical causes: we assume after things work out well that "it would have happened that way anyhow." Rather than being immersed in healing and heaven, we allow ourselves to fall back into the conventional wisdom that is actually conventional close-mindedness.

To put the whole problem briefly: *either* this is a cosmos in which there is nothing but the physical; *or* this is a cosmos in which there are things beyond the physical. Physical science can do nothing to answer this question. It is a metaphysical question, one to which we can have no certain answer. This does *not* mean that *we* can choose or change which kind of cosmos we live in: it is objectively one or the other. Once we realize that we cannot know with certainty which kind of universe this is, we understand that it is unwarranted to reject out of hand those reports that favor one view or the other. Wonders are frequently reported, and certainly not only in "ignorant and barbarous" societies. In my experience, this indicates that we are more likely to live in a universe in which things beyond the physical occur than in one in which they do not. It seems to me a universe in which miracles—or at least wonders—do occur. I do not think that the problem is likely to be solved for a long time, if ever. It remains, and bluster or rigidity by either side is not helpful.

Whether or not Hume's arguments are compelling, all future skepticism about religion is an appendix to Hume (and Locke). Hume did not say that God is impossible, only that we can have no knowledge of such an entity, and his arguments against belief in God apply the more weightily to all that derives from belief in God, certainly to heaven. If heaven is something we cannot know anything about, why bother with it?

Among many of Hume's followers a slippage readily occurred from Hume's own belief that there can be *no evidence for marvels* to the dogma that a *marvel cannot exist*. Hume's offensive placed theologians and metaphysicians on the defensive for more than two centuries. When Hume died in 1776, the general assumption by Western elites was still that Christianity was true and that the burden of proof was borne by atheists; by 1976, the general assumption by Western elites was that atheism was true and that the burden of proof was on Christians. The effect of this tectonic shift on Christian thought has up to now been wide and permanent, visible in "Liberal Christianity," "fideism," and innumerable other movements. As the authorities for heaven, such as the Bible, tradition, and theology, were undermined, ideas about heaven inevitably became more diverse. If one accepts Hume's arguments, one has no warrant for believing in heaven. On the other hand, Hume's arguments were not the last word—or the best one.

The French *philosophes* of the Enlightenment were more propagandists than philosophers, but their fiery skepticism and pointed ridicule made Christianity unfashionable among the eighteenth-century elite. The works of Voltaire, Diderot, D'Alembert, and Edward Gibbon flowed more readily and directly into minds than the dry, logical work of Hume. Some of the *philosophes*, such as Diderot and the Baron d'Holbach, were true atheists, and Jacques Offray de la Mettrie argued in *The Natural History of the Soul* (1745) and *Man a Machine* (1748) that humans are simply elaborate mechanisms with no soul or freedom of will. Others, such as Voltaire, Jean-Jacques Rousseau, the deist Thomas Jefferson, and the Unitarian John Adams, were not atheists (indeed, Adams was a firm Christian of a liberal and tolerant bent who believed in heaven).

Voltaire's famous phrase "If God did not exist, we would have to invent him" is testimony to the growing attitude of the time that religion must serve practical social purposes. The practicality of religion—even of the idea of heaven—was pursued by philosophers such as Jeremy Bentham toward the end of the eighteenth century. We need sanctions to control human behavior, so it is useful to convince people that they will be subject to judgment. Bentham argued for utilitarianism in his *Introduction to the Principles of Morals and Legislation* (1789; the word "utilitarian" is first attested in 1781). He believed that society is, and ought in future even more to be, based on the principle that pleasures ought to outweigh pains for the good of the individual and of society. For Bentham, these pleasures and pains were clearly material, whereas "spiritual" happiness is illusion and nonsense. We can know nothing about heaven, since no one has experienced it, he said, but the sanctions of heaven and hell were still desirable in order to control society. A bizarre manifestation of this attitude occurred at the height of the radical French Revolution: "the decree of May, 1794, on the Worship of the Supreme Being" decreed belief in "the immortality of the soul" on the grounds that it was useful to society.[21]

Though not all the *philosophes* were atheists, they were bound by a common hatred of the "infamy" of the traditional alliance between church and crown. When Voltaire advised the world to *écraser l'infâme* (crush the infamy), he meant the tyranny he believed that kings and popes were imposing on the mind, culture, and society. "Liberty" meant primarily breaking the bonds of this tyranny. Anticlerical and antimonarchical views dominated the revolutions of the late eighteenth and early nineteenth century. Frank Manuel wrote of Diderot's virtual crusade against Christianity and of Holbach's wish "to destroy religion utterly as a social force."[22] Diderot's encyclopedia has only a short and ironic entry on *ciel théologique*: "One imagines that heaven is far away in space. . . . The inspired authors such as Isaiah and Saint John the Evangelist make magnificent [the French *superbes* is ironically ambivalent, because

it means both "magnificent" and "vain"] descriptions of heaven. . . . The rabbis
had a number of fantasies about heaven." Diderot picked on the rabbis for the
same reason that Hume picked on the Old Testament: in France in 1780 it was
much less dangerous than picking on the Christian clergy. His entry on "paradise" (*paradis*) is similar, observing that Copernicus and Descartes had made
it difficult to imagine where heaven might be located.[23] The entry on "Bible" is
even more skeptical, laying out a historical-critical approach to the text, the
canon, and—as Spinoza had suggested—the historical context in which the Bible
was written. The question was no longer the truth *of* the Bible but the truth
about the Bible. Diderot's own education had taught him to regard heaven and
hell as "fables."

The growing interest in other cultures that was one of the characteristics of
late eighteenth-century Europe brought to light the beliefs of other religions
(except Judaism, which was even more despised at the time than Christianity,
partly because it was the origin of Christianity and partly because of anti-
Semitism). If Muslim, Hindu, or Buddhist beliefs were fables, then Christian
beliefs could be fables as well. Holbach's *Système de la nature* (1770) specifically denied the existence of heaven, the soul, and immortality, declaring all
religions "noxious" to Progress. The title of his 1756 *Christianisme dévoilé*,
(*Christianity Unmasked*) itself registers his attitude.

"Progress" was the shibboleth of the eighteenth through twentieth centuries.[24] Some Christian writers, such as Gottfried Wilhelm Leibniz, had argued
that the blessed in heaven enjoy continual progress in thought and joy. The
basic definition of "progress" is "movement toward a goal." In order to have
progress, then, one needs a goal. If we wish to get from Boston to Cairo, every
minute we get closer to Cairo we get closer to our goal. If, on the other hand,
we have no goal, then every minute we get closer to Cairo is as meaningless as
every minute we get closer to Saturn. The more we "progress," the farther behind we fall—quite literally, for the more of our life we spend without a goal
the less time we have remaining to make the journey. Some today believe that
we will invent our goals through the process of movement itself, that "the goal
is the moment," whatever that may mean. But even then—though we may
change our goal from Cairo to Sydney or Rio or Dhaka—we will still need
eventually to have a goal. If our goal turns out to be Dhaka, then the closer we
get to Dhaka the better off we are, while the longer we stay in Boston, the
worse off we are. (The objection that we might end up being happier in the
long run if we stayed in Boston is cute but specious.) And if we are moving
toward the better, it follows that we are leaving behind the less good; a more
direct way of saying "the less good" is "the worse." If on the other hand there is
no goal, then there can be no progress away from worse toward better.

The philosophical idea of Progress in its three basic aspects—the providen-
tial, the developmental, and the utopian—has a long history, with its earliest

clear proponent being Saint Augustine. Augustine's argument (in his early, optimistic days) was as follows: God must have some reason for not having ended the world at the moment when the Passion of Christ redeemed it; he must have some plan, some goal for the subsequent years. Progress is movement toward the Kingdom of God, which is the goal that God (the final cause) has for us. Providence guides us. But for many Enlightenment leaders, the final cause, the Last Judgment, the Kingdom of God, and heaven were Christian baggage to be discarded. Progress was no longer movement toward a supernatural, divine end shaped by God but toward a secular end defined by humans in time.

One may ask why the Enlightenment assumed secular Progress at all; it is certainly no logical consequence of Humean skepticism. But humans want hope, they need hope, and—unless it is thrashed out of them at an early age—they insist on having hope. If they cannot hope for a desired future in heaven, they will hope for one on earth. The old canard that belief in heaven is merely wishful thinking applies even more strongly to belief in secular Progress, which is counterfactual to what is historically observed. All the arguments against Christians—or Muslims—for being willing to sacrifice themselves and others for their goal apply equally, if not more forcefully, to followers of secular theories of Progress such as Marxist hope, capitalist hope, Leninist hope, Nazi hope, Libertarian hope, politically correct hope, technocratic hope, and even Enlightenment hope (do not forget the French Reign of Terror).

Perhaps the most common form of hope in contemporary society is the hope that "Progress" is the "good life" measured by greater and greater material satisfactions. The problem with most secular hopes is that they easily encourage those who nourish them to have hatred or contempt for anyone standing in their way. Secular hopes led to most of the cruelties and torments of the twentieth century and the ongoing degradation of the planet.[25] It is better to take the proverbial cold shower and realize that there is no hope for the overall improvement of this world; it is certainly better than forcing or manipulating others in order to further your own convictions about Progress.

The goal of the Enlightenment was human knowledge, freedom, and liberty. Religion in general and Christianity in particular seemed to be obstacles to this goal. In this view, the farther we get away from monarchy and Christianity the farther we advance toward this goal and the better off we are. Ages past were inferior to ours, and ages future will be superior; ages past were retrograde, ours advancing; ages past were worse, ours better; ages past were primitive, barbarous, and superstitious, ours rational, scientific, enlightened; previous minds, ideas, philosophies, literature, cultures, and societies were not as good as ours. It follows logically that they were worse. Past societies, except perhaps for ancient Greece, were ages of darkness and barbarous superstition. Such ideas of "primitive" and "advanced" cultures or of "higher" and "lower" cultures had quite a long history that included racist slavery and national imperialism.

Enlightenment views of Progress were propagated in France, Britain, and America. Whereas Bernard de Fontenelle had been convinced that the human mind would Progress by expanding knowledge endlessly, French economist A. R. J. Turgot declared that there were three stages of Progress, from the primitive to the metaphysical to the scientific.[26] Building on Turgot's ideas, the powerful work on Progress, *Esquisse d'un tableau historique des progrès de l'esprit humain* was written in prison by the Marquis de Condorcet while he was awaiting execution by the Reign of Terror. It was published in 1795, a year after his own death at the hands of what he had felt to be a Progressive Revolution. Condorcet believed that humans advance from crude hunter-gatherers to increasingly sophisticated societies, and that this Progress would never be reversed. He optimistically (and ironically, considering his own fate) believed that he was living in the ninth of ten Progressive ages, just before the age of perfection. Even the idea of Progressive ages was based on traditional Christianity, which assumed that we are in the sixth of seven successive ages, the seventh being the millennium or the Kingdom of God. Adam Smith, best known for *The Wealth of Nations* (1776), posited four stages of human Progress: from hunting-gathering to herding to agricultural to commercial. Edward Gibbon, in his slashing history of Christianity—which he titled *The Decline and Fall of the Roman Empire* (1776–88) in self-protection against feared Christian reactions—admitted that there could be retrograde ideas and periods such as Christianity, barbarism, and the alleged "Dark Ages." Still, Gibbon believed that "we," now aided by the light of reason, saw history as it really was. The implication of all these Progressive ideas was that betterment was to be found in material, not spiritual realms, and that implication would become explicit in the following century with Comte, Marx, and others. Progress had no room for heaven.

In America, John Adams believed that "the arts and sciences, in general, during the three or four last centuries [before his own time] have had a regular course of Progressive improvements."[27] Bad religions and societies, considered chiefly "oriental" (but certainly including Judaism and Christianity), were associated with tyranny and superstition, so that America, the uttermost West, could lead the way to universal freedom. America was the best hope for Earth. Until as late as the 1960s or even the 1990s, the very idea of America seemed a beacon of freedom to other nations. Indeed, it could sound like heaven on Earth. *The Rising Glory of America* by Philip Freneau proclaimed in 1771:

> This is a land of ev'ry joyous sound
> Of liberty and life; sweet liberty!
> Without whose aid the noblest genius fails,
> And science irretrievably must die.

'Tis but the morning of the world with us
And Science yet but sheds her orient rays

When ages yet to come have run their round
And future years of bliss alone remain

This is thy praise America thy pow'r
Thou best of climes by science visited
By freedom blest and richly stor'd with all
The luxuries of life. Hail happy land.[28]

Timothy Dwight wrote in *Greenfield Hill* (1794):

All hail, thou western world! by heav'n design'd
Th'example bright, to renovate mankind.

Warm'd by that living fire, which HEAVEN bestows;
Which Freedom lights, and Independence blows;
By that bright pomp, which moral scenes display.[29]

Such were the poignant Progressive hopes of Enlightenment America.

Enlightenment ideas often filtered down to popular literature and thus were disseminated to a wider audience than a Hume or a Kant could ever command. The Progressivism of the period found its way even into hymns and sermons. Joseph Addison believed in the eternal Progress of the soul: God has created us to be perfect, and since we do not have enough time to achieve this perfection in this world, the soul must continue to progress in an afterlife. Addison and Isaac Watts promised a commonsensical, practical heaven, with good works as well as contemplation and with a progressive community of mutual labor, duty, service, and education. Such ideas of a "social" heaven were not a major transformation, because Christian tradition had always held to the fellowship of the saints (the elect, the saved) in heaven; but the new Progressive, social heaven focused on earthier pursuits than did traditional heaven.[30] For Addison and Watts, heaven is much like earth, only better. Heaven was still full of joy, communion, beauty, love, fellowship, and refreshment as well as awe and wonder, but the emphasis was different. They believed that we might now hope for a heaven that fulfills our earthly needs and desires in another world. Why should we, in heaven, be deprived of comfortable beds, tasty meals, relaxed friendships, or sexual intercourse? This simple view, affecting millions of people for centuries, reconstructs heaven as less stressful, less fearful of judgment, homier, cozy even, full of simple joys and comforts and reunion with friends and family (and, who knows, perhaps even entertainment). It is a heaven much more accessible and reassuring to the ordinary man and woman than the great resounding voices of the seraphim in harmony around the throne of God in majesty on high. God could step down from the throne and even become our friend and, two centuries later, even our buddy, dissonant though that might be with the ancient Jewish and Christian chant: "Holy, Holy, Holy, Lord God of Power and Might, heaven and earth are filled with your glory." Naively unaware of the blasphemy, some American congregations sang of holding hands with Yahweh.

Frederik van Leenhof's book *Hemel op Aarde*, "Heaven on Earth" (1703) argued that heaven and hell are states of mind and character on Earth rather than in another world. Hendrik Smeeks, a surgeon and member of the Reformed Church, wrote a travel novel (1708) in which heaven and hell are purely fictional places; his self-proclaimed enlightened characters build a cathedral in which clergy of all world religions come together for rational discussion—but end up shouting and abusing one another.[31]

Classic views of heaven were still predominant and indeed even encouraged by some of the philosophical trends. Catholics and other traditionalists took heart from the Cartesian division between mind and matter, even though by so doing they distanced themselves even further from the original Christian idea of resurrection. The prevalent assumption that immortality was almost self-evident appears in the lines of Joseph Addison, the English poet, hymnodist, and playwright:

> It must be so—Plato, thou reasonest well!
> Else whence this pleasing hope, this fond desire,
> This longing after immortality?
> Or whence this secret dread, and inward horror,
> Of falling into naught? Why shrinks the soul
> Back on herself, and startles at destruction?
> 'Tis the divinity that stirs within us;
> 'Tis heaven itself, that points out a hereafter,
> And intimate eternity to man.
> Eternity! thou pleasing, dreadful thought![32]

As for eternity itself, Henry Vaughan "saw Eternity the other night, / Like a great ring of pure and endless light, / All calm, as it was bright,"[33] and "They are all gone into the world of light! / And I alone sit ling'ring here."[34] Light was not photons emitted by physical bodies, but a quality, a supreme quality, diffused downward from God's heaven through the primum mobile and then through all the spheres. Darkness was not the absence of photons but the absence of the presence of God.

The traditional views were yet more deeply instilled in the population at large, impressed in sermons, tracts, and, perhaps, especially hymns. Hymns, particularly Lutheran in Germany and Methodist in Britain, were the main ways in which the nonelites participated in their religion. A hymn sung weekly or even several times a year has greater power to impress than most sermons or tracts. Joseph Addison, Isaac Watts, Charles Wesley, John Wesley, Paul Gerhardt, William Cowper, and John Newton sang through millions of voices over the years.[35] In more formal music, the oratorios of Händel and the cantatas of Bach sounded the depths of the soul. It would not be until the late twentieth century that the old music lost its magic. And, when still sung, it can still move.

Isaac Watts wrote on the limitations of reason:

> In vain our haughty spirit swells,
> For nothing's found in thee
> But boundless inconceivables,
> And vast eternity.[36]

Watts could be sentimental:

> There is beyond the sky
> A Heaven of joy and love;
> And holy children when they die
> Go to that world above.[37]

Watts expresses the joy of heaven, where Christ "scatters infinite delights / On all the happy minds."[38] Watts calls on the resurrected souls:

> Ye slumbering saints, a heavenly host
> Stands waiting at your gaping tombs;
> Let every sacred sleeping dust
> Leap into life, for Jesus comes.
> Our airy feet with unknown flight,
> Swift as the motions of desire,
> Run up the hills of heavenly light,
> And leave the weltering world in fire.[39]

And he delights in heavenly bliss:

> There is a land of pure Delight
> Where Saints Immortal reign;
> Infinite Day excludes the Night,
> And Pleasures banish Pain.
> There everlasting Spring abides,
> And never-withering Flowers:
> Death like a narrow Sea divides
> This Heavn'ly Land from ours.[40]

Through the eighteenth century, both mountains and sea—today we tend to think of these as places of recreation and exploration—generally had a negative connotation as barriers blocking us from one another and often symbols of death and of sin. To go for pleasure to such places was still uncommon, and mountains and seas seldom appeared in representations of heaven.

Elizabeth Singer Rowe wrote of Jesus:

> Immortal fountain of my life,
> My last, my noblest end:
> Eternal centre of my soul,
> Where all its motions tend!
> Thou object of my dearest love,
> My heav'nly paradise,
> The spring of all my flowing joys,
> My everlasting bliss! [41]

Anonymous is the hymn remembered by my own dying mother, a professed lifelong atheist:

> Hierusalem, my happy home,
> Would God I were in thee!
> Would God my woes were at an end,
> Thy joys that I might see! [42]

English hymnody was powerfully transformed in African-American hymns, such as "We'll get home to heaven bimeby," "When I get to heaven, gonna put on my shoes, gonna walk all over God's heaven," and "Walk 'em easy round de heaven." [43]

Jonathan Edwards, the great American Calvinist preacher, understood that the essential meaning of heaven was being in loving communion with God and that it is open to any who desire it, yet closed to those who choose not to enter. [44] Emanuel Swedenborg exemplified the trend to Progressive and more earthy heavens. [45] His views had considerable currency by the end of the eighteenth century in his native Sweden and in England, France, Germany, the Netherlands, and the United States, where Latter-day Saints (Mormon) descriptions of heaven would evince striking similarities. [46] After you die, according to Swedenborg, you first come to consciousness in a "spirit world," which is neither heaven nor hell nor purgatory. There you live a life so similar to that which you have now as to be virtually indistinguishable, except that you will be able to communicate from there with those who are still living, as Luther did when Swedenborg invited him to do so. In their conversation, Swedenborg convinced the embarrassed Luther to admit that Luther's theology was faulty. [47] Your spirit passes through a variety of states of bliss or pain depending upon your character. You are gradually educated by angels (who are perfected humans who once lived in this world) and as your character develops through education, you learn more and more, and then you pass into the "natural heaven." In the natural heaven, you learn even more and become an angel yourself. (Those who because of their dark character refuse instruction by the angels choose the path to hell.) Most become ready eventually for the next stage, the "spiritual heaven," where you do good works in fellowship and justice, in the direction of the Great Commandment to love God and neighbor. At last you pass into the "celestial heaven," where you are aware of "becoming perfected in body and spirit into an interior delight, because into spiritual life, which as an interior life is more receptive of heavenly blessedness."[48] Swedenborg's heavens had all the attributes of this world, including houses, food, games, cities, friendship, love, marriage, and sexual relations (though not procreation). Such cheerful views allowed people to look forward to death and a lovely, welcoming heaven rather than fearing—as in classical Catholic, Orthodox, and Protestant theology—Judgment. "Feel-good religion" was always as attractive as it was deceptive. The authority of such views did not rest in reason, tradition, and the Bible. Instead, for Swedenborg, his followers, and, later, Joseph Smith, authority came from new and personal revelations. Legions of sects based on such revelations continued to emerge, despite the difficulty inherent (unless you possess a bizarre personal charisma) in trying to persuade someone else that God has vouchsafed you a personal revelation.

More complex and so less immediately influential on broad public opinion than Hume, Voltaire, and Gibbon was Immanuel Kant. Kant's ideas, though less easily accessible, eventually irrigated pragmatism, positivism, idealism, existentialism, and postmodernism. From Hume, Kant had learned the ideal of the Enlightenment: courageous inquiry about the cosmos and about ourselves, never surrendering our minds to the authority of others.[49] Our sole authority is our mind. The mind cannot be reduced to matter, for physical objects cannot investigate and understand other physical objects, and the mind has the inherent ability to form patterns even in the absence of physical observation. Like Socrates, Kant pointed out that we have an inborn idea of a perfect triangle without ever having seen one. He argued that "the senses must be intellectualized."[50] The mind transcends the physical, for mind is necessary in order to synthesize the impressions of our senses. But most knowledge arises from the patterns that mind organizes from our sense perceptions. Without a pattern in our mind to organize what we "see," we could not distinguish between a tree and a chair. Sensory input would be meaningless without mind to construct and organize it. We construct natural philosophy (science) in order to understand the physical universe in which we live. Ideas about heaven, Kant believed, might be true, but since Kant saw no way to test them as propositions, they belonged to a much less certain and vaguer realm of knowledge—

a kind of almost subknowledge. We are not entitled to proceed from physics to metaphysics, Kant argued, so that any "knowledge" we have of God and heaven is of a vaguer nature than the "knowledge" of a table or a city. Kant, like Locke, rejected the idea that the validity of an observation could be determined according to the credibility of the witness, thus reinforcing the hypercritical rejection of testimony and reasonableness.

The mind is transcendent—it goes beyond matter—but Kant did not say that it was "spiritual," because he believed that the very notion of spirit is unverifiable by testing. If God exists or subsists, then God is in a pure world of understanding outside the system of natural connections with which we are familiar. We experience only finite realities (so Kant believed), and therefore we cannot experience the absolute, infinite reality of God. Moreover, we can properly *think* only of finite realities, so that we cannot even properly think about God. There may be God, but it is pointless to speculate about him when we have no experience of what God would be like if he did exist. Two centuries later, Alvin Plantinga would argue that such skepticism about God and heaven needs to apply to every idea, because *all* statements about *noumena* (things in themselves) are beyond our ability to think about them.[51] We cannot intellectually understand even "penguin" in its full existence, but only our mental concept of "penguin."

Kant sharply dismissed the ontological argument for the existence of God by questioning the meaning of "to be" and of "existence." Existence, Kant said, cannot in itself be a predicate. "A horse is" gets us no farther than a Gertrude-Steinian "a horse is a horse." So, if God is defined as absolute being, the statement that God exists is tautological: Being is being, as horse is horse. But Kant believed that the statement that "God exists" is on less firm ground than that "horse exists," because (he believed) we observe things we call horses but not things we call God. Thus for Kant the idea of a necessary being has no positive, "definite content."[52] And what Kant's view implied for God applied, a fortiori, to heaven.

But Kant did not rest with Hume's skepticism or the atheism of some of their contemporaries. Although God cannot be known and the existence of God is not knowledge, God's existence is not a fantasy; the existence of God is "better founded than an opinion."[53] In fact, Kant believed, God is necessary. The necessity of God rests not on the basis of *pure reason* but on the basis of *practical reason*.[54] That God cannot be proved makes him even more necessary in that we need to have an absolute basis for our morality. That basis Kant called the "categorical imperative." The categorical imperative is that we should always act in such a way that our will to act is in harmony with universal law. Also, since we cannot prove God's existence, we have the free choice to take the responsibility of believing in him or not. Dogmatists of all kinds, Kant believed, accept one authority or another, and any such dogmatism is mental slavery. We have responsibility for our acts, and if we fail to exercise that responsibility we will become slaves (of rulers, priests, landholders, commercial interests, political fanatics). We have the freedom to choose, and Kant chose to believe in God. Kant's grounds for doing so were original: "I will that there be a God," he wrote, "that my existence in this world be also an existence in a pure world of the understanding outside the system of natural connections, and finally that my duration be endless."[55] William James would also later argue for the will to believe. The problem is that "I will that there be a God" was easily transposed later into Nietzsche's "I will that there not be a God."[56]

Kant's contribution to the Enlightenment view of good and evil was characteristically original. He sought to establish a distinction between good and evil while removing from them the expectation of reward in heaven or punishment in hell. The moral sense is a metaphysical reality apart from the physical. Morality cannot exist if there is no purpose to the cosmos, for if we cannot distinguish between worse and better, and there is no good greater than another good, then the world—or at least human affairs—will disintegrate infinitely. Objections that we form our own moralities as we go along do not work, because we then would have no way of judging one preferable to another, and we would have to conclude that Adolf Hitler and Albert Schweitzer are morally the same. Objections that fields of study such as medicine, law, or business establish their own ethics also fail, for these ethics, by virtue of not being based in absolute morality, are compartmentalized, fragmented, and often divergent. Since we are free, it is imperative that we make the best choice open to us, and that choice is to will ourselves to fit into the purpose and plan of the universe as best we can. This is a truer meaning of Progress: moral progress by developing our characters toward the greater good, unceasingly. An evil choice is one that scrapes against the greater good of the cosmos. As shown in his *Critique of Judgment* (1790), Kant's absolute esthetics is parallel to his absolute morality: in our feelings of the beautiful and the sublime we experience a harmony of our faculties, the *beautiful* being something that our imagination can readily grasp, implying "form and limitation," whereas the *sublime* is "formless and unlimited," beyond our imaginations and only hinted at by our intellects.[57] Kant's "moral imperative" had no room for the utilitarian view (of Locke, for example) that heaven and hell are necessary in order to ensure morality. For Kant, good actions must, if they are to be morally pure, be without expectation of recompense. Morality is not a means but an end in itself; heaven is the experience of cosmic harmony.

The rationalism of the Enlightenment provoked a reaction in the direction of emotions. As the world of the Enlightenment in the late eighteenth and early nineteenth centuries morphed gradually into the world of Romanticism, the shift toward feelings manifested itself in the narcissistic life of Jean-Jacques Rousseau, whose emphasis on his own feelings permeated early nineteenth-century thought. God exists because Rousseau feels that God exists. Rousseau's God is kindly and wishes to lead us in the direction of freedom and liberty. We feel that human nature is good, and we feel that anything that obstructs the goodness of human nature is bad. Like Condorcet, Rousseau believed that the impediment to human fulfillment was tyranny, particularly that of nobles and clerics. We will advance by striking down that impediment and freeing ourselves to fulfill our true feelings, which Rousseau assumed to be good. The assumption that our basic feelings are *good* is founded on no historical evidence at all. But Rousseau believed that a revolution sweeping away the past would bring about a new society in which feelings *would* be good (a sentiment to reappear in the 1960s). The trajectory of sentimentality was thus set. Heaven is not another world; salvation is not from another world; rather, we humans create our own salvation by liberating ourselves from oppressive superstition and from false feelings that superstition had imposed on us. Rousseau would have enjoyed seeing his ideas of "freedom" worked out in the Romantic movement, but he might have been bewildered by the eventual perversion of his ideas of "liberty" by Stalin, Mao, and Pol Pot.

The eighteenth-century intellectuals promoted physicalism as the only true way of approaching truth; they disenchanted the cosmos, blocking us from responding to it as a being that we can respond to with love and gratitude. But heaven transcended the limited rationality of the Enlightenment. It would also transcend the Romantic insistence on personal feelings as the criterion for knowledge. It is not on feelings but on divine reality that heaven is based. And that divine reality is to be found on Earth, every day, if we look for it in the right ways.[58]

CHAPTER 4

Ahead

Disenchantment grew greater in the nineteenth century, under the spell of alleged material Progress. Physicalism dominated elite circles and seeped down into popular assumptions. On the other hand, various idealist philosophical systems and literary movements attacked physicalism from a variety of angles. For both sides, the idea of Progress through development was central. It was believed that we humans are moving ahead to a better world, "a brave new world," and that better world would be here on earth rather than in heaven.

The word "develop" is first attested in 1656; "development" first appears in 1756. The original image was of *unwrapping meaning* and came to connote any meaningful change through time. The term "development" was so congenial to thoughtful Christians that John Henry Newman used it in his *Essay on the Development of Christian Doctrine* (1845). Still, Newman faced opposition from theologians clinging to the untenable position that Catholic doctrine had never changed. The verb "evolve," first attested in 1641, brought the image of *unwinding* a scroll. The noun "evolution" did not appear before 1832, from which time it has been used in the specific sense that plants and animals develop from earlier forms. "Progress" is attested by 1425: its root is less ambiguous than the other two terms, since it comes from Latin *progredi,* to step, walk, or move forward. By the nineteenth century, "progress," "evolve," and "develop" had gravitated close together in meaning. Although the term "Progressive" in a political sense was not used before 1865, Progress as an ideology was rooted in the late eighteenth and early nineteenth centuries. Other terms acquired new definitions or emphases. "Natural philosophy" became "science," with its exclusive sense of the study of matter and energy, and the term "scientist" was invented by William Whewell in 1833.

Change was the basic idea. Though some ancient and some non-Western philosophers denied the reality of time, most took change through time for granted: "later" is a change from "earlier." But is change for the better, for the worse, or for neither? More fundamental than the question whether change is necessarily good is whether there is any direction at all inherent in change. If there is direction, is it a designed development or a combination of chance and mechanical movement?

The debate about physicalist Progress centered on the term "evolution." One was asked to be "for or against" evolution or to "believe or disbelieve in evolution." This dichotomy harmed both science and religion. If "evolution" is taken to mean, as it originally did, the development of plants and animals through time, it would take a powerful amount of stubbornness to deny its truth. (The question how *species* develop into other species through time, however, is open.) If, on the other hand, "evolution" is taken (as many contemporary writers take it) to mean development through time *without any purpose or design*, then it is freighted with ideology and will cause angry, endless, and futile disagreements pitting Darwin and Jesus against one another in a contest for the survival of the fittest bumper stickers. It is politically, scientifically, and philosophically unfortunate that the term has been so blurred and charged, making analytical discussion difficult. Someone may eventually solve the problem, but in the meanwhile this book distinguishes between "evolution science" in the neutral scientific sense; "physicalist evolution" in the physicalist ideological sense; and "theo-evolution" in the sense of divinely-guided evolution. The roots of all are in the theories of Progress in the late eighteenth and nineteenth centuries.

In the Christian tradition, the idea of Progress assumed that humanity progresses spiritually. By the nineteenth century, Progress meant that humanity progresses materially. Both assumptions are purely metaphysical, the one as much as the other. The mathematician Pierre Laplace, famous for his comment to Napoleon that he had no need for the hypothesis of God, argued for a completely mechanistic universe that came from nowhere for no reason and in which, if we could establish the position of each particle and the forces acting upon it, we could predict everything in the future. This left a purposeless, undesigned, goalless movement that was somehow supposed to make things better. Physicalists claimed to scorn metaphysics, yet their own supposition that the cosmos is merely physical is itself metaphysical. Physicalism, linked with increasing technological sophistication in such fields as medicine, chemistry, and engineering, became the dominant faith of our own times.

The problem for physicalist theories of cosmic development prior to the very late eighteenth century was that there seemed to be no way at all for the present complexities of the cosmos to have arisen from its inception without God's having planned the whole thing. The old "argument from design," which even Hume had difficulty in dismissing, was restated by William Paley in his books *View of the Evidences of Christianity* (1794) and *Natural Theology* (1802). Paley's often-cited example was that if you are walking across a field and encounter a stone, you may reasonably consider the stone to have been constructed without design and by chance. But if you are walking across the field and encounter a pocket watch, you would be crazy to assume that the watch had appeared there constructed without design and by chance. The complexity of the watch, Paley argued, was an indubitable argument for a watchmaker, and just so the intricacy of the cosmos was an indubitable argument for a purposeful design. Though the argument was later frequently rejected (Darwin accepted it when he was young but then dismissed it) and modified, it long bolstered the belief in a Designer.

Paley's argument persists in modified forms today: it is not so passé as zoologist Richard Dawkins would have us believe, and it carried great weight as long as physicalists could provide no alternative explanation.[1] The window to that alternative explanation was opened by the discovery of vast expanses of time. It was unimaginable that the complex universe could have come about in the roughly six thousand years that had previously been assumed by biblical hyperliteralists to have elapsed since the beginning. But once it was established that the cosmos was millions, even billions, of years old, then it became possible that chance and mechanism could work, over vast ages, to produce that complexity. Though it is philosophically possible that in fact the speed of time itself has varied, so that what seem like billions of years of processes occurred only in thousands, only a very few people today would care to make such an essentially meaningless argument. If Hume had lived to know about the vast amounts of time that were beginning to emerge by the end of the eighteenth century, he would readily have employed them against the idea of Design.

The geologist James Hutton proposed the principle of uniformity—the idea that the features of Earth have been formed over vast periods of time by the same processes (such as erosion and volcanic activity) that form them today. "Uniformitarianism," the term for this principle, was coined by William Whewell in 1833. It was no longer necessary to imagine that Earth's features had been rent apart by Noah's flood or other catastrophes, for its geological features might have been changed by ages of uplift and erosion. The evolutionary perspective of the nineteenth century would further vitiate the idea of a Designer. Jean Lamarck, although he believed in Cosmic Design, argued for biological evolution in his *Philosophie zoölogique* (1809): over eons of time, organic change can produce new species. Charles Lyell argued the principle of uniformity in understanding geology in his *Principles of Geology* (1830–33). The problem for heaven in these scientific developments was that they undermined biblical and traditional views by a purely physicalist idea of Progress, which could have no logical room for heaven.

The idea of Progress in the sense of the overall material advance of humanity—in addition to technical advances in one field or another—may seem more reassuring than that of spiritual Progress culminating in heaven and/or in the Kingdom of God on Earth. It may seem reassuring because it is allegedly based on what we think we are sure of: what we can see and touch. It also seems reassuring because it dispels fear of divine judgment of our characters. Unfortunately for its adherents, it is fundamentally less credible. There is not, and cannot ever be, any scientific evidence against heaven, but both biology and history offer inexhaustible evidence against Progress. If superstition means clinging to old beliefs contraindicated by the evidence, Progress has been one of the most prevalent superstitions of the past two centuries.

Physicalist Progress was promoted in social thought by Auguste Comte, drawing upon Condorcet and Bentham. In Comte's *Cours de philosophie positive* (1830–42), the term "positive" denoted the optimistic belief in intellectual and moral Progress, but the term shaded into belief in such Progress based on knowledge derived from the data of experience. Although not all theories of Progress were couched in terms of purely material Progress, ultimately even those with some kind of idealist color tended more and more to be based on chance and mechanism. Positivism came in general to be associated with the philosophy of natural science. Comte's physicalist evolution scheme of human society was that it developed from theology to philosophy and metaphysics to science. (He believed of course that he himself was in the final and best stage.) Ultimately derived from the medieval Christian seven stages of development with God at the end and as the goal, Comte's metaphysics posited Progress toward an eventual universal brotherhood of man (or, as we should say now, "community of humankind") as the universal end and goal.[2] Schiller's "Ode to Joy," set to music by Beethoven, epitomized this generous and hopeful view.

Comte, more consistent than some of his followers, was aware that he was promoting a religion. He rejected atheism on the grounds that it claims to know what is unknowable: the existence or nonexistence of God. Strongly anti-Christian and opposed to any kind of supernaturalist religion, all of which he regarded as fictional and capricious, he proposed a naturalist religion based on science and aimed at the perfection of humanity through coherent social organization of scientific knowledge. Comte laid the foundation for sociology, inventing that word in 1843. Like Condorcet, he maintained that Progress was automatic and irreversible. There was, he thought, a fundamental instinct, a complex resultant of the combination of all our natural tendencies, which directly pushes man to ameliorate his condition incessantly in every way. A younger contemporary of Comte, and like him influenced by Condorcet and Bentham, John Stuart Mill was a utilitarian influenced by Comte. He differed from Bentham by distinguishing between the qualities, rather than simply the quantities, in the pleasure-pain balance. Mill also differed from Comte by emphasizing the individual more than society. Whatever Comte meant by amelioration, he certainly did not mean the Kingdom of God. Jacques Barzun observed that Comte's fallacy was "reducing all experiences to one condition of their origin and so killing meanings by explanations."[3]

The nineteenth century marked the full-bodied emergence of antitheism, which aimed at the unconditional elimination of God from our accepted convictions.[4] Ludwig Feuerbach in his *Essence of Christianity* (1841) opposed belief in God or gods of any and all sort, and he attacked traditional Christian views of heaven vehemently. His atheism was stronger and more complete than that of Enlightenment atheists who had merely declared that if gods exist they have little or nothing to do with human life. For Feuerbach, "God is nothing else than a product of the imagination," and so of course is heaven. The traditional idea of the resurrection of the body was so "naïve" or "ingenuous" that Feuerbach found it difficult to believe that any theologians actually credited it. The idea that the resurrected body would be both the same and different from the present body was "a fundamental contradiction, and the resurrected body can be only a thoroughly fanciful, subjective body." Any kind of immortality is nonsense, Feuerbach declared, the fantasy of "the emotive imagination, the satisfaction of" a craving for supernatural happiness, a craving that springs from a desire to escape the limitations of our bodies and our earthly lives. Heaven is simply a wish-fulfillment (as Freud would call it later), for "in heaven the Christian is free from that which he wishes to be free from here— free from the sexual impulse, free from matter, free from Nature in general."[5]

The idea that religious belief was subjective had its origins as far back as the seventeenth century, and the mere physicality of "Nature" was more and more frequently assumed by Feuerbach's contemporaries. Other powerful physicalist thinkers of the time were Pierre-Joseph Proudhon (a believer in a dynamic of Progress that replaced God as the absolute with "The Good of Humankind"), radical anarchist Mikhail Bakunin, and Ferdinand Lasalle, who promoted political socialism in the 1860s. The Romantic love of nature was sometimes transposed into individualist terms; Walt Whitman, for example, wrote "I celebrate myself, and sing myself."[6] The term "individualism" is first attested in 1827 and "individualist" in 1840.

Much of the negation of traditional heaven came from the pens of religious writers themselves in their efforts to make Christianity fit the physicalist worldview that was beginning to dominate. Heinrich Schleiermacher published *On Religion* in 1799, emphasizing experience over revelation, tradition, and reason—a theme that would be taken up by William James a century later.[7] D. F. Strauss's *The Life of Jesus* (1835) and Joseph Ernest Renan's *Life of Jesus* (1863) both declared that the supernatural portions of the Gospels were unhistorical "myths." Renan's *Future of Science* (written 1848, published in 1892) asserted that "We have destroyed both heaven and hell. Whether we have thereby done well or ill, I do not know. What is certain is that the deed is done. You cannot reseed heaven or rekindle the flames of hell. We have to stay the course, and we must make a heaven for everyone here on earth."[8] The classic study of the development of these ideas is Albert Schweitzer's *Quest of the Historical Jesus* (1906).

Such works attempted to remove miracle and myth from Christianity and to make it a template for morality and high-mindedness. Heaven, they believed, was to be realized on earth through education, science, and social programs. Liberal Christianity emphasized experience; the primacy of ethics over doctrine; and the "higher criticism" of the Bible (analyses of content and context more than the traditional textual criticism that aimed at establishing the purest texts). Higher criticism was under way as a serious intellectual approach by the time of Hermann Reimarus, who rejected miracles and went so far as to say that the biblical writers were frauds. By contrasting the "historical Jesus" with the "theological Christ," these predecessors of the twentieth-century "Jesus Seminar" deeply eroded belief in traditional heaven.

Idealists continued to offer alternatives to physicalism and Progress, thus allowing room for at least some sort of heaven. Georg Wilhelm Friedrich Hegel, the great idealist philosopher, is famous for his system of dialectical development. Hegel used "dialectic" to mean a process where a thesis is stated, followed by an antithesis, the two being resolved in a synthesis superior to the first two. In this way, Hegel believed, thought and knowledge progressed. Marx and Engels would later "turn Hegel on his head" by making the dialectic materialist rather than idealist. Hegel's *Lectures on Philosophy of Religion* (1824 and 1827) allowed for concepts of immortality and spirit, but only as symbolic realities without reference to things beyond the human mind. The immortality of the soul, Hegel reckoned, "must not be imagined as though it first emerges into actuality at some later time; rather it is a present quality. Spirit is eternal, and for this reason it is already present; spirit in its freedom does not lie within the sphere of limitation. . . . Eternity is not mere duration but *knowing*—the knowing of what is eternal" (1824).[9] "Humanity is immortal only through cognitive knowledge, for only in the activity of thinking is its soul pure and free rather than mortal and animal-like." Cognition and thought are the root of the human soul. "The animal soul is submerged in corporeality, while spirit is a totality in itself" (1827).[10] The divine principle contains the cosmos within itself, and a special place where the divine intent unscrolls is the human mind or consciousness.

Hegel's view, far from the traditional concept of heaven, gave strength to later religious idealists, pantheists, and panentheists. Ralph Waldo Emerson, romantic, optimistic, and evasive of the problem of evil, believed that we should trust ourselves and the light within. Emerson, like Liberal Protestants after him, believed in "the intrinsic goodness of human nature."[11] The problem with such a view lies in the possible explanations of such a belief, against which stands the whole of biology and human history: (1) either goodness comes from Intelligent Design (God), and so does evil; (2) or human nature was originally good but is deformed by our own fault; (3) or goodness springs from the basic nature of an undesigned cosmos, an absurdity because an undesigned cosmos can be neither good nor evil. A catchphrase of the mid-twentieth century was "God does not make junk," but we have the option of turning ourselves into junk.

Marxism arose not only from physicalist Progressivism but also from Thomas Malthus, the prophet of doom by population explosion and thus decidedly no Progressive; from the utopianism of Claude-Henri Saint-Simon, who predicted the withering away of the state; from the idealist philosophy of Hegel; and even from traditional Christian millennialism.[12]

Karl Marx and Friedrich Engels, along with their political successors such as Lenin, Stalin, and Mao, considered religion in general and Christianity in particular as antithetical to Communism. As much as both Communism and Christianity have both declined over recent decades, they were powerful antagonists. For traditional Communism as expressed by Marx and Engels in *The Communist Manifesto* (1848), *Das Kapital* (1867), and *Ludwig Feuerbach and the End of Classical German Philosophy* (1889), only physical reality has any objective existence. Ideas are merely "epiphenomena" (secondary and superficial phenomena) generated by material society, so religion is an imposture. Marx wrote, "The basis of irreligious criticism is *man makes religion, religion does not make man.*" Religion springs from a "*perverted world consciousness*" produced by perverted society. "*Religious* distress is at the same time the *expression* of real distress and the *protest* against real distress . . . It is the *opium* of the people. The abolition of religion as the *illusory* happiness of the people is required for their *real* happiness."[13] Engels was even more pointed: "All religion, however, is nothing but the fantastic reflection in men's minds of those external forces which control their daily life, a reflection in which the terrestrial forces assume the form of supernatural forces. . . . It is still true that man proposes and God (that is the alien domination of the capitalist mode of production) disposes."[14] God was a capitalist invention (the word "capitalist" first appears in 1791, "capitalism" in 1854). "Communist" and "Communism" appear in 1840, but their later specific philosophical and political meaning was first formulated in 1848 in *The Communist Manifesto*. The term "Dialectical Materialism" was coined by Marxist theorist Georgi Plekhanov and ensconced in Communist theory by *Dialectical and Historical Materialism* (1938), a book appearing under the name of Joseph Stalin. Feudalism was the thesis, capitalism the antithesis, and Communism the synthesis.[15]

For Marxists, religion is an obstacle to Progress, which is entirely material. Progress was also automatic, although human action or inaction may accelerate or decelerate it. The goal of Progress is a classless society accompanied by the withering away of the state and culminating in earthly happiness and contentment for all. For Communists, God and heaven were fantasies imposed by greedy and corrupt clergy upon the credulous masses in order to exploit them. Religious ideas were merely cognitive processes perverted by society and masking real concerns. Though Communism did little or nothing to shape the tradition of heaven, it eroded it in two ways: by the assumption that heaven and hell are not worth thinking about, and by the substitution of a material workers' paradise for heaven. A new deity, the inexorable Progress of "History," replaced "God."

Though physicalist Progressivism had the greatest impact on heaven, some nineteenth-century philosophers resisted the trend. Johann Gottlieb Fichte and other Kantians remarked that if the universe were not observed and considered by any intelligent being, it would be equivalent to the universe's not existing at all.[16] In other words, if there were no mind or consciousness to name, categorize, or understand things—even the "objective things" so favored in that century—the things would have no reality.

Take for example the geological period of time known as the Permian Period. Every textbook in geology assumes the objective reality of the Permian Period, but no creature living at the time had any sense of living in any geological "period," let alone something named "the Permian." The Permian or the Devonian or any other period has no inherent existence. The use of geological periods is simply a practical device for categorizing geological and biological developments over long sections of time. In one very important sense, there was no such thing as the "Permian Period" before Sir Roderick Murchison constructed and named it that in 1841. This is not to question the validity of geological study of that period of time. The point, rather, is that we are unjustified in assuming a correspondence between our concepts and external things or events.[17] There is no objective entity "out there" to which our concept of the Permian Period applies. Lenin's "copy theory of knowledge" is a good example of simplistic epistemology. In his view, our minds copy external phenomena. Such an error often has practical consequences. An example is "feudalism." The word first appeared in 1839 and was applied to a complex series of social relationships in the Middle Ages. No one in the Middle Ages, however, had any such concept. Just as important, the more medievalists study so-called feudalism the more they are convinced that the social relationships of the time were so diverse that the term is virtually useless in describing them. Yet a basic axiom of Marxist-Leninists is that society evolves from feudalism through capitalism to socialism. The main point here is that we tend to "reify" our ideas—to believe our ideas correspond to external realities. A joke among numismatists is

"I have found a coin with the date 60 BC on it," as if minters or anyone else at the time "knew" that they were living BC. "BC" did not exist before, well, Christ (or even perhaps before Denis the Small in the sixth century established dating by the Incarnation; Denis, by the way, miscalculated by only a few years). The "objective knowledge" claimed by eighteenth-century thinkers turns out to be not the knowledge of objects "out there," but the projection of human concepts onto "objects out there." Once that is understood, the lack of "objective evidence" for heaven becomes vastly less important than the Enlightenment believed.

The Romantic movement, a broad, diverse, ill-defined, but widespread network of opinions, originated in England with the discovery of Shakespeare as an anticlassicist genius and in France with Rousseau, and from there spread rapidly into Germany and its neighboring countries.[18] The word "romantic" is rooted in Old French *romanz,* used to designate the vernacular or vulgar language of the people in opposition to Latin; it was later used to describe fictitious stories and picturesque scenery and architecture. By 1800, the word "romantic" evolved further into a critical term used in poetics to indicate the contrast with classicism, and in 1819 the term was used to refer to the specific movement of Romanticism. Romanticism was two distinct and practically opposed movements: romantic zeal to fulfill the French Revolution and romantic idealization of the past, especially the medieval past.

This movement proved so successful in literature that it soon suffused the other arts, philosophy, and social thought. Although, as with any shift in ideas, Romanticism evolved from the Enlightenment, general distinctions can be made between the two movements. The Romantics were repulsed by the reduction of humanity to physicalist mechanism and called for the expression of truth through the esthetics of religion, art, poetry. They emphasized feeling and passion more than logic and science, and will more than reason.[19] The basic contrasts between Enlightenment and Romantic emphases are: reason contrasted with feelings, intuition, imagination; social order contrasted with individualism and change; clarity, order, and logic contrasted with the mysterious; artifice over the natural; cultivation and civilization contrasted with unique self; human fallibility contrasted with innate human goodness; principles and standards contrasted with making up personal rules of conduct.

One aspect of the movement, a philosophical concentration upon human will, as expressed by Schopenhauer in his *World as Will and Idea* (1819) would lead eventually to Nietzsche and William James. By emphasizing the importance of human will, it led eventually to the assertion of choice, especially the choice to assert claimed rights.

The other, esthetic, aspects of the movement were more pervasive: God represents beauty, love, and generosity more than causation; religion is based upon feelings of the beautiful and the sublime; morality was rooted in sentiment;

"nature" was transformed from a physical or philosophical term into something kindly and protective: Mother Nature. The sentimentalizing combination of philosophical "naturalism" with Romanticism popularized the notion of Mother Nature. The old philosophical definition of "nature" as the intrinsic qualities and characteristics of an entity was supplemented in 1662 by the sense of "nature" connoting the physical features of the cosmos or the general way that the physical nature is constructed. Darwin and other biologists in the nineteenth century thoroughly dismantled the naïve sense that nature is kind. Mother Nature is not a traditional Christian idea but a Romantic one.

Throughout the century, Romantic "I feel that" or even "I want that" trumped "I think that" or "I know that," eventually in our own time extending even to matters of external fact. "Democracy" and "rights" are what you feel them to be; "heaven" is what you feel it to be. Whatever we feel is right for us. That attitude affirms our right to our feelings, but it destroys analytical comprehension of any subject by making it infinitely malleable.

We have the right to imagine that heaven is eating endless chocolates. We have the right and freedom to believe anything we want about heaven, from "there's no such thing" to an overt assent to the descriptions in Revelation 20–22. And we have the right to define a polar bear as a pine tree—if we like. You have a legal right to call yourself a Christian even if you "feel" that God does not exist and that dialectical materialism is the best explanation of reality, but what does that mean? You have the right to call yourself a Communist while believing in the Incarnation and the Resurrection, but what does that mean? Dissolving distinctions among concepts disables everyone from understanding any concept at all. There are limits to inclusiveness.

The Romantic inclination to make religion, ethics, morals, and esthetics subjective may appear democratic and egalitarian. Its underside is dramatically illiberal and eventually made public discourse almost impossible. That you or I *feel* that heaven is this or that does not help even us to understand it and indeed impedes understanding by others. Heaven is a word (and behind the word a concept) that develops through time and whose limits are defined by the history of that development. We need a middle ground between two extremes. One extreme is that words have only fixed, essential meanings. The other extreme is that words can have any meaning we feel like assigning to them. The latter seems at first to produce maximum freedom of choice, but it in fact annuls real choice by making alternatives meaningless. The middle position grants both that words have porous meaning and also that words—and the concepts they address—do not merely represent our internal feelings but also the full meaning of the word as it has been developed over the word's life.

It is no wonder that the Romantic movement produced idiosyncratic and incoherent mythologies such as those of William Blake. Frequently these mythologies inverted God and Satan, finding the liberation of the spirit in the denial or reversal of both the Christian tradition and the rationality of the Enlightenment: for example, Blake's poems "Urizen," "Thel," and "The Four Zoas." Later, Carl Jung, Joseph Campbell, Carlos Castañeda, and others "felt that" such mythologies were validated on the grounds that they arise from deep, universal, human archetypal insights (Blake's "Marriage of Heaven and Hell," however, was a parody of Swedenborg). From the time of William Blake onward there was no limit to the diversity of views on heaven. As powerfully individualist as Blake was, he believed that experienced religion, like poetry and artworks, was a superior path to understanding:

Mock on, mock on, Voltaire, Rousseau;
Mock on, mock on; 'tis all in vain!
You throw the sand against the wind,
And the wind blows it back again.
And every sand becomes a gem
Reflected in the beams divine;
Blown back they blind the mocking eye,
But still in Israel's paths they shine.
The Atoms of Democritus
And Newton's Particles of Light
Are sands upon the Red Sea shore,
Where Israel's tents do shine so bright.[20]

Analysis was not a favorite approach to reality among the Romantics. Imagination was their high road to understanding, and Blake reserved some of his greatest emotion for a defense of imagination against mechanism. Søren Kierkegaard defended Christianity by recreating it as a personal intensity in his *Christian Discourses* (1850). Subjective experience, he believed, is prior to and superior to the objective. All consciousness was personal and subjective. Christianity was not to be intellectualized or institutionalized but lived out as the choice of the individual soul. One does not have truth; one lives it out in one's life.

Since Romantics valued feeling more than thinking, their effects upon heaven were most notable in poetry. William Wordsworth's "Intimations of Immortality" (1807) expressed our origins and destiny in God, pointing out that the practical knowledge that we gain in maturing tends to block us from deeper reality:

Not in entire forgetfulness,
And not in utter nakedness,
But trailing clouds of glory do we come
From God, who is our home:

Heaven lies about us in our infancy!
Shades of the prison-house begin to close
Upon the growing boy

Though inland far we be,
Our souls have sight of that immortal sea
Which brought us hither.[21]

Ralph Waldo Emerson wrote that "the blazing evidence of immortality is our dissatisfaction with any other solution." He also noted wryly in his journal: "Immortality. I notice that as soon as writers broach this question they begin to quote."[22] He was right, and here are more quotations: Elizabeth Barrett Browning said that "Earth's crammed with heaven, / And every common bush afire with God,"[23] and, according to Fyodor Dostoevsky, "if you were to destroy in mankind the belief in immortality, not only love but every living force maintaining the life of the world would at once be dried up."[24]

By such powerful emotional expressions of love, heaven was both strengthened and weakened: strengthened by the sense that heaven is literally innate in us, our beginning and our proper end; yet weakened by the increasing idiosyncrasies of feeling about it. Here are a few idiosyncrasies by way of illustration. Spiritualism and reincarnation, pantheism, and belief in ghosts took root and flourished, shading and stifling the older plants of Christian tradition. Spiritualists believed that the dead appeared to us when summoned (and sometimes, less agreeably, when uninvited). Mesmerists believed in a magnetic field that flowed around bodies and could be used to communicate with the dead; "somnabulists" believed that they could contact the dead in sleep. Séances in which the dead communicated with the living were popular among the educated elite such as Victor Hugo and Arthur Conan Doyle as well as among the less affluent. Hugo believed that the dead went to populate other planets after death, the virtuous to pleasant planets and the wicked to unpleasant ones. Novalis, Goethe, Charles Kingsley, and Emily Dickinson all believed that heaven was less a matter of saints than of lovers, and heaven would include intense experience of sexual love. Others emphasized happy families who would reunite in family gatherings among "homes, schools, pets, and suburbs" with good food, cookies, games, pianos, machines, and whatever else one finds useful or pleasing. Other than family interactions, one enjoyed the company of one's friends and made new ones.[25] Influenced by Eastern religions, by Swedenborg, and by Romantic ideas, these exotic blooms also drew from physicalism in unusual ways. If "truth" is entirely physical, as so many in the nineteenth century assumed, then our experiences of religion, of spirit, and of soul, must have physical bases: we must try to get "direct empirical evidence of an afterlife."[26] Eventually such studies metamorphosed into twentieth-century studies of near-death experiences, pre-death dreaming, extraterrestrials, ESP, and hallucinogenic reveries—all efforts to reconcile spiritual longings with physical science and thus sometimes confusing two proper and separate modes of thought.

Meanwhile the Christian tradition itself was fading. The rapid growth of liberalism, education, and secularism in the course of the century meant that more and more people felt entitled to question their clergy and were often disappointed in the results. The great astronomer Flammarion left the Catholic Church for spiritualism because he could find no Catholic who could explain to him "the location of Heaven, Hell, and Purgatory."[27] The church was also weakened by the belief in secular Progress, which among other things caused people to question the harshness of traditional teaching about hell and the legalisms of Catholicism with its catalogs of sins and penances sometimes humorously described as "laundry lists." The milder and more welcoming views of Saint Alphonsus Liguori mitigated the harshly rigorist Jansenism (the Catholic equivalent of Calvinism) by the 1820s to the 1840s; Liguori emphasized generosity and hope for the penitent. No amelioration of hell could match the Progressivism of the mesmerist and spiritualist Alphonse Cahagnet, who believed that on dying we immediately proceed to a spirit world in which we all shall be happy.[28]

Although the Roman Catholic First Vatican Council (1869–70) under Pope Pius IX affirmed the ancient doctrine of the resurrection of the body, the Jansenists had long been emphasizing the immortality of the soul as more credible. The increasing secularization of states (whether overt as in France or Germany or covert as in Britain and Scandinavia) removed education more and more from the churches, which had been for centuries almost the sole source of education. The ongoing struggle of secularism against Catholicism in France, for example, produced in the Third Republic a law against teaching God, heaven, or any related Christian doctrines in primary education (1882).[29]

A very large number of books were published on heaven in the mid-nineteenth century. A frequent theme of nineteenth-century views was marital and domestic bliss, a view promoted by Queen Victoria's personal chaplain, the well-known writer Charles Kingsley, and by the famous evangelists Dwight Moody and David Sankey.[30] Presbyterian sermons announced that heaven is where we meet our friends and family and enjoy their company together. Heaven, after nearly two millennia of fairly stern theology, had at last become the saccharine pie in the sky that modern skeptics so easily ridicule, a location from which (as the novelist Sharan Newman described it to me) your deceased relatives can spy on you.

Colleen McDannell and Bernhard Lang were deceived that the general trend of thought about heaven in this period was toward communalism. Rather, it was toward individual gratification, a sort of romantic sentimentalism. Classical Christian views were much more communitarian. McDannell and Lang misunderstood the traditional doctrine of the Beatific Vision, regarding it as individualistic, whereas the Christian view is that a person enjoying such a Vision does so *in the loving community of God and all the blessed.*[31]

Progress and dynamism in the other world was an ancient theme, though it was certainly encouraged by the Progressivist trends of the nineteenth century. McDannell and Lang are right that the idea of working hard in heaven seems to be a creation of the famous "Protestant Ethic" of the century. It was thought that leisure corrupts, that adoration of God is indolence, and that we cannot be happy in heaven unless we continue to do good works in the service of others, even of those already in heaven.[32] By striving, we move ahead in heaven, just as for secular Progressives we strive to move ahead in this life.

Views of heaven, whether traditional, sentimental, or intellectual, would all be challenged by the most important trend of the later nineteenth century, physicalist evolution. By the time Ernest Renan's work *The Future of Science* appeared in 1892, he could well believe that the battle against heaven had been won. As Edward Fitzgerald wrote:

> Some for the Glories of This World; and some
> Sigh for the Prophet's Paradise to come;
> Ah, take the Cash, and let the Credit go,
> Nor heed the rumble of a distant Drum![33]

CHAPTER 5

Back

I n the Christian tradition, we can look back to the perfection that was Paradise and forward to the even greater perfection that is heaven. In the nineteenth century, as evolutionary ideas developed, "back" looked less like the
Garden of Eden and more like the jungle. Evolution eclipsed heaven more
than Copernicus had done. Spreading across the intellectual landscape in the
mid-nineteenth century was the idea that time was vast enough for current
biological phenomena to exist without divine creation. Nothing in this idea
made God impossible or even unlikely, but the vastness of time meant that it
was no longer necessary to assume a Designer in order to explain how the
universe could be orderly. Theists then tended to shift their argument from
the positive necessity of God's existence to the defense that the evidence is
compatible with God's existence.

Paradise had always been a state of being to which one could hark *back*,
regain, as well as look forward to. Heaven was a return to the harmony and
happiness enjoyed by humans before original sin. But the growing strength of
ideas of Progress, while traditional religion gradually faded, meant the slow
eclipse of the sense that we could return to that primeval joy.[1] More concretely,
the origins of humanity seemed to lie not in the special divine creation of the
first humans but rather in a seamless fabric of evolutionary development all
the way from prokaryotes to Planck.

It is legendary that Charles Darwin was the fount and origin of this change.
But Darwin, the greatest scientist of the nineteenth century, was shaped by his
time as well as shaping it himself. His ideas arose from those of previous natural scientists and even more—which is sometimes forgotten—from those of
social theorists. The "development hypothesis" predated Darwin by a century.

The common term "Social Darwinism" is misleading, as it implies that theories of social Progressivism arose from Darwin. Rather, it was the other way around; "Darwinist" principles were enunciated before Darwin. They include the following: "human natures and institutions had developed through successive stages from brutish beginnings"; "the historical process was subject to laws of development"; "social evolution was a continuation of biological evolution"; "competition and natural selection [were] responsible for Progress."[2] Soon, of course, biological and social evolutionary views borrowed from one another. But evolution did not necessarily entail Progress toward a goal or even "ascending levels of general complexity."[3] Indeed, Darwin himself usually eschewed either claim, but the times were such that his ideas were readily mingled with Progressive assumptions. Only in the twentieth century did the idea that evolution had no direction at all come to dominate.

In nineteenth-century thought, heaven was not so much rejected as ignored. The most influential social theorist of the nineteenth century was Herbert Spencer, the author of *Social Statics* (1850) and "Progress: Its Law and Cause" (1857). Spencer argued for what he called "the development hypothesis" well before Darwin and Alfred Russel Wallace's breakthrough in biology in 1858–60. Spencer, who invented the phrase "survival of the fittest" and published it for the first time in 1864, was one of the founders of "social science."[4] By 1857, Spencer was already arguing for the unification of developmental principles in geology, astronomy, linguistics, and social theory according to the idea of Progress. Although biological evolutionism and political or societal progressivism had no logical connection between them, they both flowed from the fount of eighteenth-century Progressivism.[5] Spencer denied supernatural explanation for anything, gradually in his own life exchanging belief in God for belief in a "remote unknowable" and eventually for atheism.[6] Spencer's rather utilitarian view was that the standard of morality should be the liberty of each individual limited only by the liberty of all. Societies evolved through organic evolution according to material, mechanical laws, and the principal mechanism for this Progress was competition—competition among individuals, states, nations, and societies. Along with antisupernaturalism, competitive nationalism and racism were also emphasized by Malthus, whose ideas had deep influence on Darwin. Unlike Spencer, Malthus did not assume that the results would be beneficent. Spencer tied together the strands of mid-nineteenth-century thought and may have been—measuring by the breadth of his audience—the most influential thinker of his time. His emphasis on competition was implicitly a denial of the Christian virtues commended in the idea of heaven. Not love, but competition, made the world go round.

Spencer argued forcefully and effectively for the abolition of metaphysics and the study of societies by natural science, yet he unwittingly espoused the metaphysics of Progress. Rather than our being moved toward an end or goal by a metaphysical principle called God, we are moved by a metaphysical principle called Progress. Progress, Spencer announced, "is not an accident, not a thing within human control, but a beneficent necessity," a continuous advance whose chart might be graphed with temporary ups and downs but always tending to the higher.[7] Civilization will grow like "the development of the embryo or the unfolding of a flower."[8] Competition fuels Progress, and Progress will never end until humanity reaches its greatest happiness and perfection: all we have to do is to remove the obstacles to Progress, such as religion. This view provided agendas for Lenin, Stalin, Hitler, and Mao as well as for racism, capitalism, and imperialism. It now seems more difficult, given the past hundred years, to judge that happiness and perfection on this planet are drawing any nearer.

The underlying question is how or why (absent any cosmic purpose) Progress would exist at all, or why humankind should be its beneficiary. It might, after all, really be best if the entire human race were destroyed in order to make room for a more "advanced" genus or at least in order to restore ecological balance to the planet. When Darwin's theories became public, Spencer eagerly supported them, replacing "Progress" in his vocabulary with "evolution." Though geneticists have now discovered "genes for cooperation" that may ultimately benefit a species more than "genes for competition," those facts were in the future. Spencer saw in biological evolutionism a demonstration of his own theory that competition elevates "civilized" Europeans above "primitive," "mentally undeveloped," and "savage" races such as (so he perceived them) Africans.[9] Just as biological evolution weeds out the unfit, so society will automatically weed out those "of lowest development . . . the ignorant, the improvident, and the lazy," whether individuals, nations, or races. The great American botanist Asa Gray considered "the Negro and the Hottentot" "backward" peoples.[10]

Racist theories were new, and they were rooted in Progressivism. All too true, there had been many Christians and others who thought and acted in racist and anti-Semitic ways, and some unenlightened Christians argued for centuries as to whether Africans or American Indians had souls, but there were no Christian *theories* of racism, no *theories* of racism in the West, before the nineteenth century. Spencer's racist ideas sprang from Enlightenment Progressive thought. Progress would eventually result in the elimination of "inferior" races and individuals in favor of a "superior" race of individuals who would optimize liberty, freedom, and knowledge. That was a formula for a materialist, racist millennium. In his later thinking, Spencer became more skeptical, fearing that his hope for improvement might not be realized and that warring power groups might demand the creation of "rights" that could readily deteriorate into claims of privilege. By the 1890s, T. H. Huxley, Darwin's most

vocal supporter, himself came to doubt that evolutionary change was necessarily for the better; indeed, he observed that it might produce degenerate and
vicious races and societies.

It is a curious aspect of late eighteenth-century and nineteenth-century
Progressivism that at one and the same time it promoted a sense of superiority over non-European peoples *and* a growing sense that Westerners had much
to learn from non-Europeans esthetically and especially in terms of myth. The
love of non-Western myth inspired Sir James Frazer's influential *The Golden
Bough* (1890) and, later, Carl Jung, T. S. Eliot, Joseph Campbell, and many
others. But Spencer, Huxley, and their colleagues deplored the religions of
their own culture and saw in the religions of other cultures only more faiths
to deplore. Their more pessimistic reflections on the future only confirmed
their atheism, as they recognized no benevolent plan in either God or Nature. A benevolent Mother Nature seemed no more in evidence than a benevolent God.

Indeed, it seemed to many people toward the end of the nineteenth century
that advances in medical science, political egalitarianism, and liberal law meant
that more degenerates were being preserved from natural selection and that
deliberate human intervention through eugenics—engineered selection—was
necessary to enable Progress to continue. The term "eugenics," meaning human intervention to improve the human race, is first attested in 1883. (Eugenics, having lost its savor after Nazism, is again being promoted by evolutionary
engineers under other terms.) Eugenicists called for conscious intervention by
human agents in order to achieve better, superior creatures, especially to balance what they regarded as the degradation of the race by the heedless efforts
in medicine to preserve and prolong all human life, even the mentally, morally, or physically handicapped. It would be better, they thought, to select those
persons who are most desirable to propagate the species. Who determines what
is desirable and who is unfit to live is an unanswered moral and legal question,
but the historical evidence suggests that such decisions are usually made not
by dispassionate reason but by those who wield power in a given society, as did
Stalin, Hitler, and Pol Pot, all of whom made very clear decisions about who
was unfit.[11] Hitler began by eliminating persons with disabilities and then wid-
ened the scope to Jews and Slavs. The eugenicists argued that because human
medical and social policies have artificially enabled the unfit to survive and
propagate, humans must now artificially correct this imbalance.

The leader of the eugenics movement was Francis Galton, who was influenced by his cousin Charles Darwin. Darwin personally did not like his own
minutely supported biological theories to be slapped onto social agendas, but
the eugenicists generally based their arguments on what they took to be Darwinian principles. The mid-nineteenth century was the first time that philosophical arguments appeared for eugenic abortion, infanticide, euthanasia, and

compulsory sterilization, as well as for prohibitions against "miscegenation" (interracial marriage) and cousin-marriage. Laws along these lines were enacted in the United States from the 1880s to the 1920s, and some even remain on the books.[12]

Ernst Haeckel, a distinguished zoologist, was the most influential eugenicist in Germany. His ideas are painful. In line with the eighteenth- and nineteenth-century belief that physically measurable quantities were more real than qualitative characteristics such as "humanity," Haeckel argued that there was no *qualitative* difference between animals and humans. In his view, only a spectrum of quantitative differences of races descending from the most "advanced" human (a classical Caucasian) down through what he considered the lower human races through Africans to the primates and then through lesser mammals and on down. Here is the once-popular idea of "the missing link," which dates from 1859 at the latest. "The missing link" halfway between humans and other great apes, it was claimed, would eventually be found by paleontologists. Haeckel sometimes actually argued for four different genera of humans. There are many paintings from the nineteenth century of the "the four races of man," usually European, Asian, African, and "Indian."

Such widely admired writers as Havelock Ellis and Clarence Darrow advocated infanticide for eugenic purposes: killing the unfit is not murder but a benefit to society, relieving it of burdens. You help people by killing them. (It's less expensive than keeping them alive.) Death is good when it encourages natural deselection of the unfit; the death of the vanquished is a good thing. Even the death of otherwise fit men on the battlefield can be good, because it contributes to the advancement of the race (an argument that became less attractive after the slaughters of World War I).

It is a "speciesist illusion" to imagine that humans are qualitatively different from animals. For example, your mother is worth as much as her dog, which is worth as much as its flea. Ironically, the Catholic Church, often condemned for its pro-life views on abortion, was much praised by liberals in the past century for its pro-life resistance to sterilization and other programs of eugenics.[13] On the other hand, many Liberal Christians supported eugenics, for example Kenneth C. Macarthur, "pastor of the Federated Church in Sterling Massachusetts, lecturer at Andover Newton Seminary, advocate for the Social Gospel, and spokesman for the American Eugenics Society," who argued that "decent Christians have a responsibility to use 'every help which science affords' to prevent the 'feeble minded and wrong-willed' from 'pouring their corrupt currents into the race stream.'"[14]

The word "evolution" provokes a variety of responses, though most educated people will say that they believe in it without being quite sure what they mean. Most people equate "evolution" with "Darwinism," although other evolutionary theories continue to exist, and Darwin himself "did not use the term 'evolution' in the modern sense until the last edition of the *Origin* published in his lifetime," before which he preferred "descent with modification."[15]

In the history of language and of ideas, the appearance of any new concept is quickly followed by the invention of a word or phrase to denote it. Conversely, if a word is not yet developed, that indicates that the concept was not yet there to be formulated. "Physics" as knowledge of matter and energy appears in 1715 (but "physicist" not before 1840); "science" as the study of physical phenomena (1725, but "scientist" not before 1833); "geology" (1735), and "geologist" (1795); "biology" (1800), and "biologist" in its specific sense (1874); "paleontology" (1838); "evolution" in the geological and biological senses (1832). In addition to these relatively precise terms, words and phrases such as "fit" and "fittest," "adapt" and "adaptation," "uniformity," "advanced," "primitive," "descent," "higher and lower," "superior and inferior," and "favored," developed a range of new connotations.

I distinguish between the scientific theory of evolution ("evolution science") on the one hand and two metaphysical theories on the other. The metaphysical theories are "theo-evolution," which maintains that evolution is guided and intelligently designed by God, and "physicalist evolution," which maintains that the process is entirely without any cosmic purpose or design. The implications for heaven are immense, for "physicalist evolution" makes heaven nothing but a superstitious social construct that is either worthless or actually harmful to Progress. Because the metaphysics of physicalist evolution by the 1880s infused itself throughout scientific institutions, it became easy to confuse that metaphysics with science itself.

The pioneers of geological and biological evolution science were Buffon, James Hutton, Jean-Baptiste Lamarck, Charles Lyell, and Darwin's contemporaries Alfred Russel Wallace and T. H. Huxley. Lyell's *Geological Evidence of the Antiquity of Man* (1863) argued persuasively for the vastness of the geological time scale and the geological principle of Uniformitarianism. Lyell presented evidence for the existence of *Homo sapiens* thousands of years earlier than the traditional dates of creation and invented the term "missing links," even though he was not a biologist.[16] It is presently believed that hominids may go back more than six million years, and the genus *Homo* may be something like two million years old, since *Homo erectus* is likely to be our ancestor. Anthropologists differ as to when *Homo sapiens* emerged, but it seems to have been roughly a hundred thousand years ago. Wallace was a biologist, and he developed similar evolutionary ideas at the same time as Darwin, though he always generously and correctly admitted that Darwin had compiled vastly more evidence in support of their views, which came together in 1858 owing to some deft footwork in the community of biologists. That their idea "evolved" nearly simultaneously was not coincidental, for it attested to the width and strength of then-current general ideas of Progress.

Wallace was an astute observer of the specimens he collected in what is now Indonesia. He discovered the "Wallace Line" (the discontinuity between fossil types between Sulawesi and New Guinea, the reason for which—plate tectonics—was not clear before the 1960s). Wallace began with the basic observation that within a species, the fittest plants and animals tend to survive and pass on their heredity to their descendants.

Over time, as had long been known, animals such as cattle and dogs can be bred to certain specifications, producing superior individual animals and thus presumably bringing about "improvement of the race." Then Wallace moved from improvement of race to improvement of species and then to the origin of new species. He believed that given enough time and enough breeding (whether natural or artificial), a species could develop into a new species without any divine creation or intervention. This theory, Wallace was confident, would be borne out by the biological and geological evidence. Nature would reveal a "universal process of selection from lower to higher animals,"[17] a process driven by the competition for survival and for reproduction, and developing gradually and incrementally through time. Other scientists' discovery of differing species in isolated locales such as Australia and the Galapagos seemed to offer Wallace the evidence that he needed. Wallace used the terms "higher" and "lower" to indicate that more complex creatures develop from less complex creatures, and thus from less good to "better" creatures, an idea wholly compatible with that of Spencer. Unlike Darwin and Huxley, but like Lyell, Wallace refused to extend evolutionary principles to the origins of humanity, which he viewed as unique.

Though no nineteenth-century evolutionists believed in the Great Chain of Being (or any such ontological scale), its influence through the millennia remained the backdrop, encouraging a tendency to think in terms of "higher and lower" and of "better and less good" and thus turn the great chain on its side and make it chronological—while lopping off God, heaven, and the angels.[18] In 1844, a sketchy but immensely popular book, *Vestiges of Creation*, published anonymously by Robert Chambers, did much to prepare the public for Darwin's ideas, which were immeasurably more sophisticated and better documented than Chambers's.

The man on whom evolutionary ideas centered was, of course, Charles Darwin. By 1837 Darwin adopted the idea that species could evolve into different species, and by 1838 he also believed that the human species itself evolved from lower species. He linked Lamarck's idea of biological transmutation with Lyell's idea of geological transformation while eventually differing markedly from both. In 1838, having read and admired Malthus's *Essay on Population* (1798), Darwin was ready to believe that the mechanism for biological evolution was struggle for existence. Natural selection (Darwin repeatedly said that the phrase was not meant to imply the existence of any active selector) meant the survival, extinction, and modification of species through meaningless chance, competition, and struggle without any guiding principle or cosmic purpose.[19] How the mechanism of natural selection would operate was at the time unclear to everyone, including Darwin and Wallace. But eventually Gregor Mendel's discovery of genes provided the answer. (Mendel discovered genetics in 1860, although the importance of his discovery was not recognized before about 1920).

Darwin was working on his theory of speciation through the 1840s; in 1851 he met T. H. Huxley, who after accepting evolution science by 1858 became the strongest promoter of physicalist evolution through the rest of the century.[20] In 1858, by the time Darwin received Wallace's famous letter and essay suggesting material causes for speciation, Darwin had already in 1856 begun work on *The Origin of Species*. On July 1, 1858, Darwin's and Wallace's papers on evolution science were read together at the Linnaean Society under the title "On the Tendency of Species to Form Varieties; and on the Perpetration of Varieties and Species by Natural Means of Selection."[21]

The next year, 1859, Darwin's celebrated book appeared under the full title *On the Origin of Species by Means of Natural Selection, or the Preservation of Favored Races in the Struggle for Life*. Each species had earlier been believed to be created to fill a specific niche in nature, and its particular niche was fixed. Although adaptations or variations might occur within species (for example different breeds of dogs or cattle), the boundaries of species themselves were supposed to be clear in that individuals of different species could not produce offspring. The production of new species was therefore held to be impossible. Darwin thought on the contrary that variations over time would produce new species. One of Darwin's most important innovations in biology, which spread to other sciences and social sciences, was the idea that species had fluid boundaries. A species, rather than being a fixed Aristotelian entity, was simply defined as any group of beings who during a particular period of time could mate fruitfully.

By the time the famous meeting of the British Association for the Advancement of Science took place on June 28, 1860, evolution science was already celebrated. Physicalist evolution had also begun to spread and to generate opposition, and at the meeting Huxley had his famous (and later overdramatized) exchange with Bishop Wilberforce, during which Wilberforce reportedly asked Huxley whether he preferred to be descended from an ape on his grandfather's side or his grandmother's side. In 1871, Darwin published his *The Descent of Man and Selection in Relation to Sex*. Sexual selection became a necessary factor when Darwin denied Lamarck's theory that individuals could acquire biological characteristics during their lifetime. If Lamarck was wrong, that left only sexual selection as a means of change in a species.

Heated controversies about evolution have been raging since 1860, but although propagandists insisted that the problem was a war between science and theology, the roots of the matter are metaphysical. *Evolution science* itself is no problem for heaven, but *physicalist evolution* and heaven are obviously incompatible. The incompatibility is between the two opposing principles (1) the cosmos has an overall purpose and (2) the cosmos has no overall purpose. The problem is that evolution science and physicalist evolution were often fused, as if biology demonstrated physical metaphysics, and the confusion persists at almost all levels of thought, education, politics, and even law.

After a number of personal tragedies, especially the painful death of his young daughter Anna, Darwin became disillusioned with Christianity. In the first edition of *The Origin of Species*, he still mentioned the Creator, but by the sixth edition in 1872 all such references were dropped. It was the problem of evil, of suffering, that turned Darwin toward atheism: "There seems to me too much misery in the world. I cannot persuade myself that a beneficent and omnipotent God would have designedly created the Ichneumonidae with the express intention of their feeding within the living bodies of Caterpillars."[22] "Natural selection" became "natural"—physical—alone, without any room for intelligent design. The natural world had "no moral validity or purpose."[23] When thinking that way, Darwin slipped from evolution science into physicalist evolution.

Darwin occasionally mentioned his religious views in his voluminous correspondence, although both biologists and theologians considered them of tiny importance compared with the intellectual and social movements attached to his biological theory. Darwin gradually became an atheist, though he wrote that "Agnostic [a term invented by Darwin's follower T. H. Huxley] would be the more correct description of my state of mind" on the slightly disingenuous grounds that he was unqualified to make metaphysical statements. He rejected Christianity completely and could see no argument that pointed toward any sort of theism. "Science has nothing to do with Christ. . . . I do not believe that there ever has been any revelation. I had gradually come by this time [1836–38], to see that the Old Testament was no more to be trusted than the sacred books of the Hindoos. . . . The clearest evidence would be requisite to make any sane man believe in the miracles by which Christianity is supported [a statement derived from his reading of Hume late in his life] . . . I gradually came to disbelieve in Christianity as a divine revelation." On the subject of evil, Darwin was still inclined to believe that there is more overall happiness than pain in the world, but on the idea that natural laws imply purpose he declared "I cannot see" that.[24]

Christianity assumes the equality of souls in heaven, so that a person's sex, race, and intellectual or mechanical skills are irrelevant. Darwin was at different times of different minds on the questions of race. Sometimes he denied racial superiority, but at other times he wrote that "I look at this process as now going on with the races of man, the less intellectual races being exterminated,"[25] and "that 'the lower races' would soon be eliminated by 'higher civilized races' throughout the world."[26] The process of natural selection would lead "to the inevitable extinction of all those low and mentally undeveloped populations with which Europeans come in contact."[27] On the subject of eugenics, he observed that "We civilized men . . . do our utmost to check the process of elimination; we build asylums for the imbecile, the maimed, and the sick; we institute poor-laws; and our medical men exert their utmost skill to save the life of every one to the last moment. . . . Thus the weak members of civilized societies propagate their kind. . . . This must be highly injurious to the race of man. . . . Excepting in the case of man himself, hardly any one is so ignorant as to allow his worst animals to breed."[28]

Darwin and Huxley both came to realize that lack of paleontological evidence and the existence of vestigial organs posed problems for evolution science. A century and a half after the publication of *The Origin of Species*, it is still unclear how species originate, a fact that is hardly a disproof of Darwinism but could properly be a curb on physicalist dogmatism.[29] Darwin himself was no dogmatist.

"Darwinism" can be defined in quite different ways. "Darwinism" (or "Neo-Darwinism") is used by biologists to refer to evolution science, the theory that species of plants and animals develop through natural selection. This natural selection favors, through algorithmic genetic processes, variations that increase the organism's ability to survive and reproduce. In this sense it is a "process that results in the adaptation of an organism to its environment by means of selectively reproducing changes in its genotype, or genetic constitution."[30] Adding the phrase "by entirely physical means" to the above definition radically transforms the idea from evolution science to physicalist evolution, which (to repeat) is a metaphysical rather than scientific view. When used in that way, "Darwinism" is shorthand for physicalist evolution. "Darwinism" can also be defined quite differently, as a *historical movement* beginning around 1860.[31] For historians, it denotes the development of a physicalist mode of thought centered on biological physicalism but spreading far beyond.[32] The historical definition has the advantage of not reading back into Darwin's own mind what later developed from his views and enables understanding Darwinism as a varied cultural development through time with vast effects on religion, science, politics, education, ethics, and philosophy. This is the way "Darwinism" is generally used in the rest of this book.

Historically, Darwinism implied that the origin, development, and extinction of species are a natural process having no supernatural cause or purpose. There was no place for the Special Creation of humankind or for humankind's place in heaven.[33] Humans, rather than being the product of any divine intent, descended from primitive animals that descended in turn from more primitive animals, back to the beginning of life. The term "descent" was taken from genealogy, in which one is called a "descendant" of one's grandparents. "Lower," "higher," "advanced," and "primitive" were terms often ambiguously employed by Darwinists, who frequently meant by "lower" merely "earlier" or "less complex" and by "higher" merely later or more complex.

Although development goes usually from the less complex to the more complex, Darwinists were ambiguous as to whether more complex meant "better," even in the sense of "better able to adapt," let alone "better" ontologically or morally. Evolution science is morally neutral, but Darwin lived at a time when Progressive metaphysics was intellectually dominant, so that it was almost unavoidable for him to consider "the action of natural selection on the physical, mental, and moral capacity of individuals, tribes, nations, and races."[34] He sometimes agreed with Wallace that so-called higher, refined races were better than so-called lower, brutal ones.[35] *The Descent of Man* declared that European civilization was better than that of "primitive, semi-civilized, barbarous, and savage nations." Compare, Darwin wrote, the beauty of Greek artistic representations of Jupiter and Apollo with "the hideous bas-reliefs on the ruined buildings of Central America." "There can hardly be a doubt that we are descended from barbarians." It was unclear then, as it still remains unclear now, what "race" is. The difference between races, Darwin wrote, is not quite enough to consider "the Negro and European . . . as true and good species"; rather, he thought, they were subspecies. Biologically, "man [has risen] to the very summit of the organic scale [giving humanity] "hope for a still higher destiny in the distant future"; some individuals and societies are "inferior" and some "superior."[36]

"Believing as I do that man in the distant future will be a far more perfect creature than he now is,"—a belief inconsistent with his scientific views—Darwin went on to assure us in a letter of 1881: "Remember what risk the nations of Europe ran, not so many centuries ago, of being overwhelmed by the Turks, and how ridiculous such an idea now is! The more civilized so-called Caucasian races have beaten the Turkish hollow in the struggle for existence."[37]

Curiously from his physicalist point of view, Darwin claimed that belief in the soul was a sign of superior societies; "the barbarous races of man . . . possess no clear belief of this kind. The idea of a universal and benevolent Creator does not seem to arise in the mind of man, until he has been elevated by long-continued culture."[38] Darwin's kind words for the immortality of the soul are to be taken as a social observation rather than an expression of personal belief, for Darwin had lost any belief in heaven himself.

Physicalist evolution's most determined proponent was T. H. Huxley, "Darwin's bulldog," for whom "Natural Selection took the place of divine Providence."[39] Huxley defended Darwin's views at the famous meeting of 1860 and explained them fully in his own book *Man's Place in Nature* (1863). Huxley, who coined the word "agnostic" in 1869 or 1870, argued that humans are machines with the illusion of consciousness. It is curious that physicalists were so taken with the idea of animals and humans as machines, given the fact that machines themselves are the product of purposeful intention and design.

By the 1870s, evolution science was widely accepted by educated people in Austria, Britain, Germany, and the United States. By the end of the 1880s, thanks in large part to Huxley, it dominated biological thought so much as to squeeze away other ideas, which were branded as "unscientific."[40] For example, "Intelligent Design Theory" is currently declared "unscientific" on the grounds that no article supporting it is published in a scientific journal—and no article supporting it is published in a scientific journal for the reason that it is "unscientific." We may be permitted to wonder if this is a roundabout without an exit. Evolution science has been the basis of innumerable and enormous scientific achievements, but the insistence of Huxley and others upon *physicalist* evolution ensured at least a century and a half of dispute.[41] Most people brandished weapons in the dispute with only blurry ideas of what it was about.

By the 1880s Darwinism had taken on the metaphysical as well as the scientific senses. Huxley and his fellows rejected God and any cosmic purpose. Rejecting two-and-a-half millennia of natural law, they believed that morality was founded on biologically-developed intuitions and could vary among societies.[42] They believed that physicalist evolution has no goal or "directional tendency." Huxley rejected every sort of teleology (the belief that we are moving toward a goal), and he specifically and indignantly dismissed Comte's "Positive Philosophy."[43] For Huxley, "life is progressive realization of its inherent potentialities . . . Progress . . . is the way which leads to ever-fresh realizations of new possibilities for living substance."[44] But as clear as they tried to be in affirming lack of tendency, they could not avoid being caught up in the Progressivist metaphysics of their time. "Few Victorian thinkers of any persuasion could tolerate the idea of evolution as anything but an essential Progressive system: evolution *had* to have a purpose in which the emergence of man played a key role."[45] Following several decades of confusion in the early decades of the last century, the "Neodarwininan Synthesis" or "Modern Synthesis" was established in the 1950s by Ernst Mayr and his colleagues.

What physicalist evolutionists had in mind about Progress were the eighteenth-century assumptions that we are advancing to greater liberty and understanding and justice—none of which are in fact in any way implied by evolution science. Huxley later changed his point of view, asserting that Progress could be achieved only through a human struggle to master nature rather than by going with the flow.[46] Thus there were two schools of Progressive evolutionary thinking: one claiming the biological inevitability of "Progress," the other, more sophisticated, claiming that humans can and must use rationality to press evolution into moral "Progress." Despite the pressures of Victorian Progressive ideas, a markedly different school (including Darwin himself) resisted the assumption of any future betterment for humanity at all. In a climate where such ideas were in play, heaven could only be dismissed as rank superstition.

The profound antitheism of the physicalist evolutionists created something that had not existed before, the corrosive idea of an age-old warfare between science and religion. Advancing into a battle that they had provoked, such writers as John W. Draper, William Whewell, and Andrew Dickson White laid about with their broadswords against religion as enemy of humanity and in so doing fixed some falsehoods in the public mind.[47] On the other hand, agnosticism seldom sprang directly from evolution science or indeed any scientific discoveries. In her study of nineteenth-century scientists who turned agnostic, Susan Budd found only two who abandoned Christianity on account of evolution.[48] Most agnostics, like Darwin himself, moved away from Christianity because of personal problems that challenged their belief in a good and omnipotent Deity. This is particularly understandable in the context where the core Christian belief in the saving suffering of Christ was fading in the churches themselves.

Of external intellectual promptings to atheism, another of the most influential was "higher criticism" of the Bible, which undermined traditional views of the authorship of the Bible, its accuracy as a scientific document, and its account of miracles. The narrower the religious upbringing, the stronger the reaction against it and the firmer the later agnosticism. Later, some people raised in dogmatically atheist families would open their minds in the opposite direction. Of course, few people other than clergy, scientists, professors, and other intellectuals took part in these private or public agonies, but doubts about the authority of the Bible trickled down and by the middle of the twentieth century had formed a vast water table. Physicalism often served as an alternative source of assurance about the future in that we had nothing to worry about after death.

The care that Huxley and his fellows took to deny the existence of design in the cosmos evoked three main reactions on the part of thoughtful Christians. In the short period between 1858 and 1871, a revolution occurred in Western thought. Though evolution science has nothing to say about God and heaven, physicalist evolution challenged all the tenets of traditional Christianity, including heaven, the creation of the cosmos by God, the creation of fixed species (an Aristotelian as well as a biblical view), the Special Creation of humankind, the Incarnation, the Resurrection, miracles, revelation, and above all the idea that the universe has purpose and that God cares about humans.

This comprehensive challenge was entailed in the view promoted by Spencer and Huxley. By 1900, which happens to be the year of Nietzsche's death, heaven had been eclipsed.

Religion and natural philosophy had cooperated for centuries. Many nineteenth- and twentieth-century thinkers, however, desired to see them as antithetical and as a zero-sum game where any gain of the one is a loss to the other. The proper methods of science include observing accurately, inferring, predicting, classifying, developing questions and hypotheses, and conducting controlled experiments. The success of such methods in understanding the physical cosmos is one of the great human achievements. In contrast, their success in understanding societies is open to doubt. A great historical irony is that both physicalist evolution and its religious opponents equally base their positions in faith, and physicalist evolution is an ideology as much as Christianity or Marxism.[49] A lucid, valid explanation of the relationship between science and religion was issued in 1985 by the U.S. National Academy of Sciences:

> At the root of the apparent conflict between some religions and evolution is a misunderstanding of the critical difference between religious and scientific ways of knowing. Religions and science answer different questions about the world. Whether there is a purpose to the universe or a purpose for human existence are not questions for science. Religious and scientific ways of knowing have played, and will continue to play, significant roles in human history.[50]

The current heated insistence of physicalist evolutionists that their position is scientific rather than metaphysical may be an understandable result of their dismay that after a century and a half, in America at least, only about 10 percent of the population accepted physicalist evolution.[51] Both the physical evolutionists and the Christian rejectionists cleaved to dogmatic views, encouraging the myth of an age-old conflict between science and religion. One source of muddle was the attitude of dogmatists on both sides to the Bible, since both wanted to read it in the overt sense: some claimed that it is "true," others that it is "not true," with little sense on either side of the varieties in the meanings of "truth."[52] Charles Harper of the Templeton Foundation has called the diametrically opposed dogmatic positions of physicalists and hyperliteralists photographic negatives/positives of one another. Right-minded people are of course always against wrong-minded people, whoever we think is which.

Physicalist evolution is a religion, as sophisticated students of religion such as Raimundo Panikkar, a Roman Catholic scholar of Hinduism and Buddhism as well as of Christianity, and Ninian Smart, a pioneer of religious studies, argued, and it is a kind of religion that narrows down rather than opening up. For heaven, the main issue was whether the cosmos is created with divine purpose or whether it arises by accident with no Purpose at all. Secondary points were whether revelation had occurred, whether humankind was created specially by God, whether humans have immortal souls as opposed to the mortal souls of animals (which Wallace came to believe, to Darwin's disgust), and whether miracles occur. Evolution science can have no response to these questions, and whether the cosmos has Purpose is not a scientific question. But physicalist evolution certainly had its answers, and it had no place for heaven other than in a zoo of useless superstitions.

Not only species were in question but life itself. By 1940 it was suggested that all life began with "a process of chemical evolution through levels of increasingly complex organization."[53] No creation of the species, no special creation of humanity, no special creation of life, no creation at all, in fact, only the blind and pointless groping of chemicals that happened by chance to produce life. When one looks "back" with the mind's eye, one sees only a swirl of particles rather than the splendor of Paradise.

Christians had a number of options: they could abandon their religion and embrace physicalist evolution. They could reject evolution science as well as physicalist evolution, a disastrous strategy. They could argue for the "God of the gaps," the belief that God is active wherever science lacks an answer, another vulnerable strategy. They could embrace evolution, as many had embraced Progress, and argue for theo-evolution, divinely guided evolutionary process. Christian responses to evolution were numerous and diverse. Among these were the following: God sets up all creation just as it is now without development of species and with Special Creation of humankind; or God is a remote and passionless prime mover; or God knows all time and space in eternity but works with evolution—development through time; or God intends species to begin and to end; or God intervenes to create new species; or God is constantly involved in creating every moment; or God himself develops along with the cosmos. At first the idea of the *extinction* of species bothered many Christians more than the origin of species, for it seemed outrageous that God should exterminate a species once he had created it; but on some reflection it was seen that extinction was compatible with the biblical view, where God both creates the world and brings it to an end. Further, the personal extinction of you and me has always seemed more important to you and me than the eventual extinction of species. But it certainly extended the seventeenth-century problem of animal souls as well. If animals have souls, do the individual animals of each species have souls, or do species themselves have souls? If so, what happens when species develop? What could the soul of a trilobite be? It seemed more simply consistent to believe with Wallace that human beings are created with souls distinct from, though related to, the other animals.

The chief problem, once again, was evil. Christians, Jews, Muslims, and all monotheists have always had a difficult time with theodicy, the effort to reconcile the goodness of God with his absolute power.[54] The question that moved the physicalists much more deeply than any scientific evidence is whether the nature of the observed cosmos is compatible with *a benevolent purpose.* It can cogently be argued that it is not, but the Christian response is that God suffers every pain and suffering with us in the Passion of Christ.

Some Christians refused to accept evolution science at all, partly because they feared (not without grounds) that evolution science was prone to morphing into physicalist evolution. But many thoughtful Christians readily adopted evolution science, including Adam Sedgwick, Charles Kingsley, Asa Gray, Cardinal John Henry Newman, Robert Baden-Powell, and the entire Jesuit Order. The official attitude of the Catholic Church was ambiguous. The *Syllabus of Errors* issued by Pope Pius IX in 1864 and confirmed by the First Vatican Council in 1870 condemned pantheism, "rationalism," and socialism, and it declared false the proposition that the pope ought to reconcile himself to "Progress, liberalism, and modern civilization." Yet it did not condemn evolution in any form.[55] The main (and understandable) fear of the conservative pope and his council was "higher criticism" of the Bible. The otherwise very strict pronouncement of a later pope, Pius XII, *Humani generis* (1950), declared that evolution was an open question to be seriously explored, and neither *The Origin of Species* nor *The Descent of Man* ever appeared on the Vatican's lengthy *Index* of books prohibited as being harmful to the faith. On the other hand, books by Catholic writers supporting evolution sometimes did.[56] In 1996, John Paul II accepted theo-evolution, including the evolution of human beings from previous species, so long as the special creation of the human soul was retained. Benedict XVI observed that "we are not some casual and meaningless product of evolution. Each of us is the result of a thought of God. Each of us is willed, each of us is loved, each of us is necessary."[57] Meanwhile, many Protestants and Catholics continued to affirm the resurrection of the body, a theological doctrine to which the origin of species is almost irrelevant:

> Man's spirit will be flesh-bound when found at best,
> But uncumbered: meadow-down is not distressed
> For a rainbow footing it nor he for his bones risen.[58]

Evolution, it seemed to many, was further indication of God's enormous generosity; earlier theologians had already argued that God's generosity in pouring himself forth into the cosmos implied a "plenitude of forms," the idea that somewhere in time and space God will have made every kind of possible creature. A complementary idea was famously expressed by the late (agnostic) astronomer Carl Sagan: if Earth were the only inhabited planet in the galaxy, it would be "an awful waste of space," an idea rightly implying that intelligence and consciousness are infinitely more valuable than the hugest galaxies. That an enormous amount of time elapsed between the Big Bang and God's creation of humankind posed no problem for those who believed that God "sees" all time and space as one: God does not "sit around waiting" to create humans; they simply exist in a particular region of spacetime according to his eternal plan. Only hyperliteralists who insisted on reading the Bible overtly as a scientific and historical document found themselves insisting that evolution was impossible because the world is only several thousand years old.

A common illusion continues to be that the Western world is divided between "evolutionists" and "creationists." In fact, "creationism" is almost as slippery a concept as "evolutionism." The problem is that the word "creationism," in the general and proper sense of the belief that God designed the cosmos, was gradually hijacked in the late twentieth century by "Creation Science" or "Scientific Creationism," which rejected evolution science. Are Darwinism and Creationism opposed to one another? Absolutely, if Creationism is defined the way a small extreme section of Christians define it, and if Darwinism is defined the way extreme physicalists define it. But why abandon the definitions to the extremes? Only an extreme antitheist will claim that the geological and biological evidence *disproves* the existence of God, and only an extreme Christian will demand that geology conform to Genesis presentations of time.

"Creationism" in the currently used sense implies hyperliteral, overt reading of the Bible as valid historically and scientifically, hence denial of development through long ages of time. At its extreme, "creation science" joined biblical hyperliteralism insisting that life is at most ten thousand years old. This "Creationism," which has now spread from America into various parts of the world, was first enunciated by George McReady Price and given wide publicity in 1961 by the publication of *The Genesis Flood*, a book by John C. Whitcomb and Henry M. Morris. From the 1970s to the 1990s, proselytizers for "scientific creationism" gradually co-opted the term "creationist" for their hyperliteralist views. By 1993, despite persistent efforts by evolutionists of every stripe, an amazing 47 percent of Americans believed in recent (i.e. the past ten thousand years) special creation—special creation not only of the human soul, and not only even of the human body, but of all species and of life itself. By the 1990s, "creationism" had come to designate this particular doctrine, depriving theo-evolution of a good one-word term for itself.[59] "Creation Science" is not science but a metaphysical theory opposed to all three evolutionary views: evolution science, physicalist evolution, and theo-evolution. Dogmatic "creationists" and dogmatic physicalists have created an opposition where no opposition need exist.

By the late nineteenth century, educated Christians, whether Catholic or Liberal Protestant, tended to accept theo-evolution. Theo-evolution leaves both heaven and scientific evolution intact. Theo-evolution entails some sort of special creation of the human soul, but the infusing of an immortal soul at some point in human evolution is not a physical event and so does not conflict with evolution science. Heaven remains the eternal home of our souls, whatever the direction of human evolution has taken or will take. Nonetheless, the prestige and power of the scientific establishment intimidated many Liberal Christians, preventing them from understanding that physicalist definitions of "reality" are themselves based on metaphysical assumptions. There were many exceptions, of course, notably the Church of Jesus Christ of Latter-day Saints (Mormons), whose elaborate and sensuous view of heaven drew from Swedenborgian and similar movements. Even so, the heaven revealed to Joseph Smith had much compatibility with the classical Christian tradition.

The nineteenth-century revelations to Joseph Smith and his followers were in seventeenth-century English, apparently God's peculiar idiom, and arranged in book, chapter, and verse according to the template of the Bible. For Mormons, there exist several spirit worlds that are stages in life after our death on this planet, stages centered on families living amidst pleasant towns and countrysides and continuing to work and serve happily for the good of all. At the end of the world, Jesus will return to Earth and rule for a thousand years, when the saints will be busy with many things. Few take activity in heaven as seriously as do the Mormons.[60]

Traditional heaven was most damaged by sentimental, popular, saccharine writers who liked to describe children as little angels and to set heaven in pleasant bourgeois surroundings. One of the most influential was the novelist Elizabeth Stuart Phelps, who as a twenty-four-year-old American in 1868 wrote *The Gates Ajar*, a best-selling novel that assumed ease of entry into heaven and enjoyment of personal satisfactions there, where everyone gets what he or she wants. It is understandable that the traditional view had difficulty competing with this hedonistic heaven. *The Gates Ajar* was just what the urban reading public who romanticized children, happy families, and Mother Nature wanted to hear:

> Why should we not have pretty things in heaven? If this "bright and beautiful" economy of skies and rivers, of grass and sunshine, of hills and valleys, is not too good for such a place as this world, will there be any less variety of the bright and beautiful in the next? . . . Just such sunrises, such opening of buds, such fragrant dropping of fruit, such bells in the brooks, such dreams at twilight, and such hush of stars, were fit for Adam and Eve, made holy man and woman. How do we know that the abstract idea of a heaven needs imply anything very much unlike Eden?"[61]

Drawing upon Swedenborg, Phelps proposed "houses, but more beautiful; in them are parlors, rooms, and chambers in great numbers; there are also courts, and round about are gardens, shrubberies, and fields."[62] The cuteness of nice little girls and sweet little boys pervades Phelps's writing, and the more popular such ideas became, the more contempt heaven excited among skeptics and agnostics.

A few Christians, as well as a number of agnostics such as Arthur Conan Doyle, attempted to reconcile science with religion by means of spiritualism—communication with those "on the other side."[63] "Vitalism," another popular view in the late nineteenth century and early twentieth century, invoked against the physicalists the theory that a "life-force" entirely different from any physical process was needed to explain life in general and human life in particular. A leading proponent of this view was Henri Bergson, who had abandoned Spencerian thought as too mechanistic. A variety of religious movements influenced by Transcendentalism and known as New Thought adopted the belief that there are a variety of "planes of existence" on which we humans can exist, some being more in touch with spiritual reality than others. Neither Vitalists nor New Thinkers advocated traditional heaven.

Almost all writers and thinkers of note were influenced by Progressivism and physicalism. Some feared that physicalism would eat away at the foundations of society, as did Matthew Arnold in his famous threnody on the fading of civilization, "Dover Beach":

> The sea of faith
> was once, too, at the full, and round earth's shore
> Lay like the folds of a bright girdle furl'd;
> But now I only hear
> Its melancholy, long, withdrawing roar,
> Retreating to the breath
> Of the night-wind down the vast edges drear
> And naked shingles of the world.[64]

Mark Twain combined satire with skepticism verging, in his most depressed moments, on nihilism. Twain's *Captain Stormfield's Visit to Heaven* is biting:

> [A preacher says] that the first thing he does when he gets to heaven, will be to fling his arms around Abraham, Isaac, and Jacob, and kiss them and weep on them. There's millions of people down there on earth that are promising themselves the same thing. As many as sixty thousand people arrive here every single day, that want to run straight to Abraham, Isaac, and Jacob, and hug them and weep on them. Now mind you, sixty thousand a day is a pretty heavy contract for those old people. If they were a mind to allow it, they wouldn't ever have anything to do, year in and year out, but stand up and be hugged and wept on thirty-two hours in the twenty-four. They would be tired out and as wet as muskrats all the time. What would heaven be, to *them?* It would be a mighty good place to get out of.[65]

Twain also unjustly remarked that "There is no humor in heaven" and that "[Man] has imagined a heaven, and has left entirely out of it the supremest of all his delights . . . sexual intercourse! . . . His heaven . . . has not a single feature in it that he *actually values.*"[66] Here Twain was mocking the immortality of the soul rather than classical resurrection. Twain's depressive journey into nihilism, *The Mysterious Stranger*, was a dark beacon for the new century: "There is no God, no universe, no human race, no earthly life, no heaven, no hell. It is all a dream, a grotesque and foolish dream."[67]

Poetry spoke more deeply to audiences in the nineteenth century than philosophical disquisition or indeed any other medium. Alfred, Lord Tennyson, poet laureate of Queen Victoria and beloved throughout the English-speaking world, typified the complex struggles of Christians accommodating physicalist Progressive ideas. His long poem *In memoriam*, begun in 1833 and published in 1850, contemporary with the work of Herbert Spencer, coped with the new era "when Science reaches forth her arms / To feel from world to world, and charms / Her secret from the latest moon."[68] The purpose of the Divinity and the course of "Nature" seemed at odds:

> Are God and Nature then at strife
> That Nature lends such evil dreams?
> So careful of the type she seems
> So careless of the single life
>
> "So careful of the type?' but no.
> From scarped cliff and quarried stone
> She cries, 'A thousand types are gone;
> I care for nothing; all shall go'
>
> Nature, red in tooth and claw
>
> O life as futile, then, as frail!
> O for thy voice to soothe and bless!
> What hope of answer, or redress?
> Behind the veil, behind the veil."[69]

Despite that pessimistic comment on nature, Tennyson believed in theo-evolution:

> That God, which ever lives and loves,
> One God, one law, one element,
> And one far-off divine event,
> To which the whole creation moves.[70]

He affirmed in "Crossing the Bar" that "I hope to see my Pilot face to face / When I have crost the bar."[71]

Gerard Manley Hopkins knew that the cosmos is alive with God:

The world is charged with the grandeur of God.
It will flame out, like shining from shook foil;
It gathers to a greatness, like the ooze of oil
Crushed. Why do men then now not reck his rod?
Generations have trod, have trod, have trod;
And all is seared with trade; bleared, smeared with toil;
And wears man's smudge and shares man's smell: the soil
Is bare now, nor can foot feel, being shod.
And for all this, nature is never spent;
There lives the dearest freshness deep down things;
And though the last lights off the black West went
Oh, morning, at the brown brink eastward, springs—
Because the Holy Ghost over the bent
World broods with warm breast and with ah! bright wings.[72]

Among influential philosophers the spectrum ranged from mild skepticism to nihilism. In his *Three Essays on Religion* (1874), John Stuart Mill suggested that immortality was as likely to be true as not; William James too was inclined to believe in immortality in some form and promoted the spiritualist idea of communication with the deceased. James rejected both traditional theology and physicalism, emphasizing that religion is valid experience and that belief is an act of will. James replaced the old proofs of God through reason with demonstrations from religious experiences, a view that fit American pragmatism—and depth psychology—better than traditional philosophy. Humans are not so much rational animals as irrational, emotional animals. We have the right to adopt beliefs but not to dogmatize about them—much less punish heretics—a rule that James applied to atheists as well as to Christians.[73]

The nineteenth-century philosopher who eventually had the most impact on the twentieth century was Friedrich Nietzsche, who coined the famous phrase "God is dead."[74] Nietzsche was no friend of either Progressivism or physicalism, but he was absolute on the point of religion. He told a tale of a man who rushes out in public to declare the death of God but finds that he has come too early and is dismissed as a madman. By "the death of God" Nietzsche meant not only that God had no reality for him, or for contemporary civilization, or even that God was dead for science or for language: he meant that there is absolutely no meaning to the cosmos and that any attempt to find or establish any would be totally vain.[75] It might have been more accurate for Nietzsche to have said that God "is unalive" than that God "is dead," for Christians always believed that God could die and rise again; for Nietzsche, God was never alive. He believed that we can obtain no absolute knowledge of any kind, and we wander "through an endless Nothingness." Nietzsche insisted that heaven, God, idealism, metaphysics, Platonism, transcendence, absolute standards of morality, and being itself is illusion. Theology was nonsense, Romanticism was self-indulgence. Because the meaning of the world, if there is any, is forever hidden from us, we must create our own reality by using our will to create value and meaning. But any value and meaning that we create must be rooted in the human experience of suffering and despair; morality consists of facing and incorporating our own evil. Though Nietzsche respected the courageous authenticity of the human Jesus himself, Nietzsche considered the religion *about* Jesus—Christianity—a slave ideology based on weakness, fear, pity, and submission, and he had no room for anything remotely resembling heaven. "One experiences only oneself," he claimed, and individuals must assert their power to make their own meaning.[76] His focus on only the immediate present further vitiated the traditional thought that one can look back to human creation as good and look forward to a divine future.

Nietzsche's ideas would be the springboard for twentieth-century Existentialism and for a number of other movements from Deconstruction to "Death of God Theology" to Nazism. Nietzsche's death in the last year of the nineteenth century is an emblem of the growing eclipse of heaven in that century and introduces its further eclipse in the twentieth.[77] Heaven, joy, love, beauty, morality would all freeze in that long eclipse, be downgraded to illusions; or be reduced to toys for humans to create, mold, and adjust to fit their fancies. The nature of fancy itself would be the center of attention in the new century of depth psychology.

CHAPTER 6

In and Out

F ew of the dominant intellectual trends of the twentieth century had any place for heaven. Darwinists, Marxists, Freudians, and almost all leading thinkers dismissed it from their various points of view. Like a number of great waves coming together and reinforcing one another in battering a city, twentieth-century trends came together to nearly obliterate the City of God among intellectual elites. Where Galileo had weakened the metaphor "Up," and Darwin "Back," Sigmund Freud weakened that of "In"—internal spiritual reality—and Max Weber that of "Out"—the community of humans in God. Where Nietzsche had granted the power of will and William James had granted the validity of interior religious experience, Freud and most of his psychoanalytic followers denied the reality of either. Three of the four traditional bases of Christian belief—the Bible, tradition, and reason—had already been weakened, the Bible by higher criticism, tradition by the rejection of apostolic authority, and reason by the substitution of rationality for reasonableness. Freudian psychology seemed to pull down the fourth—experience—by dismissing religious conviction as neurotic. Freud has been under attack from a variety of viewpoints—not only Christian but also feminist, Marxist, multiculturalist, pragmatist, and psychiatric. Many criticisms are well founded, but one has only to read Freud's own work without ideological blinders to realize that one is encountering a genius. His brilliance accounts for his influence.

Freud, who believed that civilization itself springs from the repression of primal urges, also believed that civilization was necessary and desirable, for it produces the arts and sciences. But while some aspects of civilization are creative, he considered religion to be destructive. For Freud, religion was irrational and cognitively immature because it is an illusion. Freud sometimes distinguished between "illusion" (belief in something, however unlikely, that is rooted in external reality—some people actually do win the lottery) and "delusion" (a demonstrably false illusion rooted in no reality other than that of a disordered mind). Sometimes, however, he blurred the line and considered religion delusional. On the basis of a number of patients who were both religious and neurotic, and on the basis of his own deep personal animosity toward religion, he came to believe that religion itself was a sort of group neurosis. In the individual, religion was a projection of infantile fantasy and a sign of personal immaturity, though not necessarily of serious neurosis. Heaven did not correspond to any external reality; more than that, its internal roots within the individual, far from arising from the Holy Spirit or any experience with the divine, were a fictional compensatory belief for the misery of life on Earth.

Religion's roots, Freud believed, were in the "primal horde," where young men, sexually desiring their mothers and therefore hating their fathers, conspired to kill the father. Torn between love of the father, hatred of him, fear of him, guilt for killing him, and terror of his all-consuming wrath, they created totems—animal spirits—upon which they could project these powerful feelings and which they could worship and propitiate. The animal totem was sacred as the supposed father-ancestor of the tribe, and it forbade incest and imposed other taboos. Eventually these totems were replaced by animist spirits inherent in animals, plants, waterfalls, the sea, mountains; and then by gods, who were in charge of these forces of nature. Farther on in time, the gods were exchanged for one God who controlled the universe and who was, like the Ur-father, at the same time loving and stern, reassuring and terrifying. Freud believed that such events actually occurred, or that at least the very fantasies of such events were enough to push people into totemism. God is an "exalted father . . . a transfiguration of father . . . a likeness of father . . . a sublimation of father . . . a surrogate of father . . . a substitute for father . . . a copy of father," and even God "really is the father."[1]

Meanwhile, Freud continued, powerful and contradictory feelings provoked by the original Oedipal revolt are constantly being reinforced because all humans have Oedipal desire for the parent of the opposite sex, and envy and hatred of the parent of the same sex, whom they perceive as their competitor. Too weak to actually compete with the envied parent, children nonetheless feel the fear and guilt that the mere desire to kill the parent arouses. As time went on, the original taboos engendered more and more taboos, creating the often complex moral codes found in many religions. Since the Oedipus complex generates hatred of the father both in the individual and the race, the analogy of attitudes toward the father to attitudes toward God is powerful: we both love and hate God; we thank him for his generosity and curse him for our misery. Our desire to kill our earthly father produces desire to kill our heavenly Father, the mere wish producing terror of punishment. For Freud, the feared punishment for Oedipal transgression was castration, but it can be extended to mean death as well. Our ambivalence about God, analogous to our ambivalence toward our father, leads us to fear retaliation.

The Oedipus complex, rooted in fear of punishment by the displaced father, produces religion's false assurance that death can be overcome. Freud's followers expanded the sense of the Oedipus complex as a set of contradictory unconscious feelings *both* positive and negative toward *both* the mother and the father. The complex is "twofold attitude toward both parents: on the one hand a wish to eliminate the jealously hated father and take his place in a sensual relationship with the mother, and on the other hand a wish to eliminate the jealously hated mother and take her place with the father."[2]

According to Freud, the religious urge was the product of the Oedipus complex and has no root in external reality; moreover, since it is irrational, it blocks the way of the Progress from animism through religion to science. For different reasons from those of Marx, but even more strongly than Marx, Freud believed that religion must be overcome, though he was pessimistic about its ever being so. By freeing ourselves from religion, we would free ourselves from irrationality and from the burden of taboos in order to advance scientific knowledge and prosperity.

Freud's views, though owing something to both Darwin and Sir James Frazer, were imaginatively original. Since religion is *nothing but* the projection of internal neuroses upon the external world, God and heaven are simply infantile fantasies that shackle us with promises of happiness in another world. Mature adults cannot believe in them, and if they do, it is a sign of personal psychopathology. Freud's assumption that religion is false denied any rational foundation of religion whatsoever, and it entailed dismissal of any religious person as irrational and even neurotic.

The view seemed to be that if we want something very much, such as heaven, it cannot be true. It can be argued to the contrary that the intensity of desire is probably the result of yearning for an actual object of desire and that loving, committed sexuality is itself a sign of the intensely erotic hope to merge with the cosmos in God. We long to merge yet hold ourselves back in fear; we long to understand the cosmos, other people, and ourselves, but we are unable to do so. These are deep longings for fulfillment, and our deepest longings may be for the deepest reality: God in heaven.

Whereas Marx's critique of religion was that it was produced by cognitive processes aimed at producing true beliefs but distorted by the viciousness of society, Freud's critique was that it was "produced by processes that are not aimed at the production of true beliefs" at all but rather by fear and guilt.[3] Freud, who rejected his own religious beliefs in his twenties, had by the beginning of the twentieth century become harshly critical of religion, labeling it as "fairy tales."[4] In *Totem and Taboo* (1913), *The Future of an Illusion* (1927), and *Civilization and its Discontents* (1930), Freud dismissed religions as "patently infantile . . . , psychical infantilism . . . , mass delusions . . . , distorting the picture of the real world in a delusional manner." He asserted that defenses of religion by philosophers were "pitiful."[5] Freud recognized "nothing about religion's efforts to understand the universe, to relate to a transcendent reality, to acknowledge human limitations and fragility while wondering about mysteries exceeding the powers of the intellect"; in short, he reduced religion to a symptom.[6] In these views Freud was compatible with his contemporary sociologists and anthropologists, who located religion in rite rather than in belief. Anyone giving more than token assent to religion was deemed compulsive and obsessive. Freud failed to observe the distinction between conscientiousness and compulsiveness. He also neglected the fact that most religious people are far from being compulsive about practicing their religion.

For Freud, Christianity arises from the repression of libidinous energy; it arises from the masochistic desire of the son to expiate his guilt against the father. Christian heaven is a projection of what we hope and long for upon an allegedly external reality that is in fact entirely fictional. Christianity, said popularizing Freudians, is a crutch—an odd characterization of a religion based on consciousness of sin and judgment, the agony of its founder, and alleged obsession with punishment and hell. Surely atheism is more comforting than that.

Freud himself, however, was much less a physicalist than many of his followers, including his closest disciples, made him out to be. His reputation for materialism in the English-speaking world was in part based upon the standard translation of his works by James Strachey and Anna Freud, who in an effort to make Freud more acceptable to the English-speaking physicalists of the day, deliberately rendered Freud's simple German terms into abstruse materialist English. Freud's *Seele*, "soul," for example, became in Strachey's translation "mental apparatus," and Freud's *das Ich* ("the I" or "the me"), *das Es* ("the It"), and *das über-ich* ("the Upper-me") became the jargon "ego, id, and superego."[7] Freud himself was less a physicalist than a secular humanist influenced by the Romantics and Goethe in particular, and a humanist with an extraordinary ability to think metaphorically and symbolically, even poetically.[8] Freud, in other words, was more than many of his followers made of him.

Whereas for Freud, religious experience was a symptom of neurosis, for his followers, any intense personal religious experience (especially of a monotheist kind) could be dismissed as a sort of psychotic break rather than the expression of any sort of reality. Recently, however, such religious experiences have found physiological confirmation, which is unsurprising given that the reality of such experiences is reported by millions.[9] Although many analysts

are more open to religion than Freud was, religion remains for most Freudians an illusion. Freud's imaginative fantasies were not weighty arguments
against religion, but by providing an alleged physicalist alternative to revelation and theophany, he encouraged those already inclined to antitheism. The
God within—the Holy Spirit—might be a delusion, and doubt about that
weakened the metaphor "In."

Carl Jung split with Freud on a number of issues, including the validity of
religion. Jung himself had a powerful religious experience in 1944 and was not
inclined to question its reality. He thought that religion was a necessary part
of the individual psyche, of civilization, and indeed of human nature, and he
considered expressions of religion psychologically valid. Although it is true
that Jung thought of God and heaven as "myths," he followed Frazer in considering "myths" to be not mere fictions but stories presenting truth in terms
of powerful and omnipresent psychological realities. Author Joseph Campbell
and religious historian Mircea Eliade shared this view. Psychological whole-
ness, health, and indeed holiness, consist in integrating unconscious elements,
which Jung believed were not simply the debris of repression but rather a deep
source of meaningful creativity when integrated with the conscious in the light
of reason. The physical structure of the brain is similar in all human beings, so
that it produces similar "archetypes" in unconscious thought, representing
universal, timeless, human understanding. We must all come to terms with
the contents of our collective human unconscious as well as that of our own
personal consciousness. The conjunction or coincidence of opposites—Jung's
model for both the psyche and the cosmos—produces the All, the Whole, the
Complete.

The influence of such universalistic beliefs was augmented by the growing
interest in Asian religions, especially Buddhism and Hinduism, an interest that
crested about 1970. Islam is often (falsely) believed to be an "Eastern" religion
when it is in fact an Abrahamic monotheism, but it never caught on in the
West in the 1970s and '80s when so many other religions were being imported.
Now with the recent increase of Muslim immigration, it is better known than
it was. Still, it has attracted few converts, possibly because its strict rules seem
as unattractive to the hedonistic Western public as those of Calvinism or
Jansenist Catholicism.

Unlike Liberal Christians, Jung believed that the internal sense of religious
truth grasped by introverts is more fundamental than religion's external and
extraverted interpersonal aspects, and Jung particularly disdained the "posi-
tive-thinking" and minimalist forms of Christianity. God is ultimate reality,
but our ideas of God, heaven, and other supernatural entities are projections
of our limited human minds upon the absolute. We cannot know heaven in
itself but only through images that we create according to the archetypes.
Heaven may not be an external reality, but it is an internal reality, and for Jung

that meant it is inherently real. Jung and Jungians have been ambivalent as to whether the archetype of God derives from a transcendent source or whether it is entirely a human construct. For Jung, the closest we get to heaven is through "individuation," the term he used to denote the self that fully integrates the conscious, the personal unconscious, and the collective unconscious in a whole, open, and joyful personality.[10]

In the twentieth century, deeper and deeper psychologizing became a substitute for exploring and loving God, cosmos, and neighbor. Psychologizing—especially that sort that seeks to categorize human behavior in terms of the DSM (Diagnostic and Statistical Manual)—remained a dominant trend at the beginning of the twenty-first century. Diverse as twentieth-century intellectual and social movements were, most shared a number of common characteristics undermining heaven. These characteristics were denial of God; denial of the good, true, and beautiful; rejection of tradition; denial of natural law and justice; denial of wisdom; denial of the soul, including even denial of consciousness and personality; assertion that the material is more "real" than the spiritual; use of jargon and sloppy writing to disguise muddled thinking; assertion of the pointlessness of life (along with the contradictory belief in Progress); the reduction of religion to a matter of personal belief (what one might call egology rather than theology); assignation of "rights" to power groups (as Spencer had already feared); and ethics based on pragmatism rather than on principles.[11]

Pragmatists considered heaven an entirely useless idea. The movement of Pragmatism derived from the thought of the logician C. S. Peirce, who argued at Harvard from about 1878 that metaphysics and speculative thought were pointless and that only practical considerations are of importance. Its core belief was "the theory that a proposition is true if holding it to be so is practically successful or advantageous."[12] Although not all pragmatists were atheists, Pragmatism was based on physicalism and amounted to atheism in practice. Unlike the Enlightenment, which wished to advance truth, unlike the natural scientists, who sought to discover and understand the world, and unlike the socialists, who wished to improve society, pragmatists were concerned with "adaptability" (a term they adopted from Spencer and Darwin). By 1950, a common criterion of judgment was whether a person was "well adapted" or "well adjusted" to a society and whether a society was well adapted to manipulate and control the world for its purposes. As historian Leonard Marsak comments, it was not a great leap from Pragmatism to the technological success of the Holocaust death camps.

Implicit in Pragmatism is the view that our cognitive faculties do not exist to discern truth but rather to assist our reproductive fitness. The idea of "Truth" is itself false, and natural selection does not reward truth but only adaptability. Beliefs may cause behavior, but only through physiological reactions to the chemical effects of beliefs, which are themselves real only as chemical reactions. Technique replaced philosophy, technology replaced wisdom, process replaced goal, and all value was construed as entirely subjective. John Dewey, author of *Experience and Nature* (1925), the pragmatist with the greatest influence on education, asserted that "there is no such thing as the disinterested pursuit of truth."[13]

A pragmatist saw no value in any aspect of religion except occasionally as a means to manipulate people into what pragmatists consider "right-thinking"— that is, adaptive—behavior. "But if you ignore the depth-meanings of religion, what you have remaining is not religion at all, but sabbatical play-acting."[14] For pragmatists the substitute was "adjustment" to society. Pragmatism was a good program for Nazis and Stalinists, who adapted well to their societies but scarcely appropriate to followers of the New Testament, which advocates the opposite of adjustment to society ("He has scattered the proud in the thoughts of their hearts. He has brought down the powerful from their thrones, and lifted up the lowly; he has filled the hungry with good things, and sent the rich away empty" (Luke 1:51–53). Christianity at its best has "spoken truth to power," to use the Quaker phrase. Pragmatism's dismissal of moral values entailed the abandonment of the Enlightenment as well as of Christianity. The erasure of fundamental moral values left some serious problems: Is it all right for an Aztec to rip the heart out of a living sacrificial victim but not all right for a Franciscan missionary to do so?—indeed, is it all right for a missionary adjusted to his own Christian culture to try to prevent the Aztec from "adjusting to his own culture" by cutting out the heart? Relativism, however attractive it is to multiculturalists, does not work on the most basic levels of human thought and behavior.

Related to Pragmatism was "Behaviorism," a term coined in 1913 by an American psychologist, John B. Watson, author of *Behaviorism* (1925).[15] According to Behaviorists, psychology is the value-free, objective study of human behavior; some behaviors may be less adaptive than others, but none is intrinsically better or worse than any other, for human minds are objectively nothing but patterns produced by the physical brain for which we (there really *is* no *we*) are not responsible. Criminals should be grateful for the influence of this view in the law. The mind was undermined. The mind was nothing but the physical brain. The perennial question was revived whether the consciousness is a construct of the physical cosmos or whether on the contrary the physical cosmos was the construct of consciousness. Of course, if there is no real consciousness, there is no soul, and no heaven.

The "social sciences" were invented in this period, with the first professorship in psychology established at the University of Pennsylvania as early as

1888. Religion was increasingly addressed from the outside, imposing psychological and sociological categories on religious beliefs and dismissing Christianity as well as other religions first as primitive, then as merely functional, and then as actively dysfunctional. Max Weber, the coiner of the phrase "disenchantment of the world" and a distinguished founder of sociology in such works as *The Protestant Ethic* (1905) and *Economics and Society* (1922), argued that religion is intrinsically nonrational and therefore must be investigated only through external rationalities such as social psychology. Weber himself recognized the dangers of disenchanting the world and replacing the charisma of authority with the bureaucracy of popular power. His "disenchantment" was not a prescription but a description of the tendencies of twentieth-century society toward bureaucratization, depersonalization, fragmentation, and anomie. Technique lacking underlying values, Weber feared, could create virtually any sort of social control, a fear in which he was amply justified by world events after his death in 1920.

The leading sociologist Emile Durkheim, who invented the term "sociology of religion" in 1898, believed like Marx that religion was retrogressive and infantile in that it blinded people to their real needs. Durkheim repeatedly declared that sociology was objectively independent of philosophy and metaphysics, but in fact his sociology was filled with thinly masked metaphysical atheistic assumptions. Durkheim believed that religion is essentially ritual with social functions. This externalization of religion excluded it from interior human experience and made it into an exterior phenomenon, a human artifact that could—or for Durkheim's followers, *must*—be studied only "objectively," "scientifically," from the outside. In this way, the "sociology of religion" was based on two conflicting assumptions: declaring that is an "objective science" free of the contamination of metaphysics, while at the same time metaphysically insisting that religion has no internal reality. Religion, Durkheim thought, had in the past played a constructive role in understanding the world analogous to the role that science played in his own time. It was of historical and sociological importance, and it was now a subject of observation like Permian fossils. Belief in heaven as an actual state of being today was an irrelevant, silly diversion of people's real need to understand in true, scientific terms.[16] But historians know better than sociologists how the "certain" knowledge of "today" is sooner or later displaced.

Weber and Durkheim embraced a view of society virtually the opposite of the traditional Christian one. For Christianity heaven is the model for human society. Human laws and governments should be modeled on truth, justice, and love. Insofar as they are not (as everyone always admitted was usual), they fall short of their model and need correction and revision. The human state or city or nation or church was to reflect the ideal of the City of God. Looking *out* to that ideal permitted judging the degree to which society succeeded or failed to meet that ideal. The modern abandonment of the search for that ideal meant that societies would be ruled by groups asserting their own ideas of justice and truth on the basis of power alone. The more intellectuals insisted that "power" was the basis for human behavior, the more headway unexamined power made. Deliberations over the delicate balance of justice were replaced by the shouts of mobs demanding "justice," which for them meant only doing things the way *they* wanted. The abandonment of divine truth, justice, love, and beauty took its toll.

The social sciences were founded on the premise that human behaviors can be legitimately studied and understood only from the outside, and that behaviors follow certain regularities that are measurable. This view relegates individuality, ideas, and even consciousness to epiphenomena, to "secondary characteristics" (in the seventeenth-century phrase). Technology came into play in the social sciences, though in blurrier form than in the natural sciences. Adopting Pragmatism, social scientists came up with endlessly diverse sets of plans to improve society, some of which worked well, some of which worked while having adverse unintended consequences, and some of which did not work at all. Governments (that is, taxpayers) and corporations (that is, consumers) pay for such insecure schemes. As with investors in junk bonds, their bets sometimes pay off, but the odds are usually long.

If the physicalist paradigm of society that social scientists invented should be shown to be flawed—if in other words there should be interior, even spiritual, means of understanding humanity—the value of social science would be dramatically reduced.

Hostility to and ignorance of religion continue to pervade the social sciences, for if there is actually anything *to* religion—if, that is, it has internal reality as well as its external forms and functions—then the entire sociology of religion is pushed back into a corner (though still a spacious one) of religious studies. From the time of Durkheim, departments of social science have been maintained on the assumption that religion has no intrinsic truth or meaning beyond that which can be socially measured. It is not surprising, then, that the proportion of academics who take religion seriously in itself is lower in the social sciences than in other fields. There is a good-sized stake for social scientists to continue to teach that God and heaven are untrue.

There were exceptions, such as the distinguished sociologists Robert Nisbet and Rodney Stark, whose work is beginning to have the impact it deserves. Stark pointed in dismay to an anthropology textbook by Anthony Wallace written for undergraduates: "The evolutionary future of religion is extinction. ... Belief in supernatural powers is doomed to die out, all over the world, as a result of the increasing adequacy and diffusion of scientific knowledge."[17] Religion, according to social scientists, is based on ritual rather than belief (but the creeds are exactly what define historical Christianity). Religion is to be understood socially, not intellectively, and rituals ostensibly meant to unite believers with God are actually rituals to promote social cohesion. Stark commented that "one must be a highly trained social scientist to believe such [unlikely] things."[18] With Durkheim and the physicalist sociology of religion, Stark argued, "began a new social science orthodoxy: Religion consists of participation in rites and rituals—*only*."[19] Another widespread fallacy continued to be that "primitive" people invent gods to explain natural phenomena. Aside from the dubious concept of the "primitive," so-called primitive people did not think of phenomena in this way, and the gods were not devices. Their whole universe was alive; it pulsed with godness.

The physicalism implicit in social-scientific views implied the denial of consciousness, a view that would be actively pressed by the end of the century. All knowledge is empirical; since one has no empirical evidence for the consciousness of a lover, child, friend, or neighbor, one is not obliged to treat them as if they had consciousness. Fortunately most physicalists usually act *as if* their lovers and children have consciousness, and such a course of action may be socially and biologically adaptive, but it commits them to behave daily in a manner whose validity their intellect denies. They must daily *pretend* that consciousness, love, suffering, and humor exist while knowing in their minds (or rather, the chemical reactions in their brains that seem like minds) that it is all an illusion. This view might be an example of unwarranted certainty beyond the boundaries of both empirical knowledge and physical theory. It is an example of cognitive dissonance.

The great scientists of the past century were not all physicalists. Though it is uncertain what Einstein meant in his frequent references to God, it was unlikely to be physicalism, for he said that "Science without religion is lame. Religion without science is blind."[20] The confident mechanistic certainties of late nineteenth-century science were opened up to vaster and more complex worlds by Relativity and by the quantum dynamics developed by Max Planck and others in the first half of the twentieth century. Any system will contain more truths than the axioms can yield.[21] Still, the impressive advances of the physical and life sciences and of technology too easily slid down into the metaphysics of physicalism, which assumed that (1) "the scientific method is the only reliable path to knowledge" and (2) "matter (or matter and energy) is the fundamental reality in the universe."[22] Reflection might reveal that the terms "scientific method," "reliable," "knowledge," and "fundamental" are open to question. The popularization of science also produced massive misunderstandings, the most pervasive of which is the common illusion that "Relativity" is connected with "relativism" and the second that quantum mechanics provides a basis for spirituality. Also, the knowledge that the sun is not at the center of the galaxy (1909) along with Edwin Hubble's discoveries that our galaxy—the Milky Way—is only one among many galaxies (1924) and that the universe is expanding (1929) led to the common illusion that the center is somewhere else and that we are on the periphery. Instead the cosmological fact is that there is *no* center of the universe, so that we are as much the center as anything else. In fact, unless intelligent life exists elsewhere, we are *more* the center than anything else.

Although many modern intellectual movements were physicalist, conclusions drawn from physicalism were diverse. Schools known as "Logical Positivism" and "Analytic Philosophy" dominated Anglo-American professional philosophy from the 1930s to the end of the century. Positivism's basic assumption was that all knowledge is empirical and based in sense-data, a perspective drawn from British empiricism and Comte, under the influence of Spencer. Logical Positivism further emphasized logical analysis and dismissed the historically perennial questions of humanity—"the Great Conversation"— that the Greeks and Hebrews had begun to ask two and a half millennia earlier. The leaders of Logical Positivism—Bertrand Russell, G. E. Moore, and Ludwig Wittgenstein—rejected the idea that truth could exist beyond language. They sought to establish logical and mathematical analysis of language as the only sure way to get beyond verbal language itself to what they considered the language of languages: mathematically logical and precise propositions.[23] Russell, the eloquent translator to the general educated audience of the complex program of mathematics and symbolic logic that they invented, was also one of the great publicists of physicalism. He wrote as early as 1918:

> That man is the product of causes which had no prevision of the end they were achieving; that his origin, his growth, his hopes and fears, his loves, and his beliefs, are but the outcome of accidental collocations of atoms; that no fire, no heroism, no intensity of thought and feeling, can preserve an individual life beyond the grave; that all the labors of the ages, all the devotion, all the inspiration, all the noonday brightness of human genius, are destined to extinction in the vast death of the solar system, and that the whole temple of man's achievement must inevitably be buried beneath the debris of a universe in ruins [is] so nearly certain that no philosophy which rejects them can hope to stand.... Only within the scaffolding of these truths, only on the firm foundation of unyielding despair, can the soul's habitation henceforth be safely built.... Blind to good and evil, reckless of destruction, omnipotent matter rolls on its relentless way ... [man must] preserve a mind free from the wanton tyranny that rules his outward life; proudly defiant of the irresistible forces that tolerate, for a moment, his knowledge and his condemnation, to sustain alone, a weary but unyielding Atlas, the world that his own ideals have fashioned despite the trampling march of unconscious power.[24]

This statement, allegedly an assertion of human freedom, sounds more like a groan of despair. It shows every sign of its historical context—Spencer, physicalist evolution, the collapse of Europe in World War I. It was a powerful expression of the attitude of much of the intellectual leadership of Russell's time, and it continued to exercise power over the educated public for a long while after.

Russell's *Religion and Science* (1935) was a brilliant attack on a number of beliefs but especially Christianity. Against Progressivism of any kind (other than that which he favored arbitrarily, Soviet Communism), he wrote, "There is no law of cosmic Progress, but only an oscillation upward and downward, with a slow trend downward on the balance owing to the diffusion of energy [the principle of entropy].... From evolution, so far as our present knowledge shows, no ultimately optimistic philosophy can be validly inferred."[25] Consequently he denied theo-evolution and rejected Liberal Christianity, including "the social gospel," as completely as he did tradition. He of course denied immortality, the existence of "soul," and the reality of personal consciousness other than as a fabric of memories.

About heaven and hell Russell was explicitly scornful: "As the belief in hell has grown less definite, belief in heaven has also lost vividness.... Less is said of [heaven] in modern discussions than about evidences of Divine purpose in evolution.... The belief that this life is merely a preparation for another, which formerly influenced morals and conduct, has now ceased to have much influence even on those who have not consciously rejected it."[26] G. E. Moore argued in *Principia ethica* (1903) that morality is nothing more than a human concept, that there is no natural law, that ethics are relative and relate only to the practically useful, and that good and evil do not exist. Still, Moore felt entitled to assert two positive goods for humanity: human interaction and esthetics. A. J. Ayer declared that ethics are entirely practical, that there are properly no morals in ethics, and that morality was based on mere emotion.[27] Wittgenstein, though late in life more open to religion and astounded by the fact that anything exists at all, argued that the only genuine statements other than tautologies are scientific statements. Therefore he held that human values are properly banned from philosophy, whose proper study is linguistic analysis.[28] Even more astounding, one may think, than the fact that the physical universe exists at all is that humans understand so much about it, especially if they are the products of blind evolution.

Ayer and Wittgenstein agreed that the nature of language itself renders the terms "God" and "heaven" meaningless. The only valid language, they maintained, is overt: it is "literal and universal and has a unique relation to truth. ... It is the proper vehicle for science."[29] I. A. Richards distinguished between a "valid" statement—namely a scientific proposition or fact—and "pseudo" statements of a personal, emotional, subjective, value-laden kind. One example: "O rose, thou art sick" must be translated to "aphids are infesting this particular bush" in order to be meaningful. Ferdinand de Saussure, hero of late twentieth-century "postmodernism" and (with Peirce) founder of semiotics, went further. In semiotics, signs (such as words and concepts) have meaning only in relation to one another within the same system and have no reference to other systems or to any putative external "reality."[30] This view creates quite as much a difficulty for physicalism as for Christianity.[31]

Philippe Ariès, whose books have been modified and corrected but are still classic, described the shifting attitudes toward death and immortality over the centuries.[32] Saints Paul and Augustine were certain that death was a bad thing deriving from original sin and doing at least temporary violence to the unity of soul and body, but they also believed that there is a remedy for death. Christianity developed a communal idea of death in the communion of saints and the continuous presence of angels. That is to say, all the blessed, past, present, and future, are all together with the angels and with God. However, with growing individualism from the time of the Reformation and with the decline of external communities and their submersion in industrial cities, death became more frightening, even "solitary and shameful."[33] By the twentieth century, the dying were removed to hospitals and nursing homes, mourning was shortened and eventually almost eliminated, and survivors demanded to get on with life, declaring indignantly that "life is for the living" and leaving the frightening details to "undertakers" or "funeral directors"—euphemisms that reveal the growing horror that people felt for the subject. Young people especially tended to encounter death only in fiction and films, usually violent and insensitive ones. Real death was too depressing to think about. Death was seen as a failure of doctors and family to keep the patient alive rather than as a natural event. Death, Ariès observed, replaced sex as the most taboo subject. Death was an impossible negation that we do not choose to face—until we are inevitably faced with it. As the old American folk song puts it, "You got to walk that lonesome valley, you got to walk it by yourself; nobody else can walk it for you, you got to walk it by yourself." Or do you?

That you do was the view of the Existentialists of the mid-twentieth century, many of whom declared that neither God nor death is open to human understanding. Existentialism and its intellectual relations were more powerful in France and Germany than in English-speaking countries, where analytical philosophy reigned. Existentialist leaders included Martin Heidegger, Karl Jaspers, Jean-Paul Sartre, and Albert Camus, the last of whom stands out for his refusal to adopt Communism or any ideology.[34] Jaspers, a bridge from Nietzsche, objected to the depersonalization inherent in physicalism and believed that true existence consists of the realization of oneself through the exercise of free will. Heidegger, the most original existentialist, questioned whether "being" actually meant anything. To say that "God is" or "the cosmos is" or even "you are" or "I am" is, he thought, problematic. What was real for him was what he called *Dasein* (no translation works well because of the enormous fuzziness of the term). *Dasein* is not a state of "objective" or external existence but rather a state in which only humans are "real," because they alone of all creatures consciously face the problem of existence.[35] Heidegger's thought was complex and dense to the point of impenetrability, for its subtleties necessarily required going beyond simple language. By the beginning of the twenty-first century, existentialists began to recognize that heaven too requires going beyond simple language, arguing that heaven may be "real" without "existing" in the traditional, ontological sense.

For Sartre, who spread the Existentialist Word through Western society more effectively than the complex Heidegger, truly authentic Being—being-for-itself—consisted of "Becoming" through Action. Traditionalist thinkers were indignantly puzzled at the refusal of so many twentieth-century "Activist" intellectuals to investigate or even to care about the perennial questions of being, morality, esthetics, law, and truth. They were amazed by the refusal of Activists to examine, reflect upon, or question, their own assumptions; or to accept any limiting principles. They were appalled that Activists did not refrain from self-righteous denunciation of people who expressed other views than their own. Yet whether one admired or deplored "Activism," it was a phenomenon rooted in its time. "Activism" seemed self-evident to some and self-refuting to others, but it could scarcely have existed without its historical context in Existentialism. For Sartre, a person creates his or her own being in an "objectively" absurd and pointless world by the use of free will in unique and crucial circumstances. We can, he argued, courageously create our own meaning in the face of death.[36] Perfectly aware that external circumstances usually circumscribe actual choices, Sartre insisted that we have at least the freedom to say *no*, to refuse to submit ourselves to existing tyrannies. Although derivative from Nietzsche's Will to Power, the Will to Action was a courageous position to take during the Nazi occupation and the fascist Vichy regime in France, and Existentialists promoted the freedom to say *no* not only to Nazism but also to capitalism, racism, imperialism, elitism, conservativism, and other perceived evils of the times. "Perceived," because nothing for Existentialists could actually be good or evil. That there are in Existentialism no principles upon which one can distinguish between good and evil did not bother Existentialists because perception and subsequent action are more important than the essence of the deed in itself. If God "existed," his existence would be his action, not his essence, but since Sartre denied God, he believed that it is our own action that is the ultimate reality. Several generations acted accordingly.

Sartre famously said *no* to Hitler but later *yes* to Stalin, an apparent aberration unless one considers the internal consistency of Sartre's views. For Sartre, there was no inherent good or evil but only the arbitrary perception of it that we create with a free will uninformed by principles. Since we are urged to use that free will to take action according to that arbitrary perception, then we may freely say *no* to any view at all. But saying *no* to some views necessitates saying *yes* or at least *not no* to others. Sartre was less determined in his search for individual freedom than Nietzsche had been; it is difficult to imagine Nietzsche embracing either Nazism or Communism. The Romanticism of feeling was extreme in Sartre. He used his own freedom to resist some sorts of tyranny but to accept another that he "felt" to be "Progressive." Sartre *felt* that Communism represented continuous action against entrenched tyranny; and he did not *feel*—he "did not get it"—that people under Stalin's rule were trying (and dying) to say *no* to Stalin's tyranny, torture, deportation, murder, genocide, and terror. Sartre's acquiescence in Communism cannot be judged wrong by any of his own precepts, for he *felt that* Stalin's "excesses" were justified in the struggle against aristocracy and capitalism, so long as he *felt* them justified in the name of Progress. The principle of saying *no,* while often useful, has no inherent limiting principle, so that one could with as much justification say *no* to philosophy or Justice. One can even simply redefine them as one pleases by saying *no* to what some people called "the tyranny" of traditional language. One can say *no* to gratitude, generosity, kindness, and love; Goethe's Devil, Mephistopheles, did just that: "I am the spirit that always negates."[37] The Devil is against heaven both in principle and in practice.

Phenomenology, which had more of a run on the Continent than in Anglo-American circles, provided an undervalued alternative to physicalism and opened a way to understanding the reality of heaven and other phenomena. Phenomenology was developed by Edmund Husserl from Kant and, earlier, from Italian philosopher Giambattista Vico.[38] Husserl held that consciousness is all that we know immediately and therefore all that is certain. We know what we think infinitely better than we can know anything outside our minds, including the physical functions of our brains. Therefore phenomena—when the word is used in the sense of *things as we perceive them*—are more "real" than externals. The reality of "In" had returned. We cannot grasp truths in themselves, but we can be "intentional" toward them by opening our understanding in the direction of truth. We cannot know for certain that an external thing is real, but we can know that our mind's experience of it is real.

Another sort of alternative was offered by Alfred North Whitehead, who, though he worked with both Russell and Wittgenstein, deplored the decline of speculative philosophy in Anglo-American academia and accepted the reality of metaphysics—but not Christianity. God, Whitehead maintained, is both simplicity and multiplicity. "The actuality of God must . . . be understood as a multiplicity of actual components in process of creation. This is God in his function of the kingdom of heaven."[39] Whitehead's was an original variant of pantheism in which God and the cosmos develop together, and it became the basis for a school of thought known as "Process Theology."[40]

Christians in the early twentieth century faced ever more intensely the quandaries they suffered in the late nineteenth. They could affirm Scripture and Tradition while ignoring the various intellectual challenges to them. Or they could compromise their beliefs in the direction of the dominant philosophical trends. Or they could adjust their beliefs to fit those trends (a course that usually led to practical agnosticism). Or they could in a Jamesian or Jungian sort of way "try to uncover and retrieve the experiences embodied in the tradition."[41] Or they could uncover the metaphors that point to deeper reality.

By the mid-twentieth century, religions tended to emphasize the idea of "encounter." Rudolf Otto's persuasive book *The Idea of the Holy* (1917) argued, somewhat like James, that the essence of religion was the experience of a radical Other, "something" totally different from anything familiar, "something" that instills a sense of awe and wonder. Among Roman Catholics, the work of Jacques Maritain and Pope Pius XII continued to elucidate traditional views. In 1950, Pius issued the document *Humani generis* against the tendency of some theologians to compromise with modernism; later the same year he issued the document *Munificentissimus Deus* claiming infallibility in pronouncing the bodily assumption of the Blessed Virgin Mary into heaven. The heaven of Pius XII was closer to the classical view of Augustine or Dante than to that of the great Protestant theologians who were the pope's contemporaries. While creating considerable stir among Protestants as to the position of Mary in Christianity (the Eastern Orthodox, nearly one quarter of Christians worldwide, venerate Mary even more than do Roman Catholics), this document reaffirmed that heaven is not the home of disembodied spirit but of a unified soul in which body and spirit are eternally united.[42]

A variety of Protestant views appeared in the same period. The great Protestant theologian Oscar Cullmann confirmed that the core Christian belief about heaven is the resurrection of the body rather than the immortality of the soul.[43] Reinhold Niebuhr, Paul Tillich, and their Catholic contemporary Karl Rahner argued for a "reversion" to the sense of heaven: the encounter with God. For Tillich, heaven was neither a place nor a state of being, and we are not in a position to say *what* it is; we share in it, but how we do is unclear.[44] The Jewish philosopher Martin Buber pointed out that there are "two types of faith": assent to a proposition, and trust in another person.[45] Your faith is how you act. Rahner believed that we will be emptied of our personality at death and that the vast void will be filled in by the grace and glory of the Savior. This view left in the foreground the question how "we" are to be "we" if emptied of our personality.[46]

The ideas of heaven appearing in such theology have been called "symbolist compromise." However, these theologians were following the coherent tradition of Christianity, exploring and expanding depth-metaphors for heaven, opening them out. The difference was that these modern theologians were doing it in modern terms.[47] Negative metaphorical language had been used explicitly for at least fifteen centuries and is reviving at the outset of the twenty-first. Such language is "negative" in that it denies that we can ever know what God or heaven are in themselves, and metaphorical in that it claims that we can know what God and heaven really are through metaphor.[48]

"Encounter" was the term *du jour* of mid- to late-twentieth-century religion and psychology, not only in Christianity but in Judaism as well. Martin Buber's *I and Thou* observed the chasm between the attitude that "I" am real amid objects and people that I treat as things to manipulate, as opposed to the attitude that in other people and creatures I encounter "Thou," that is, other authentic, independent beings. Of these the most wholly Thou, the most wholly other, is God.[49] The substance of encounter theology was not entirely different from that of Existentialism, for they both shared the view that humans inevitably face what is absolutely beyond their understanding. But the chief difference was that whereas Existentialists believed that there was nothing beyond the abyss, the theologians believed that ultimate reality is always beyond and beneath the abyss, catching Reality in his hand. Rainer Maria Rilke, the German lyric poet, wrote:

> *Die Blätter fallen, fallen wie von weit,*
> *als welkten in den Himmeln ferne Gärten;*
> *sie fallen mit verneinender Gebärde.*
>
> *Und in den Nächten fällt die schwere Erde*
> *aus allen Sternen in die Einsamkeit.*
>
> *Wir alle fallen. Diese Hand da fällt*
> *Und sieh dir andre an: es ist in allen.*
>
> *Und doch ist Einer, welcher dieses Fallen*
> *Unendlich sanft in seinen Händen hält.*

> [The leaves fall, fall as from afar,
> As if distant gardens in the skies were turning to autumn,
> falling in a gesture of denial.

> And in the night the heavy earth falls
> from all the stars down into loneliness.

> We all are falling. This hand here is falling.
> And look at others; it is in all of us.

> And yet, there is One who without end
> holds this falling softly in his hands.][50]

Meaninglessness is made meaningless by meaning.

Several other competing trends existed in mid-twentieth-century religion: Protestant Neo-orthodoxy, the Social Gospel, and higher criticism. The leader of Neo-orthodoxy was Karl Barth, a Calvinist who constructed a huge summa of theology that was unequalled in the century. For Barth, away with feasts, banquets, singing, and dancing, away with the whole idea that heaven is a happier continuation of this life; we must expect to be absorbed by God in some way that surpasses any understanding.[51] Heaven is not any space that we can conceive of, but rather "Divine Space," which is "utterly concealed from man." As God is ultimately beyond us as a *deus absconditus* ("hidden divinity"), it is not so much that we go to God but rather that God breaks through to us in Jesus Christ, both in his incarnation two thousand years ago and in the eschatological moment at the end of time. Barth, like his contemporaries, insisted that the substance of Christianity is not the comfortable and the familiar but rather the awesome and even frightening encounter with the wholly Other. Barth's views on heaven are difficult to understand. Heaven, he said, although it is metaphorically "nearer" than Earth to God, is not identical with God. It is, rather, a dynamic relationship between God and humanity: "the nature of heaven [is] the divine action and attitude." Earth is the human sphere, but "heaven is the boundary which is clearly and distinctly marked off from man." It is "the place in the world from which God acts to and for and with man. . . . But . . . it is incomprehensible and inaccessible, outside the limits of human capacity," not merely unknown but unknowable. The Bible has "no intention of instructing us concerning the nature of heaven," yet the Bible "gives us some idea of what is meant by heaven," and even if heaven's "nature is unknown, we are not wholly ignorant of its purpose, function, and direction. . . . [It] is unitary but not formless, collective but not without individuation, total but not uniform or monotonous."[52]

The difficulty in a view of heaven as diffuse as Barth's was that without some definition, meaning leaks out onto the sand. Barth's understandable quandary was the difficulty of expressing "heaven" in modern idiom—in any language. It is almost impossible, even for those who try to block from their minds the thought of the past five hundred years, to return to the unqualified assent to heaven as Augustine, Aquinas, Dante, Luther, or Calvin understood it. Today, even when one assents to the traditional view, one cannot help (and should not try to help) filtering it through important later ideas.

More practical and influential than Neo-orthodoxy, the movements known as Christian Socialism and the Social Gospel dominated Liberal Protestant thought by mid-century, and by the end of the century much Catholic thought as well.[53] These movements achieved much good, such as resistance to Nazism and (sometimes) Communism; civil rights for minorities in the United States; attempted alleviation of world poverty; resistance to unbridled capitalism; and the rebuilding of Europe on liberal lines after the world wars. These movements, however, had no place for heaven. Walter Rauschenbusch, the most prominent leader of the Social Gospel movement, specifically rejected heaven as blocking progress toward the Kingdom of God, which would be achieved on earth by social action—a view tied to the secular Progressivism dominant in the early century. The emphasis upon the immanence of God, social Progressivism, and Jesus as Teacher rather than as Divinity, all gradually upstaged Trinitarian and Christological theology. Social service displaced much of Christian theology in Liberal seminaries and congregations. The most basic ideas, such as the Trinity and the Incarnation, let alone heaven, hardly touched the consciousness of most Liberal Christians, and certainly of agnostics.

Heaven and (even more so) hell nearly vanished from sermons; when they did appear they were often accompanied by a deprecating gesture or phrase. Banners and other removable artworks symbolizing fundamental Christian teachings gradually disappeared, for example, from many churches after the 1960s; and belief in heaven, as opposed to "right-thinking" social activism, became in many congregations a tolerable but amusing idiosyncrasy. Many people in Western culture no longer denied traditional heaven; for them it was simply no longer on stage.[54]

The Social Gospel later gradually seeped into the sand as Activists found less demanding movements than Christianity in which to express their "Progressive ideals," but what would *not* run into the sand was "historical biblical criticism." Skepticism about the Bible's authenticity had gone back three hundred years and beyond, but it had not had a strong basis in scholarship before the late nineteenth century. Biblical criticism had always existed because there had been from the very beginning of Christianity a variety of manuscripts with variant readings, and the point of traditional criticism was to establish the best possible biblical texts. It also took almost four centuries (until 367–82) to reach agreement as to which books belonged in the canon (the official version) of the Bible and which did not. This traditional variety of criticism, called "textual criticism," was conducted according to sophisticated and painstaking methods drawn from linguistics, archeology, and paleography. Criticism was different from interpretation, for its task was to establish the text, which could then be properly interpreted.

But historical biblical criticism, often simply called "higher criticism" as opposed to the allegedly "lower" textual criticism, was less criticism than interpretation, for it imposed contemporary and often ephemeral sociological, anthropological, psychological, and political assumptions on the texts. Higher criticism (which encompassed source criticism, form criticism, historical criticism, and other variants) eventually came to regard the Bible as nothing but a diverse set of ancient texts to be subjected to historical and literary analysis like any other historical texts—just as Spinoza had proposed in the seventeenth century.

Higher criticism hit Protestants particularly hard, since they had from the time of the Reformation attempted to dispense with tradition by relying upon "Scripture Alone." They felt either pressed toward capitulation to secular views subjugating the Scriptures to rationalism, or else resisting any criticism beyond textual criticism. Roman Catholics and Orthodox Christians found themselves in only somewhat less exposed positions, because while accepting the importance of tradition as well as the Bible, they always believed that their tradition was based in the Bible and that the Bible was God's direct revelation to humanity.

"Moderate criticism" sought to avoid all metaphysical assumptions—whether physicalist, relativist, or traditional—in studying the Bible and related subjects. Moderates approached biblical studies by reserving or "bracketing" questions such as accounts of miracles, that is, by treating them without assuming a priori that they are either true or false. This approach had great virtues, but it relied upon a degree of objectivity in scholarship that may not be attainable and certainly has never yet been attained. Alvin Plantinga observed another problem with moderate criticism: if we proceed only on the basis of what all scholars agree on, we will have a precariously narrow base (if any at all), because—among other problems—the critics have wide divergences of opinion.[55]

Extreme higher criticism reduced Christianity to simply one of a number of sociological phenomena of religion, of no more importance than any other phenomenon except for its bizarre (to the critics) persistence and growth for two thousand years. Extreme criticism, in other words, was based upon metaphysical assumptions denying that the Bible is revealed and that Christian tradition is invalid. With these assumptions as axioms, they then interpret texts according to the axioms. Then they argue from their interpretation of the texts back to the original assumptions. Such circularity places the critics in the category of apologists as much as those who begin with different assumptions.

Extreme criticism insisted on the empirical tradition founded by Locke and Hume. It excluded any reality other than that established by natural, empirical reason, an insistence that rests on presuppositions that may be false but are certainly undemonstrated. Extreme criticism declared that uniform laws of nature apply to humans; that cause and effect always work the same; that revelation and other miracles cannot occur.[56] These were not arguments but a priori axioms *precluding* divine action. Once the axiom that divine action cannot occur is declared, the corollary follows necessarily that it does not occur. Following the axioms, no evidence of divine action can be true; no evidence of such action is admissible; therefore we must eliminate all divine action from the Bible and Tradition. In other words, divine action can't happen because we know that divine action can't happen.

Rudolf Bultmann, the most notable twentieth-century "extreme critic" (though in later life he became more conservative), made his name by calling for "demythologizing" Christianity through the process of removing the miracles and other supernatural events from theology. In his view, the meaning of Christianity was an existential decision to accept Christ as the divine breakthrough in the past, the future, at the end of time, and most importantly in the present moment in which each person chooses whether to meet the radical demand that Christ makes of each person. Heaven does not occur after death but in a state of being "above" us, into which we can enter when we "realize that our individual existence cannot find its authenticity in this world. . . . Translation to a heavenly world of light [as] spiritual body" is "meaningless."[57] But demythologizing yielded some ground later in the century to "remythologizing," an understanding of the richness of the texts and the deep meaning of "myth" more as Jung and Eliade saw it: systems of stories representing profound reality.

One problem with extreme criticism is that reflective historians know that historical views change from generation to generation, so it is naïve to believe that the tenets of "the Jesus Seminar" or any other group of historical scholars today are what they are going to be in half a century, and when another century has passed, they will be relics. Again, Christianity is what it is, not what a given small group of critics says at any given time. "Why should we suppose that [current critical scholarship takes] us closer to the truth than [traditional biblical scholarship]?"[58] Another problem was that extreme criticism was a two-edged sword. It prompted—and produced—a great body of evidence, textual, archeological, and other, that developed understanding of the historical setting of the Bible. It is useful as social history. On the other hand, by pushing traditional biblical criticism out of the way, it narrowed down understanding of the metaphorical and spiritual understandings of the Bible. For example, the whole field of typology was banished to the point of disappearing until it was recently revived by Catherine Brown Tkacz, who has shown that typology was never far from the New Testament mind, and it indeed influenced the text of the New Testament to a hitherto unrecognized degree.[59]

The impact of higher criticism can scarcely be exaggerated. Demonstrating "what the Bible says" was replaced by theories first about what the various authors of the Bible supposedly meant to say and more recently by what scholars can make of the texts regardless of what the authors meant to say. This approach has called into further question the perennial question of what Jesus meant by "The Kingdom of Heaven," of what the evangelists intended, and of what Saint Paul meant by "heaven" and the "third heaven," as well as what was intended by the various words interpreted in English as "soul," "spirit," "body," and "flesh." It cannot, according to higher criticism, even be established that they meant anything coherent at all or whether the authors cobbled the texts together from various sources. Old Testament texts and the apocrypha (works usually excluded from the biblical canon) were at least as much criticized. It became possible to argue that Jesus was whatever you want him to be, as we have no knowledge that anything ascribed to him in word or deed is at all accurate. Some critics went so far as to say that virtually nothing is known about Jesus at all. The best-confirmed archaeological discoveries can do nothing to budge such a taproot of skepticism. Even were a scroll uncovered that dated to the time of Jesus and contained Jesus' own writing or dictation, with his signature in Hebrew or Aramaic, skeptics would be obliged on their own principles to deny its authenticity. Despite their frequent claims to objectivity, they will allow no evidence of whatever quality or quantity to overcome their obdurate skepticism. The really curious question is why so many scholars expend such time and effort in trying to grasp a Jesus whom they believe is ungraspable.

One of the bases of higher criticism was historical: from this point of view nothing that Jesus is alleged to have said and done could possibly be authentic if it did not fit the social context of what people in general thought and believed in first-century Palestine. But this view begs the question of whether Jesus could have had any original ideas at all. Another base was philosophical: since miracles are impossible, it is impossible that Jesus performed any, another example of begging of the question. Yet another base was literary, distinguishing various pieces sewed together by the New Testament, including preaching models, miracles, narratives, and miscellaneous sayings. It was argued that we have no grounds for believing that the Bible was revealed or even inspired by God. The implications were clear for all of the concepts appearing in the New Testament: none of them is reliable, and the same was true of the Hebrew Bible, or Old Testament.

All of these views make unnecessary assumptions and are therefore not as significant as many educated people suppose. Part of higher criticism is based on the primitivist fallacy. The primitive fallacy is that what things *really are* is what they were in their earliest form. Thus, if the earliest form of Christianity could be determined, then that would be the true Christianity. The fallacy that origin is reality is found elsewhere among historical writers but is usually identifiable as nonsense, as if a constitutional scholar should argue that the "real" British Parliament is its original form (if indeed that could ever be determined) or the "real" Russia is an ancient Muscovite principality. That mistake turns out to be even worse than it seems, because it will also always be impossible to determine what Christianity "originally was." This is for two chief reasons: first, the documentation is unclear and incomplete, and second, the definition of Christianity is developed over the decades after the death and resurrection of Christ. The only secure position from which to defend Christianity was that the Bible is the word of God and that God knows what he means and that the evangelists and Paul knew what they meant because God inspired them. Whether it is ultimately right or wrong to take such a position can be determined only by—well—God, not by any historical or literary criticism of ancient documents. But whether that position be right or wrong, without it Christianity eventually would evaporate, as would Islam if Muslims ceased to accept the Qur'an.

Further, the notion that every scholar can create his or her own Christianity is to render the term historically and philosophically incoherent. But in the meantime, one can get a lot of media attention by saying one is a Christian while denouncing Christianity.

The complexities of biblical scholarship are immeasurable, but the underlying question is simpler: is Christianity what contemporary scholars say that it is at the moment, or is it what it has been traditionally over the centuries? This is not a question of whether the conclusions of this or that group of scholars about biblical texts is more valid than those of others. It is a question of the actual underlying meaning of concepts. What heaven "most really" is, like any other human concept, is the roughly coherent concept of what it has traditionally been considered to be. To argue that Christianity is "really" something other than what it has always been (based on the Bible and tradition) is to impose an *external* view *onto* Christianity. There are a plethora of external views of what Christianity is—Marxist, say, or Freudian—but to impose these on the subject from outside is rather like the College of Cardinals or the president of the Latter-Day Saints defining what Marxism "really" is. Even stranger is the tendency of some intellectual Christians to argue that Christianity *ought to be* what their own academic speculation seems to suggest to them at the moment. Such an argument is self-referential and leads only to confusion.

It is no wonder that, given these challenges to the meaning of heaven, a strong reaction should have set in among Christians at the end of the nineteenth century and into the twentieth century. Among most Roman Catholics before the 1950s, the tendency was to hunker down in the trenches of papal authority and even infallibility in order to combat "modernism." But as early as 1943, in his document *Divino afflante Spiritu*, Pius XII recognized the value of moderate criticism, a pronouncement reaffirmed by the Pontifical Biblical Commission of 1948, prompting a flood of strong Catholic biblical scholarship.[60] Among Eastern Orthodox Christians, the tendency to withdraw from the world of external criticism was even more pronounced. An influential Protestant view in the last century was that the Bible is a particular variety of history, *Heilsgeschichte* or "salvation history," the record of God's doings with humans rather than a philosophical, scientific, or historical account. That point of view is certainly more in accord with the bases of biblical religion.

The most vigorous efforts to grapple with higher criticism occurred among British and American Protestants. These efforts were manifold, and only the most important and general can be mentioned. One was "evangelicalism," originating among eighteenth-century British Evangelicals (the term derives ultimately from the Greek *evangelion* ("Gospel" or "Good News"). They typically rejected higher criticism and the notion that whatever is currently scholarly opinion ought to be set above revelation, and they tended to read the Bible in a more overt sense than many other Christians. Evangelicals tried to erase two thousand years of Christian tradition by claiming to revive the true, original religion of Christ and the apostles. They affirmed the divine law underlying morality and the atonement of sin by the suffering of Christ. They were strong supporters of good works, though in often different areas from those of the Social Gospel: they were the foremost abolitionists and among the foremost missionaries. For Evangelicals, as well as for Pentecostals and Fundamentalists, the authority of the Bible guaranteed the reality of heaven, while the authority of the Bible was guaranteed by God. The Pentecostal movement (the term derived from Pentecost, when the Holy Spirit descended upon the apostles), which began in 1906, differed from Evangelicalism mostly by emphasizing the immediate presence of the Holy Spirit in inspiration and healing, an emphasis that flowed into the "charismatic movement" of the 1970s among both Protestants and Catholics. Pentecostals expect the millennium and the end of time at any moment; this immediate view of eschatology flourished in the early Church and has been revived time and again throughout Christian history. In this view—sometimes called Dispensationalism and increasingly popular in America at the turn of the twenty-first century—the Holy Spirit is working through believers at all times; therefore everything true believers do is through the Spirit (a dangerous assumption). Christ will come again now; the faithful departed will rise victorious and the faithful living will be carried off to heaven in "the Rapture"; other Christians will pass through tribulation; Armageddon will be fought and won; the millennial reign of Christ will come, followed by the Last Judgment and the establishment of the New Heaven and the New Earth.

The term "Fundamentalist" has become an indiscriminate label we stick onto anyone who has deeper religious beliefs than we do. Properly used, "Fundamentalism" denotes a broad movement that began among Protestants opposed to physicalist evolution and higher criticism. In 1895 a conference of such Protestants issued a statement at Niagara in New York State, which set forth five "fundamental" points insisting on the inerrancy of the Bible, the divinity of Jesus Christ, the virgin birth of Christ, his resurrection, his bodily return to earth at the end time, and his atonement for original sin through his suffering. In the period 1910–15 a series of tracts were published to support these "fundamental" (meaning "basic") Christian beliefs, and in 1919 the "World's Christian Fundamentals Association" was founded. The term "fundamentalist" first appeared in 1922; "fundamentalism" in 1923.

Originating in Evangelicalism, the Fundamentalists affirmed that the Bible is to be read "literally" or overtly, leading some to reject not only physicalist evolution but even evolution science and to deny that life developed over billions of years. Evangelicals tended to believe in the "inerrancy" of the Bible (though they defined that term variously), a view that sometimes could unhelpfully turn the Bible into an authority on science and history. Their view of heaven was more strictly biblical than either classical or Liberal.[61] It seems puzzling to many elitist intellectuals and commentators that anyone takes theology seriously, but Fundamentalist leaders do, and their reaction against atheism, secularism, and the trend toward "feel-good Christianity" was historically understandable and almost inevitable.

Among other things that the Fundamentalists felt obliged to resist was the decline of Christian institutions. Many Christian leaders and congregations capitulated to secular Progressivism, and the trend was clear in educational institutions. The mottoes of great universities, such as *Dominus illuminatio mea* (Oxford), *Veritas* (Harvard) and even *Fiat lux* (California), are emblematic of their religious roots. By 1900 a kind of liberalism began to prevail in universities, but elements of anti-Semitism, anti-Catholicism, and racial segregation did not vanish before the 1970s, and anti-Catholicism has experienced a virulent revival among the Politically Correct.[62] By the 1920s to the 1950s, secular ideas had ousted most of the religious values in higher learning. Though a few institutions such as Notre Dame (Roman Catholic), Baylor (Baptist), Emory (Methodist), and Brigham Young (Mormon), persisted, by the 1970s all of these but Brigham Young University had deliberately diluted their religious orientations. By the 1980s, real liberal values such as individualism, careful research, and avoidance of propaganda, had followed religious values into the rubbish bin. The "disestablishment of religion has led to the virtual establishment of unbelief or the near-exclusion of religious perspectives from academic life."[63] One of the surest ways to lose an appointment or a promotion in the humanities and social sciences in most leading universities is to be known as a believing Christian: it is considerably more dangerous than being known as a Buddhist, Hindu, Orthodox Jew, or Muslim, though agnostics and Marxists are preferred to any of the above. Many intellectuals believe that it goes without saying that anyone practicing his or her religion is either stupid or perverse. Similar difficulties beset religious people working in the mainstream media. Of course such discrimination is not stated policy, any more than torture of suspected terrorists is stated policy. Discrimination was as hotly denied as it was vigorously practiced. In the 1980s when George Marsden wrote about universities, they were still allowing "individuals free exercise in parts of their lives," but by the 2000s any such views had to be carefully hidden in order to avert subtle (or not so subtle) reprisals.[64] Marsden observed that the curious thing is that "few think it odd that this religious prejudice and metaphysical ideology" should be identified with "academic freedom and free inquiry."[65] Orwell, as usual, was right.[66]

Church architecture and liturgy, which would undergo so much change in the late twentieth century, continued to be dominated by the traditional in the early part of the century, though a strong (but short-lived) liturgical reform movement was prominent in the Roman Catholic Church in the 1950s and 1960s. Not a great deal can reasonably be said for Christian art in the period. It was predominantly of the greeting-card and calendar variety, whereas the leading characteristics of the arts during the century were abstract, solipsistic, relativist, and self-promoting, deliberately dismissing religion, science, humanism, and meaning. This tendency was occasionally relieved by "revolutionary" political art but very seldom by serious Christian motifs. There were exceptions, but few will think of them without labor. Christian art and architecture tended to be pastiches of earlier works, such as the beautiful but imitative cathedral of St. John the Divine in New York and the National Cathedral in Washington, D.C. Beautiful icons and mosaics were created in the Eastern tradition, and a few soaringly original works of architecture arose, such as Antonio Gaudi's Sagrada Familia in Barcelona, but it can hardly be argued that many important buildings of the early or mid-century were religious. The dominant dogma of art by the 1940s was "whatever you think is art is art," and by the end of the century that included urinating or vomiting on the floor or videotaping orgies, and who was to object? What you think is art *is* art. Of course, the current artist elite define "you" as themselves; if *you*, actually, personally, think that something they declare is art is not art, they label you an ignorant dimwit. But when religion was the subject, it was almost always treated with irony or open hostility. Was Rouault the last important artist to treat heaven seriously? An agnostic colleague of mine in Art History bemoaned the fact that students, even after being repeatedly coached about Christian motifs in the history of European art, still were simply unable to understand or even identify them. The nihilistic works of Pollock and Warhol seemed more easily understood by the modern mind.

In literature, the dominant trends were toward atheism with a pronounced tendency to cynicism. In order to be original, it was held, it was necessary to be un-Christian, as the Bloomsbury and Auden Circles in Britain, along with Existentialism in Germany and France, symbolized. What was clever trumped what was true. Some brilliant, original authors, though in the minority, were overtly Christian, such as T. S. Eliot, Graham Greene, C. S. Lewis, Evelyn Waugh, J. R. R. Tolkien, Dorothy Sayers, and Charles Williams. Among the most notable was Flannery O'Connor, who can seldom be cited any longer because her satires of racism are now considered by the very sensitive to be racist. On the subject of heaven, O'Connor's unforgettable story is "Revelation," in which a comfortable, insensitive, self-satisfied white woman, Mrs. Turpin, thanks Jesus that she was not born "Negro" or "white trash" and subsequently is shocked and enlightened by a revelation that everybody precedes her into the Kingdom of Heaven.[67] Gratitude is one of the chief attributes of a heavenly character, but it can be less than perfect. If, like Mrs. Turpin, we express gratitude for being better than other people—stronger, cleverer, richer, more sophisticated, more religious, less religious, a better athlete, linguist, musician, or whatever, that is less thankfulness than boastfulness and a source of one of the besetting evils of humanity: arrogance. Even being grateful that one has survived a disaster that others have not survived can have a dark tinge to it; gratitude that one survived is fine, so long as it is not tinged with relief that it was someone else who did not. Feelings of guilt, though psychologically natural, also usually fail to accomplish much good. If Emily is miserable, for example, it does not help her one iota for Claire to try to feel less happy, though it might make both of them happier to do something positive to assist John. Pure gratitude is being thankful for every moment, especially every beautiful, true, and joyful moment that is bestowed upon us without discrimination between ourselves and others. One can be grateful to God, or gods, or creatures, or Nature, or a living cosmos, but one cannot be grateful to a purposeless universe of stuff, which has no remorse, gentleness, decency, or justice. The only responses to purposeless stuff are anesthesia or rage. For ourselves, and possibly for the whole cosmos, one moment of grateful joy is worth a galaxy of lifeless stars.

Though a number of powerful novels criticized physicalist Progressivism, including those by George Orwell, Aldous Huxley, and Arthur Koestler, none showed any inclination to traditional religion. Albert Camus, although an agnostic, wrote an extraordinarily fair and sensitive examination of the problem of evil (*The Plague*, 1947). But nihilism and denial of the meaning of life prevailed in the works of writers such as Franz Kafka, and *Waiting for Godot* (1955) by Samuel Beckett had a huge impact. Beckett said that "Nothing is more real than nothing," and Edward Albee, Jean Anouilh, and Harold Pinter were prolific in perpetuating such views. Some might ask how long proclaiming the meaningless of life can be illuminating, or interesting, or even thought to be interesting.[68]

Occasionally there was even the clever joke about heaven in the spirit of Mark Twain. Perhaps the best was by Rupert Brooke, "Heaven," an adaptation of Xenophanes' ancient saying that if horses had gods, the gods would have manes and tails. Brooke's satire took the point of view of fish:

Mud unto Mud!—Death eddies near—
Not here the appointed End, not here!
But somewhere, beyond Space and Time,
Is wetter water, slimier slime!

And there (they trust) there swimmeth One
Who swam ere rivers were begun

And in that Heaven of all their wish,
There shall be no more land, say fish.[69]

The second half of the twentieth century, though less marked by genius and originality than the first, would prove to be even more various. It would also produce a few florets of hope both in the soul and out in society (insofar as hatred and envy can be minimized). Every sign of gratitude is a sign of hope.

CHAPTER 7

Forward

In the late twentieth century, it was as hard to look forward to the Kingdom of God as it was to look back to Paradise—perhaps even harder. The dead were generally believed to be just that, quickened (if at all) by photographs, videos, genealogies, and other nostalgic endeavors. It had become difficult to believe that they are as much living, feeling, thinking as their survivors; difficult to imagine where and with whom they might be. Reflection, prayer, meditation faded when every hour was filled with activity, noise, and entertainment, and when networking and group identification replaced talent and accomplishment.[1] The old hopeful epitaph *May She Rest in Peace* seemed less attractive or relevant than *May She Be Eternally Entertained*. If consumption of material goods is the ultimate end, then Westerners at the time of the millennium were as close to glory as humans are ever likely to come. The dismissal of the sanctity of life; the erosion of the meaning of words and the shift from words to images (especially rapidly moving images accompanied by noise); the fragmentation of coherent thought; the virtual disappearance of principles (as opposed to opinions); the loss of transcendence; the insensitivity to spirituality were characteristic of culture by the end of the twentieth century. In such soil heaven could hardly flourish.

The decline of heaven in the twentieth century was revealed by surveys that indicated the growth of atheism and indifference on the one hand, and the fragmentation of religion on the other. The decline is clear in the declining percentage of Western population (except in the United States) that affirms any belief in any kind of heaven. The fragmentation is clear in the growth of the percentage (especially in the United States) defining heaven each in his or her own way. Though polls are always questionable, the data were gathered over time for this country by the National Opinion Research Center at the University of Chicago, and for the other countries by the World Values Surveys coordinated by the University of Michigan. "Do you believe there is a life after death" was the central question, and related questions explored respondents' attitudes toward heaven on whether they thought it to be primarily "a life of peace and tranquility" or "a life of intense action"; "a life like the one here on earth, only better" or "a life without many things that make our present life enjoyable"; "a pale shadowy form of life, hardly life at all" or "a spiritual life involving our mind but not our body"; "a paradise of pleasure and delights" or "a place of loving intellectual communion"; "union with God" or "reunion with loved ones." Some believed in heaven as eternity rather than life after death; some believed in God but not in heaven; some even claimed to believe in heaven but not in God. A whole menagerie of the beliefs of nonbelievers could be collected in any industrialized nation.[2]

Individualism and technology came to dominate American values rather than tradition and community.[3] "Success" meant "getting ahead," which implies leaving others behind if not actually thrusting them down. Tony Walter discovered that many people who either affirm heaven or deny it have little idea of what it is they are thinking about, but a few generalizations were possible. In countries with high levels of social services, such as The Netherlands, Denmark, and Estonia, and in large cities, the decline of heaven was particularly notable.[4] A hypothesis might be that the more secure people feel in their present life the less they are concerned about another one. More women than men believed in heaven (possibly because women are less likely to erect rationalist walls against experience); more elderly people than younger people; more people with college degrees than without them. Among Christians, many more believed in the immortal soul than in bodily resurrection, and the number affirming beliefs about heaven that are biblically and/or traditionally based was quite low.[5] As Walter observed, the growth of belief in reincarnation in the second half of the century shifted the meaning of "life after death" significantly away from traditional Christian ideas.[6] Additionally, solemn attention to self (the shibboleth of the 1990s was "self-esteem") grew as reverence for God and for Nature shrank. No matter how many people or what proportion of people continued to believe in heaven by the end of the century, it became virtually irrelevant in law, the arts, corporations, philosophy, politics, journalism, and society in general. Principles were washed away in floods of opinion and rejection of transcendence.

There was no place for heaven in either of the two dominant worldviews at the end of the century: physicalism and deconstruction, which—though in opposition to one another—both drained the world of meaning. The first reduced reality to only one of its aspects; the other denied reality altogether.

Physicalism was by the end of the century the most widespread dogma among the educated, despite the fact that there is no *"single system ('the organisms and their physical environment') which contains all the objects that anyone could refer to."*[7] Physicalism is the metaphysical belief that the only valid statements about reality (other than mathematics) are statements about physical objects, movements, and forces; there is no real world other than the physical world. Although of course not all statements about the physical are true, no statement about anything other than the physical *can* be true or make sense at all. Ideas, beliefs, will, and consciousness itself are nothing but the functioning of neurochemical states. Physicalist statements often use the trademark words and phrases "only," "just," "merely," and "nothing but." Consciousness is nothing but neural reactions in the brain that will someday be entirely predictable and controllable.

The biologist E. O. Wilson wrote:

> Everything can be reduced to simple universal laws of physics. Ideas and feelings are merely linkage among the neural networks. It can all eventually be explained as brain circuitry. Everything that is knowable but not yet known to science is open to being explained by science.[8]

The evolutionary biologist Douglas Futuyma:

> By coupling undirected, purposeless variation to the blind, uncaring process of natural selection, Darwin made theological or spiritual explanations of the life processes superfluous. Together with Marx's materialist theory of history and society and Freud's attribution of human behavior to influences over which we have little control, Darwin's theory of evolution was a crucial plank in the platform of mechanism and materialism—of much of science, in short—that has since been the stage of most Western thought.[9]

The geneticist Richard Lewontin:

> We take the side of science . . . because we have a prior commitment, a commitment to materialism. It is not that the methods and institutions of science somehow compel us to accept a material explanation of the phenomenal world, but, on the contrary, that we are forced by our *a priori* adherence to materialist causes to create an apparatus of investigation and a set of concepts that produce material explanations, no matter how counter-intuitive, no matter how mystifying to the uninitiated. Moreover, that materialism is absolute, for we cannot allow a Divine Foot in the door.[10]

The leading spokesman for physicalist evolution Richard Dawkins:

> Nature is not cruel, only pitilessly indifferent. This is one of the hardest lessons for humans to learn. We cannot admit that things might be neither good nor

evil, neither cruel nor kind, but simply callous—indifferent to all suffering, lacking all purpose.[11]

The philosopher Daniel Dennett:

> My own spirit recoils from a God Who is He or She in the same way my heart sinks when I see a lion pacing neurotically back and forth in a small zoo cage. I know, I know, the lion is beautiful but dangerous; if you let the lion roam free, it would kill me; safety demands that it be put in a cage. Safety demands that religions be put in cages too—when absolutely necessary.[12]

E. O. Wilson again:

> We have come to the crucial stage in the history of biology when religion itself is subject to the explanations of the natural sciences. As I have tried to show, sociobiology can account for the very origin of mythology by the principle of natural selection acting on the genetically evolving structure of the human brain. If this interpretation is correct, the final decisive edge enjoyed by scientific naturalism will come from its capacity to explain traditional religion, its chief competitor, as a wholly material phenomenon. Theology is not likely to survive as an independent intellectual discipline.[13]

These writers seem to agree that their own brains are more advanced than those of anyone who is religious.

Since there are no scientific means by which physicalists can know that the cosmos has no plan or purpose, such statements violate the fundamental principle of science that science is based upon testable hypotheses and that a good hypothesis is one that can be disproved or proved. Physicalists used axioms in place of arguments as if materialism were self-evident. A journalist once asked me if it couldn't be argued that God is an illusion created by the human mind, and she seemed unwilling or unable to grasp that that is not an argument but the declaration of an axiom. If the axiom is that all reality is physical reality, then it is an inevitable corollary that God does not exist, but the question is simply being begged. "Materialism itself is an idea, just as immaterial as any other."[14] If no idea is better than any other idea because they all proceed from purposeless neural interactions, then astronomy can be no better than astrology.

Reduction of all ideas to neural impulses also means that no moral or ethical concept is better than any other. If no behavior is better than another, why bother about whales and rainforests? What is wrong with raping children or with genocide? What is wrong with faking scientific evidence? Appeals to "good sense," "right-mindedness," and "you can't really think *that*" are simply evasions of the basic principles of reductionist thought. According to biologist

E. O. Wilson, we need the "illusion of free will" as biologically adaptive; we need the "self-deception" of altruism.[15] One may doubt that good—moral, intellectual, or evolutionary—can come out of illusion and deception.

Physicalists such as Richard Dawkins, Daniel Dennett, the biologist Stephen Jay Gould, the astronomer Carl Sagan, and the physicist Brian Greene put forward complex arguments in clear, accessible style to a public willing (because of its trust in technology) to take them seriously, whereas when a theologian or philosopher wrote accessibly about complex ideas, the public often assumed that they were merely simple-minded. Westerners were caught in the headlights of the blinding power of technology run by scientists paid by corporations and governments; anyone who criticized the technological imperative to do any thing we are able to do was consigned to the zoo set aside for antimodernists.[16] Even Progress in technological fields is not always a good thing: a famous figure in technological *Schlimmverbesserung* (making things worse by trying to improve them) is Thomas Midgley, Jr., whose lucrative inventions of tetraethyl lead gasoline and of chlorofluorocarbons remain at the top of the all-time list of products both hugely profitable and enormously toxic to humanity and to life in general. It is only partially true that "we have modified our environment so radically that we must now modify ourselves in order to exist in this new environment," for if humans engineer themselves too far they will cease to be human in any sense other than the genetic.[17]

There is increasing evidence for what has been called (usually ironically) the "God Gene," a gene for a sense of transcendence.[18] Darwin himself had speculated that humans had an innate disposition to worship, comparing it to the dog's innate desire to please its master. If in fact such a gene does exist (as it seems to), then physicalist evolutionists have to consider the options. If it serves some evolutionary purpose, what sort of purpose? With relief, physicalists can sidestep the question by explaining it away as one of the multitudes of useless genes that occur in the human genome.

Daniel Dennett's book *Darwin's Dangerous Idea* rightly pointed out that the real issue in debates over evolution was not whether life develops through time, which everyone except biblical hyperliteralists accepted, but whether it *does so through intelligent design*. Dennett showed that it is possible for the cosmos to have developed without intelligent design; although such views had been discussed for twenty-five hundred years, it was only recently that they seemed to be supported by an understanding of some of the mechanisms involved. In the name of these mechanisms and their alleged complete description of things, the physicalists dismissed the argument that intelligent design is demonstrably true—or even arguable.

But physicalists took a broad leap farther than simply denying that there is conclusive evidence for intelligent design. They denied that there *could be* evidence for intelligent design. Dennett cited "[Richard] Dawkins' . . . unrebuttable refutation" of the existence of God and invited those who did not agree to stop being boring and just change the subject.[19] A Designer does not exist; therefore there can be no evidence that a Designer exists; so no evidence need apply. What Dennett did not note is that his argument against intelligent design is itself defeated: first, by the unwarranted certitude of his view (for the only certainty is that those claiming certitude are wrong); second, by its circularity; and third, by failing to point out the inherent unlikelihood of the main alternative to intelligent design: physicalism. Still, Dennett denounced "greedy reduction of values to facts" by Dawkins and others,[20] and he ended his book with a beautiful image: "The Tree of Life is neither perfect nor infinite in space or time, but it is actual [and] a being that is greater than any of us will ever conceive of in detail worthy of its detail. . . . I could not pray to it, but I can stand in affirmation of its magnificence. This world is sacred."[21]

Many physicalists feel that they must struggle fiercely against "religious people," whom they seem to regard as darkly subhuman savages skulking out of the misty forests to attack mindlessly with Bible-shaped cudgels. "The religious faithful tend to assert, often with a tinge of smugness, that something must have started it all. . . . People who believe themselves ignorant of nothing have neither looked for, nor stumbled upon, the boundary between what is known and unknown in the cosmos."[22] It is curious that physicalists feel that they must perpetrate such stereotypical caricatures. After all, the question is quite simple (if possibly irresolvable): does the cosmos work without a cosmic Designer or does the cosmic Designer work through natural events?

Why do so many natural scientists fear and loathe the idea that a Designer works in and through the cosmos? Partly the answer is historical: they have inherited Auguste Comte's views of Progress. Another historical answer is that they see the past in terms of an eternal struggle between science and superstition, and for them superstition is almost synonymous with religion. But this perception of theirs is only partly true, mostly untrue, and very seldom true at all for the period earlier than the nineteenth century. Before the invention of physicalism, religion and science usually worked hand in hand. Another answer is the terror that religion will drive science out of education. Terror of this threat encourages unceasing pressure to ban any worldviews other than physicalism from public education. Surely it is better to allow the evidence to speak and encourage students to listen and be critical rather than insisting on propagandizing "the one true belief." It might even be intellectually and morally wrong to shirk open and honest debate.

To these answers may be added others less abstruse. To begin with there is an innate human dislike of having one's ingrained certainties questioned; when uncurbed by self-reflection and humor, dislike becomes hatred and leads to fanatical insistence on crushing such questions. To this almost universal human trait physicalists add the fear that in certain countries (notably the United States) pressure from certain religious lobbies will impede scientific development.

Because of the increasing cost of technology, and technology's demand for ever more resources, science has for a century increasingly depended on money from corporations and governments whose interests are almost entirely concerned with the profit in power and wealth that science may yield. It is notorious that research that does not seem to promise "practical" results is not easily funded, and it is a cliché among scientists that research projects are heavily influenced by where the money comes from.

If the technological paradigm were questioned, making grants less lucrative, and universities were to return to the ideal of liberal education achieved by encouraging students to investigate a variety of worldviews, some groups would lose a lot of income and power. Institutions from physics departments to Catholic dioceses to congressional districts have a vested interest in maintaining whatever status quo benefits them. Meanwhile, only elite universities profit from elitism; in many smaller universities and colleges, teachers are required to teach so many students over so many hours that the instructors have little time or energy for research or even for keeping up with their fields. Any academic in any field in any college knows what the pecking order is. The point of this seeming digression is that powerful interests in academia, government, and business are highly invested in keeping the physicalist paradigm on top. Hadrons bring in more than heaven any day.

Toward the end of the twentieth century a school of thought called "Intelligent Design" arose in science, first in biology, then in cosmology.[23] The best-known and persuasive "Intelligent Design" writers were Phillip Johnson and Michael Behe.[24] "Johnson's contribution to the argument was that philosophical naturalism restricted all possible explanations of new genetic information to purely unguided, unplanned, random mutations. . . . Behe's contribution was the discovery of a number of molecular machines in biology having the feature of irreducible complexity."[25]

Intelligent Design was a scientific approach entirely in harmony with evolution science; what it challenged was physicalist evolution. Intelligent Design theorists argued that there is no scientific reason to exclude the possibility of intelligent design in the development of the cosmos and that people who do so are making a metaphysical rather than a scientific statement. They argued that scientists ought to be open to search for evidence for intelligent design and that, in fact, scientific evidence for intelligent design has been presented but ignored or contemned by the physicalists. And they argued that much more such evidence might be uncovered if the prior metaphysical insistence that it is impossible to uncover it is abandoned. Intelligent Design argues that *"there exist natural systems that cannot be adequately explained in terms of undirected natural causes and that exhibit features which in any other circumstance would be attributed to intelligence"* (italics in original).[26] When examining all the evidence without prior blinders on, one concludes that the arguments for Intelligent Design are as strong as those for physicalist evolution, but so long as such arguments and evidence for them are vigorously suppressed by vigilant physicalists, it is likely to be a while before minds are opened. Meanwhile, it might help if all sides avoided the reduction code "nothing but"—as in Intelligent Design is *nothing but* religion in disguise, or evolution is *nothing but* a theory.

Intelligent Design has been denigrated as religious propaganda, misrepresented as "creationism," and even insulted as "fundamentalist" by its opponents, who confuse it with "creation science," which is no science at all. In fact, Intelligent Design simply opened scientific inquiry to include questions relevant to theism. One of the foremost contemporary atheists, Anthony Flew, recently declared that he was convinced by Intelligent Design.[27] Intelligent Design has been receiving more and more attention, both favorable and hostile.[28] The importance of Intelligent Design for the history of heaven is not that it demonstrated the reality of God and heaven: it never claimed to. However, it did undercut the assumption that physicalism is the obvious, common-sense, right-thinking position, which only stupid, ignorant, or malicious people could possibly question. Thus Intelligent Design restored a balance that had been heavily weighted toward physicalism for the past century: no longer were theists alone in having to defend their position; now atheists had to defend themselves as well.

Metaphysical physicalism claimed to oppose metaphysics yet disingenuously promoted its own metaphysics to the public as science.[29] Physicalists denied ultimate value; at the same time they assigned great value to their own work and assumptions. If the cosmos really does lack intrinsic meaning, the physicalists' niche in the cosmos can be no more meaningful than any other. Physicalists denied the existence of consciousness. They evaded problems of suffering and evil and the gifts of ecstasy and joy, offering futility and despair on the one hand or baseless hope for ultimate technology on the other.[30] Carl Sagan did not himself deny affective realities, as he pointed out in his line, "Prove it": I love my father, prove it; I grieve for my dead child, prove it; beauty does not last, prove it; I am the Bread of Life, prove it. But some physicalists were moved by a perhaps understandable terror that antiscientific storms would sweep them away.[31] As the famed philosopher Owen Barfield wrote,

> Listen attentively to the response of a . . . literal mind to what insistently presents itself as allegory or symbol, and you may detect a certain irritation, a faint, incipient aggressiveness in its refusal. Here I think is a deep-down moral gesture. You may, for instance, hear the literal man object suspiciously that he is being "got at." And this is quite correct. . . . An attempt is being made, of which

he is dimly aware, to undermine his idols, and his feet are being invited on to the beginning of the long road, which in the end must lead him to self-knowledge, with all the unacceptable humiliations which that involves. Instinctively he does not like it. he prefers to remain "literal." But of course he hardly knows that he prefers it, since self-knowledge is the very thing which he is avoiding.[32]

One of the increasing difficulties of physicalism is the anthropic principle (a phrase coined by Brandon Carter in 1974), which comes in many forms.[33] It relies on the uncontested fact that the cosmos is minutely tuned in such a way that we exist and can observe it in great scope and detail. Among the details are: The universe contains slightly more matter than antimatter. The universe is open-ended and will never contract, but it has one beginning point about 13.7 billion years ago. Disconformities appeared directly after the beginning that broke the symmetry of the universe and made the formation of atoms, stars, earth, and life possible. The total mass density of the universe is exactly right: if it were less, only hydrogen and helium could exist; if it were more, only heavy elements could exist. The lowest energy level at which the nucleus of an atom remains cohesive is sensitive: for helium, carbon, and oxygen, a difference of only 4 percent would mean that the universe would have too little carbon or too little oxygen. The constants for all four fundamental forces (electromagnetism, gravity, the strong nuclear force, and the weak nuclear force) must fall within very narrow ranges for atoms to exist. The conversion of hydrogen to helium must release exactly .007 percent energy, not .006 percent or .008 percent. The universe must be the approximate age and size that it is in order to support even one occurrence of life. Recent observations of extrasolar planets ("exoplanets") indicate that most if not all planets must circle late, metal-rich stars, which compose only 2 percent of the stars in the galaxy. Most planets cannot support life because they are too close to their star or else have eccentric orbits drawing them in and out of the life zone, beyond which a planet is either too cold or too hot to support the growth of complex organisms. A star that can support a planet with life must be between the arms of a galaxy, because otherwise it would get too much radiation from nearby stars, or planetary orbits would be rendered irregular by the gravity of those stars. The sun has the appropriate mass and relatively stable output of energy. The cooling of the Earth by means of the carbonate-silicate cycle has closely matched the increase of 35 percent in the sun's energy output since 3.85 billion years ago, keeping the temperature in the life zone. A large planet such as Jupiter is needed in order to sweep in comets and asteroids, but if Jupiter were closer to the Earth or more massive than it is or in an unstable or eccentric orbit, it would pull Earth out of the life zone. Earth needs a large, single moon, or else the tilt of the Earth's axis of rotation would become unstable. Earth needs a molten interior, which generates a magnetosphere that herds destructive solar particles away from most of the planet's surface. Exactly the right amount of ozone exists in the troposphere, mesosphere, and stratosphere: if there were less, we would be sterilized by ultraviolet radiation; if more, the nutrient cycle would not work. The random emergence of a protein from amino acids is even less likely than any of the above.

Perhaps these conditions are coincidence, but the likelihood of chance producing such closely calibrated coincidences is roughly equivalent to your chance of winning the grand prize in an intergalactic lottery—and, as Robert B. Parker's fictional detective Spenser says, you don't get anywhere by assuming coincidences.

Either there is cosmic purpose or there are endless numbers of multiple universes, all without purpose. It is possible in terms of mathematics and theoretical physics that multiple universes may exist, but there is no empirical evidence for it. The idea seems charged with the needs of metaphysical physicalists to assume that the cosmos has no intelligent design. The constraints for the existence of conscious life are enormously too great to take seriously the idea that our existence is random.[34] Anthropic principles must not be taken as proof of anything, but they ought to give pause to those disdaining Intelligent Design.

The possible explanations seem to be (1) the cosmos is designed to the last detail, including the design to produce humans; (2) it is pure chance that humans exist, and as fantastically unlikely as that seems a priori, that one chance has indeed happened, because if it had not, we would not be here to marvel at it; (3) the unlikelihood of the second explanation is only apparently mitigated by positing the existence of an infinite number of multiple universes, of which we inevitably occupy one (as opposed to the ones without hydrogen for example). Explanation number three is simply a trope on number two in an effort to fend off divine purpose. In 2003 it was empirically established by the Wilkinson Microwave Anistropy Probe, CWMAP, that there are no multiple universes in the time dimension, because the universe is open-ended in time, fading into higher and higher entropy rather than coming together in a "Big Crunch" and starting anew.

It is still possible that there are multiple universes in space (whatever "space" may mean in that context), but it turns out that there is more evidence for cosmic purpose than there is for multiple universes. As for the proposition that the cosmos is a result of chance either directly or indirectly from initial randomness, that proposition seems on reflection to be no explanation at all. The only phrase that can properly follow "from" in the previous sentence is "absolutely nothing." Random what? Initial what? Quantum particles popping in and out of existence need explanation. "Potential" matter and energy need explanation.[35] Perhaps the universe began, as some theoretical physicalists suggest, with a nonzero-value Higgs Field emerging from a zero-value Higgs Field.[36] And where did the zero-value Higgs Field come from? Physicists may consider that a stupid question, as it cannot be answered by science, unless of course yet another physical entity should be postulated beyond the Higgs Field. The problem of physicalism is that no physical construct *can ever, by the definition of science,* answer how something came from absolutely *nothing*—not some *thing* we call "nothing" but *really absolutely nothing.*

Although no reasonable person would conclude that this limitation of physics demonstrates the truth of Christianity or the reality of heaven, clearly the question is much more open than intellectual elites have been assuming. Physicists are quite right to work on the premise that "God" is not an explanation in physics, but that premise is in no way contradictory to the idea of God—or of heaven. Psychologists are quite right to work on the premise that extraterrestrials are not an explanation in psychology, but that is in no way contradictory to the existence of extraterrestrials. It is simply the *limitation of the field.* If you choose to believe beforehand that the cosmos has no purpose, nothing stops you from making that act of faith; and if you choose to believe that it does have purpose, nothing stops you from making that act of faith either. However, both science and religion, when they are honest and not self-serving, try to search for truth, and it seems that in the absence of any possibility of proof one way or the other, the preponderance of the evidence has come to favor theism over atheism.

In the late twentieth century, extraterrestrials were commonly presented as performing social functions similar to those of Christian angels, descending to earth and ascending again for good or ill. Yet E.T.s are in fact much less likely than angels. There can be no scientific evidence for or against angels, whose existence is based on the Bible and classical tradition; on the other hand, scientific evidence is the single and only way to approach whether E.T.s exist. But the scientific search for E.T.s, however extensive, popular, and attractive, has so far produced absolutely no empirical evidence at all for their existence. Whether you believe that E.T.s or angels seem more likely to exist depends on your presuppositions about the nature of the cosmos and the nature of knowledge.

A number of philosophers from antiquity through Giordano Bruno in the sixteenth century, and Kepler (*The Dream,* 1634) and Fontenelle (*The Plurality of Worlds,* 1686) in the seventeenth century had mused about life on other physical bodies than earth. Christiaan Huygens in his book *The Discovery of Celestial Worlds: Theories about Inhabitants, Plants, and Products of Planetary Worlds* (1690) described how observers on another planet would view the universe.[37] Three centuries later, in 1961, the astronomer Frank Drake presented a famous equation for the number of E.T.s in the galaxy, spurring books and movies such as Carl Sagan's *Contact* and actual ongoing scientific searches. The problem is that six of the eight terms of Drake's equation are (so far)

fantasy. The Drake equation states that the number of technological civilizations in our galaxy is equal to the product of the following: the rate of star
formation yearly *times* the fraction of stars that have planets *times* the number
of habitable planets *times* the fraction of habitable planets on which life actually develops *times* the fraction of those planets on which intelligent life evolves
times the fraction of those planets on which civilizations arise that engage in
interstellar communication, *times* the average lifetime in years of communicating civilizations. The equation sounds impressive, but even with the hun-
dreds of billions of stars in this galaxy, the product is likely to be exactly "1:us."[38]
Technological society has existed on this planet for a few hundred years at
most, and so it is vastly improbable that the technology of any other society in
the galaxy could overlap ours in time. Further, unless some way is found of
communicating faster than the speed of light, dialog with extraterrestrials,
even if any existed, would be almost impossible because the nearest possibly
life-sustainable planets are many light-years away. Still, the philosophical need
to continue the search is no less for that, and some astrophysicists are more
optimistic about the odds.[39] It is moving to watch dreamy-eyed scientists say
that they are certain that intelligent life exists out there somewhere. I hope it
does; it would be fascinating; the odds, however, are against it.

Theologians properly and justly consider the origin and development of
God's cosmos an important aspect of theology. On the other hand, theologians need to be cautious in adopting any particular scientific cosmologies for
theological purposes, especially since scientific cosmology is far from being
settled in itself. Classical Christian concepts of cosmic origins are not incompatible with quantum concepts of cosmic origins, but these sets of concepts
scarcely reinforce one another. To the contrary, by definition they are not able
to reinforce one another, since they ask different questions of the cosmos.[40]

Despite its limitations, physicalism permeated almost every aspect of Western culture in the twentieth century. Yet its domination is scarcely secure. Biblical hyperliteralists exhumed the old delusion that evidence from physics and
biology indicates only that the universe *seems* to be ancient. God *might* have
created all that deceptive evidence only thousands of years ago (in order to
test our faith?), but this is an idea that really does seem a contender in the
absurdity competition. On the other hand, in education the idea of a liberal
curriculum stimulating students to critical thought was replaced by a Left curriculum in the humanities and a technological curriculum elsewhere. The
number of students majoring in physics and other hard sciences dropped after 1990. The elision of old liberalism into Leftism almost destroyed the traditional meaning of "free" or "liberal," both of which imply open-mindedness in
opposition to dogmatism.

Education "has been emptied of any coherent world-view; the tie between
information and human purpose has been severed; 'information' has been el-

evated to a metaphysical status; schools and universities have become structures for legitimizing some parts of the flow of information and discrediting
other parts."[41] It had been many centuries since education last actually de-
tracted from understanding. The newer kind of education might better be
called "induction" of ideology, because the root of "education," the Latin
educere (to "draw out") wisdom, was lost. Contemporary students and their
educators have difficulty placing themselves in space (either astronomically
or geographically), time (either historically or cosmologically), or ethical context. Few, to offer a few examples, have much idea about the location of other
countries, about the U.S. Constitution, or about the brightest stars in the sky.

The arts continued to be de-Christianized. It is rare to find an author who
combines Christianity, talent, and a wide audience. Frederick Buechner, Wendell
Berry, Annie Dillard, and Scott Peck are outstanding Christian authors, but
more widely read writers such as Truman Capote, Tom Wolfe, or T. C. Boyle
comment on the absurdity of the human condition with varying degrees of
hopelessness. Examples of outstanding Christian art and architecture in the
late twentieth century are also rare, with exceptions such as the Annunciation
Greek Orthodox Church in Wauwatosa, Wisconsin, designed by Frank Lloyd
Wright; Eero Saarinen's North Christian Church in Columbus, Indiana; Le
Corbusier's Notre-Dame du Haut in Ronchamp, France; "The Crystal Cathe-
dral" in Garden Grove, California, by Philip Johnson; Thorncrown Chapel in
Eureka Springs, Arkansas, by E. Fay Jones; and Marcel Breuer's Saint John's
Abbey in Collegeville, Minnesota.

Psychology, under the influence of behaviorism, was drawn closer to biology and computer science, leading to a partial eclipse of analytical psychology.
In the middle of the century, the Harvard psychologist B. F. Skinner published
Beyond Freedom and Dignity after its accompanying widely read if clumsy novel,
Walden Two. This marked the beginning of a movement toward social engineering (a euphemism for the discredited "eugenics") and toward a mechanical view of consciousness itself.[42] In 1961, Skinner stated that people are
machines without liberty or choice, and could be freed from suffering and
induced to happiness by means and methods prescribed by Harvard professors—
or at least one of them.[43] The impressive efforts (which may eventually suc-
ceed) to construct a "thinking machine" led to a reconsideration of what is
meant by thought itself. Physicalist psychology claimed that what we experience is illusory; we just think that we think; thought is the product of material
forces; the human brain, like a computer, is nothing but a "complicated slew
of activity."[44] Any such view fails to engage the two essential poles of human
existence: suffering and gratitude.[45] It is realization of suffering in the particular, not merely in the abstract, that is at the foundation of our sense of justice;
it is gratitude that, despite suffering, reconciles us with the cosmos. Both entail a need for heaven.

Daniel Dennett argued that by physicalist assumptions (which he says are the only valid ones) there can be no absolute moral standards. He continues, however, that we should try to find "the best solution *we* could come up with, given our limitations."[46] Dennett is silent about the question who "we" are, a question that entails the deeper question of *who decides* what "we" come up with. At the moment, the *who* are the defenders of the pervasive orthodoxy (having its basis in what?) of political correctness. There were a large and varied number of plans to construct ethics without absolutes, all of which boiled down to one or another form of utilitarianism, which then left unanswered on what basis a solution might be called "the best." British sociologist Tony Walter observed that "ethical debates increasingly discuss earthly consequences, because these constitute the only form of reference that all can share," yet he pointed out that without deep-rooted change "some other basis for ethics, yet to be developed, will be needed."[47] The conundrum that relativist ethics face is that they need to be based on some degree of human consensus, whereas human consensus has on the one hand never been reached and is unlikely to be, and on the other hand where it has come close to being reached in societies such as Nazi Germany or Maoist China it has proved destructive. Another problem is placing ethical consensus in the hands of committees of physicalists. Such efforts are bound to be blundered no matter how seriously the professors take their burden. For example, microbiologist Richard Losick, in considering the ethical limits of biotechnological research, observed that the goal of his committee "is to review the research to see if something being proposed would clearly fall in a realm many people would agree is unethical."[48] This leaves unanswered the questions of what group the phrase "many people" refers to and, even more to the point, on what basis those "many people" judge what is "unethical."

Though physicalism was the most powerful and predictably the longest-lived intellectual trend at the end of the century, another trend was "Deconstruction," also called by a number of different names such as "Critical Thought," "Textual Studies," "Literary Theory," or "Postmodernism." No one actually knows what these amorphous terms meant (Deconstructionists deliberately rejected definitions), but they dominated academic thought in the humanities. Deconstruction amounted to a sophisticated defense of relativism and solipsism. If Deconstructionists held any views in common, among the foremost was the belief that everything is a political statement, that everything is equally true, good, or beautiful, and that any text (political, historical, scientific, financial, administrative—any text at all, including graffiti in the toilet) can be interpreted in any way the reader chooses. These views entailed the rejection of objectivity, the rejection of truth, the rejection of classical epistemology, the rejection of tradition, and the rejection of science.[49]

Notable Deconstructionists included Jean-François Lyotard, Michel Foucault, Richard Rorty, and above all Jacques Derrida. The philosopher Thomas Carlson summarized Derrida's view: "the signatory of a text delivers the text up to dissemination without return. The signatory of a text abandons it, as an orphan, or is dispossessed of it."[50] A text and its author disappear into a "vast, free-floating matrix of signs."[51] As the random motion of particles produces the cosmos, the random motion of signs produces a poem—or a memo from the Water Board (which can be construed as a call for monarchy or an encomium of syphilis if either suits our political agenda). Derrida's famous aphorism was "there is nothing beyond the text, *il n'y a pas de hors-texte.*" Truth, according to Rorty, is merely what the majority of one's peers think. Noam Chomsky bridged physicalism and deconstruction in his argument that mental states are physical and computational, and that languages are merely constructions of linguistic particles. Dennett, a physicalist who could not be accused of being a Deconstructionist, nonetheless allowed the idea to go a step farther in his argument that culture consists of conceptual particles he called "memes."[52] These alleged particles, being infinitely manipulable (within the limits of the human genome), could be arranged and rearranged to construct or deconstruct any mentality or worldview.

The implications of such views were not long in unfolding. If an author's intent means nothing and every view of every critic is equally valid and any text can be interpreted in any possible way, then the only determination of the meaning of a text is political power. Each text has no meaning other than however some earthly power chooses to construct it. This view makes it rather hard to fault Hitler and Stalin. In a world of complete relativism, any statement—as well as any political program—is as true as any other and also true in whatever way somebody chooses at the moment. (If a test of one's beliefs is one's actions, it is safe to say that almost no one actually believes this; intellectuals enthusiastically promote their own views above others.) Deconstructionists argued that their views gave the individual limitless freedom to interpret and believe what he or she wants, but in fact Deconstruction produced closed-minded suppression of thought in humanities and social-science academic departments and university administrators. Where only the politically correct is in practice tolerated, the reader's—or the student's—choice is not freed but severely *limited*. When applied to the physical sciences, the results were ludicrous; they carried even less weight in schools of engineering or medicine.[53]

Allegedly free on principle to read texts as they pleased, academics were actually intimidated by ridicule, isolation, and implied threats about degrees, hiring, fellowships, and promotion. "Liberal education" thus became illiberal, narrowing down rather than opening up; worse, it was based on hypocrisy about "equal opportunities." "Liberal arts" became an outmoded, quaint term; and the term "Liberalism" was transmuted into a term for Leftist Activism.

Narrowing down deprives one of a treasure of alternative worldviews. "What is true" becomes merely what is labeled as true by the standards of society, which can be changed by political-action groups (whether "Left" or "Right") to suit and benefit themselves. As Alvin Plantinga ironically observed, "if we reject the very idea of truth, we needn't feel anxious about whether we've got it."[54] Religion in modern society became "personally meaningful but socially irrelevant."[55]

The significance of Deconstruction does not lie in any inherent value of the approach or in any contribution to enduring thought. To the contrary, its absurdity will soon be recognized by everyone, and it will be remembered only as one manifestation of a deteriorating Western culture. Its significance lies in the fact that language and history departments deprived generations of students of the ability to encounter, understand, commune with, and argue with great ideas and great writing. When students have no connection with Augustine or Dante, with Calvin or Donne, they can have little sense of heaven.

Some people claim that they can as individuals construct a set of firm standards for themselves to live by. That would have to mean the indwelling of the Holy Spirit or the imprint of Natural Law. If this were not the case, it would simply mean an arbitrary selection of standards that happen to appeal to them at a given moment. Since it is unlikely that anyone can think of standards that have not been thought of before, that leaves the further question of why people choose the standards that they do select from the buffet of standards set before them. We seem caught between the hard rock face of physicalism and the crevasse of relativism. There is a way out: to cease struggling and allow in the peace of joy and gratitude. That is not giving up, it is opening up. Gratitude is the key. Every day without gratitude is wasted. It is possible to feel gratitude to others and to God, but it is difficult to feel gratitude to randomness (unless, of course, you have just won the lottery).

Whereas Julian Huxley believed that morality lay in Progress toward the emancipation of thought from mechanical causation, the tendency at the end of the century was in the opposite direction.[56] As the late media critic and author Neil Postman observed, societies function when there is a belief in a transcendent authority, and by the beginning of the 2000s Western society was attempting to operate as if there were none.[57]

In politics and law, the natural law that for over two thousand years had characterized the political culture of Cicero, Aquinas, Locke, and Jefferson faded. The concept of absolute justice was replaced by rights manufactured on the basis of power by interest groups, including commercial, sexual, racial, corporate, union, and other pressure groups. Law became a vehicle for social engineering to achieve "Progressive," "right-thinking" values, but since there are no principles establishing these values or even what they are, open discussion or debate about them was discouraged and wherever possible quashed by the rhetoric of resentment. Liberalism was replaced by egalitarianism. Egalitarianism slipped from the principle that no person is better than another to the claim that no one has more ability than another. This led to the claim that no one *can* be better than another, and finally to the assertion that no one *ought to be better* than anyone else. And that includes God: what makes him superior, anyhow? No one was supposed be a better poet, mathematician, painter, philosopher, statesman, or musician than another—all are equal. Tellingly, this fantasy (which hardly anyone really ever believed and even less frequently acted upon) was never extended to sports, where the Dallas Cowboys were (correctly) assumed to be better football players than the West City High Gophers. Fortunately, efforts to extend the fantasy into engineering, medicine, and the physical sciences did not get far; efforts to extend the fantasy into the humanities and social sciences have succeeded beyond expectation.

Metaphor's privatization, common since Blake and the Romantics, overwhelmed the arts, while censorship, once imposed on sexual expression, was now imposed on political incorrectness instead.[58] Esthetics were even more unpopular than ethics, despite increasing scientific understanding that the cosmos itself is esthetic, while liturgies became more and more kitsch and "horizontal" (human to human rather than human to God), rather more like meetings of the Rotary Club than occasions for worship.[59]

Roman Polanski, David Lynch, and other filmmakers perpetuated the view that life has no meaning. One great exception was the work of Franco Zeffirelli. Some might wonder how long telling audiences that life was meaningless could be original, illuminating, or interesting—or even thought to be interesting. However much influence serious writers and directors have had on views of Christianity, mockery and sarcasm affect popular beliefs more. In that way Woody Allen and Monty Python (however funny they may be), with their witty flippancies about religion, probably undermined heaven more than Sartre and Beckett, though without Sartre and Beckett in the background, they probably could not have produced the sort of work they did. The mood of the late century was epitomized by Monty Python's movie *The Meaning of Life* (1983), yet another statement that there is no such thing. It was difficult to find a serious literary work treating heaven (or even God) respectfully after the time of C. S. Lewis, who wrote: "We want . . . to be united with the beauty we see, to pass into it, to receive it into ourselves, to bathe in it, to become part of it."[60]

The Dispensationalist millenarian "Left Behind" novels by Tim LaHaye and Jerry B. Jenkins, inspired by Hal Lindsey, had sold around sixty million books by 2005.[61] The novels based their stories about the end of the world on an overt interpretation of the Book of Revelation (Apocalypse) as predicting actual historical events to come. Although cut out of cardboard with blunt scissors, they may have had more influence on current beliefs about heaven than any contemporary historian, critic, or theologian. This influence might be ephemeral, but it responded to what seemed an immense thirst for the comfort of certainty as against the discomfort of critical thought. Other hugely popular books attesting to the interest in heaven current in the United States were Alice Sebold's *The Lovely Bones* (2002) and Mitch Albom's *The Five People You Meet in Heaven* (2003).

Deep spiritual tradition was also deconstructed and reconstructed as brand-new religions were created, often in direct opposition and hostility to Christianity.[62] Witchcraft (Neopaganism) defined its identity "in terms of its *difference* from, and its *opposition* to, the Christian-based culture and religion of the West . . . in particular with its monotheism and its transcendence."[63] Since the early 1990s, the cultural mix of MTV, electronics, comic books, fantasy literature and games, and movies and TV shows such as *Buffy the Vampire Slayer* (1997) and *Charmed* (1998) melded with the "counterculture," "New Age," and pop culture, expanding Neopaganism from a tiny niche of romantic (and often amiable) misfits into an increasingly established alcove as a minor yet recognized religion. Witchcraft has been recognized by the U.S. military, the U.S. courts, and many American colleges and schools as a valid religion. These fads are ephemeral, coming and going with the fashion of a year or at most a decade, yet each contributes to the swirl of pop culture.[64] Very few worshippers of Buffy and her kind could possibly have taken their "religion" seriously; they were doing it for camp, coolness, and kicks. But that is the point: the current spirit of the early twenty-first century encourages taking religion of almost any kind as an ironic pose. Less understandable to the rational mind is that people such as the woman who claims to channel a prehistoric warrior named "Ramtha" still had followers serious enough about her to part with both their money and their senses in support of a popular movie in 2004.[65] Heathen replaced Heaven.

Unlikely though it seems that Wicca (witchcraft) will become a major religion, it has proved to be no mere fad, and its anti-Christian media message is particularly effective with preteens, teens, and young adults. But witchcraft is only one part of a general religious movement that has been called "The New Religious Synthesis."[66] Among current beliefs that, however various and incoherent, oppose the Christian tradition are: occultism (spiritual elitism with allegedly ancient secrets known only to the initiated), syncretism, astrology, numerology, gnosticism, goddess-worship, channeling, crystals, divinity of the self, psychics, magic and sorcery, reincarnation, and pantheism. In other words almost anything other than physicalism, Marxism, or Judeo-Christian religion.

Many people who considered themselves too sophisticated to believe in the miracles of Christ subscribed to at least some of the "New Age" beliefs on this list. The prevailing anti-Christian culture of the early twenty-first century in both the academic and entertainment industries meant that Christianity had become the *real* counterculture.

In a deracinated culture where traditional Christianity was transmitted perfunctorily or not at all to the young, a vacuum was created where the basic narrative of Judeo-Christian religion was disappearing and where new religions were created and dissipated at personal will and whim. Many contemporary Western persons, conceived in and suckled on materialism, were simply deprived of the imaginative basis for understanding heaven. Their lives were individual, functional, sensual, and indifferent, taking away their capacity to imagine a heaven of spiritual depth and shared ecstasy. They were also deprived of a sense of need for heaven, since they were convinced that they would live longer and longer, enjoy more engaging employment, be ceaselessly entertained, and acquire increasing numbers of toys. Christian metaphors were ignored or (worse) drained of their content to be mixed incoherently with New Age images. Although this New Age brought as little comfort to physicalists and classical philosophers as it did to Christianity, Christianity became a prime target of bigoted hate-speech.[67]

On the other hand, serious efforts were made to bridge science and religion, among them books by Stephen Jay Gould, Willem Drees, John Polkinghorne, R. W. K. Paterson, and Stephen M. Barr.[68] The Templeton Foundation was established to encourage creative exchange of ideas between science and religion. There were two basic issues: one was the insistence by both fundamentalist physicalists and fundamentalist theists that each keeps the only gate to reality; the other was the question of cosmic design, for it seemed difficult to find an answer that reconciled both ultimate design and the absence of ultimate design. Philosopher Michael W. Tkacz wrote that chance and design are not incompatible, yet the compatibility of the two as principle of the cosmos was tenuous, and Tkacz's contemporary Stephen Toulmin enjoined skepticism about all myths, including physicalist ones, pointing out that concepts and even rationality change with time. Skepticism is necessary, Toulmin observed, but skepticism can turn into radical skepticism and finally cynicism, which obliterates all meaning.[69] Cynicism is usually accompanied by a peculiar kind of naiveté in that cynics assume that anyone adhering to standards other than their own is a hypocritical fraud.

Willem Drees noted that "scientific explanations are provisional human constructs" that cannot be independent of their social and intellectual contexts, but he ended, like Stephen Jay Gould, in denying religion any claim to the natural world.[70] Gould argued that science and religion are two completely discrete entities—he famously called his plan NOMA, "No Overlapping Magisterial Authorities." The problem with this proposed solution is that religions actually do exist to describe a real, outside world, whether their descriptions are right or wrong: they do not exist to describe feelings but to express knowing and conviction. "God," Michael Arbib and Mary Hesse observed, is "more like gravitation than [like] embarrassment."[71] John Polkinghorne wrote that "to regard the divine as being simply an internalized symbol for individually chosen value" cannot in any helpful way be called Christian belief, and that religious tolerance and openness "cannot mean that there are no limits to what may with honesty be contained within the description 'Christian'. . . . [It is not] helpful to evacuate Christian theism of content to make the phrase too vague to be usefully discriminating."[72] Efforts to be "relevant" (to what?) lost touch with the essential coherence of the system.[73]

The notion that there is a *real* Christianity as opposed to a fake one that was put forward as Christianity for millennia is an ancient fantasy that reduces the term to meaninglessness. That Christianity ought to be what it is not is problematic enough; that it properly *is* what it is not—a view put forward by gnostics for centuries and still advanced by some—implies oddly that God defines Christianity differently from how Christians do. Perhaps he does, but how could we know?

On a variety of different paths, Buddhist philosopher Alan Wallace argued for the validity of "subjectivity"; Polkinghorne said of religious experience that we should take "what witnesses say seriously, unless we have reasons to doubt their testimony"; and Frank Manuel wrote that "the mythic cannot be exorcised without danger to the soul of man and without his utter spiritual impoverishment."[74] Hilary Putnam found an inviting middle way between physicalism and deconstruction in what he called "critical realism." He observed that "there is no such totality as all the objects there are, inside or outside science." Putnam spoke out for "the open texture of the notion of an object, the open texture of the notion of reference, the open texture of the notion of meaning, and the open texture of reason itself."[75] In other words, our concept about anything is fluid and changeable, yet also necessarily has coherent threads that hold it together. For example, though "democracy" is very fluid, it has enough coherence that to apply it to, say, absolute monarchy makes no sense. In the same way, the concept of heaven, though its borders are fluid, necessarily retains a degree of coherence. To use heaven as a synonym for "reforestation," for a wild example, would make "heaven" meaningless. What is needed is a view of reality that both recognizes meaningful boundaries and also is open to development within those boundaries. Giving up alleged certainties requires generosity of both mind and spirit.

Until the spread of Islam into Western society at the beginning of the new millennium, religion was on the defensive against physicalism, despite a brief surge of interest in the 1970s.[76] The most original movement was the religious feminism originating among writers with a Christian background such as Mary Daly and Rosemary R. Ruether, and in anthropological views such as those of Marija Gimbutas postulating ancient matriarchal societies; the Wicca movement was also predominantly feminist.[77] Feminist religion centered on God as the mother who makes space for the cosmos in her womb, on spherical images as opposed to linear, "phallic" ones, on critiques of "rationality" and of logic, on "self-development," on rejection of both science and traditional religion as "patriarchal," and (especially relevant to heaven) on birth and "natality" over death and immortality.[78] The worship of Gaia (Earth-spirit), the nature that enwombs and fosters us, was a form of pantheism with connections to feminism. The aim of religion, it was argued, is not a codified system of truths but rather becoming divine—an idea that had been emphasized (however differently!) for centuries by the "patriarchal" Eastern Orthodox churches, whose wisdom has long been overlooked in the West.

Expanding upon Progressivism and the philosophy of Alfred North Whitehead, a movement called Process Theology developed in the late century with the work of Charles Hartshorne and others.[79] The essential point was that God is in the process of creating himself and that humans participate in the emerging nature of God by co-creating their own characters. The basis of the relationship between God and the cosmos and among humans is love expressed in persuasion rather than coercion. The whole process of creation is good; the suffering inherent in sentient life is a necessary part of the creative process; and God suffers everything that his creatures suffer. John Polkinghorne observed that the philosophical and Augustinian view that all time and space are eternally present in God had not easily been reconciled with the biblical God who is intensely involved in human events. He pointed out that it is not written that "God is causation" but that "God is love."[80] In the view of Process Theology, heaven is the omega, the end point of the divine self-creation, or else becoming consciously one with the process of the cosmos. The whole physics of spacetime opened up new questions in the twentieth and twenty-first centuries. "The idea of an atemporal stratum [a timeless layer] in the world's structure reappears recently in some important models of fundamental physics. . . . Physical models teach us that atemporality does not necessarily mean static, motionless state; dynamics and timelessness can go together."[81]

As Western culture grew impervious to Christianity, Christian sectarianism became the equivalent of niche markets, especially that sort of sectarianism that provides comfort and reassurance. It became difficult for those who wanted to think about Christianity seriously to find information, dialog, or imaginative help, even in the churches themselves.[82] Christians struggled in a pluralist world to affirm Christianity without capitulating to relativism on the one side or retreating into dogmatic insensitivity on the other. Liberal Christianity gradually faded, although theologians such as Gordon Kaufman expressed disbelief in sin, judgment, resurrection, and heaven. Kaufman went so far as to say that belief in heaven really represented a lack of faith, in the sense that it indicated an expectation and therefore a failure to place oneself unreservedly in God's hands. For theologians such as Kaufman, traditional

Christian heaven was actually un-Christian.[83] Kaufman, John Hick, and others developed theologies with little place for Christ.[84]

Conservatism was based on the Bible and the tradition that grew from the Bible. Pope John Paul II issued the intellectually powerful pronouncements *Veritatis splendor* (1993) and *Fides et ratio* (1998), which affirmed both revelation and the use of reason to elucidate revelation. Fresh blood was infused into the classical view by a statement by Catholic and Protestant leaders affirming that sanctification is a process "of the whole person, involving the mind, the will, and the affections."[85] Quite early in the twenty-first century there was talk of an "Emergent Church," a concept that seems to be an effort to recover much of the traditional wisdom of ancient and medieval theology and spirituality while exploring new routes in liturgy and worship, and de-emphasizing denominational and ideological differences. It is possible that it will encourage restoring spiritual and theological wisdom across denominational boundaries as an alternative to institutional, lowest-common-denominator ecumenism. That would help restore the truth of heaven as the warm heart of the living cosmos, Jesus Christ.[86]

Among Protestants and some Catholics, a variety of radical theologies arose on the basis of earlier skeptical movements. According to these, the statement "I believe in God" had no referential meaning because the term "God" had no external reference, and neither did the term "I." God does not exist; you do not exist. Why, then, consider yourself a theologian? The "Death of God"[87] theology promoted by Thomas Altizer did not last long in itself, but it did help prompt a deeper intellectual movement toward "negative theology," which attempted to get beyond both "being" and "negation."[88] In negative theology, the propositions "God exists" and "God does not exist" are both pre-empted by the proposition "God does not *not* exist." That peculiar phrase is not necessarily meant to be an affirmation that "God exists," however, but rather a denial that the word "exist" in the original two propositions is sufficient to apply to God. For Thomas Carlson and others, asserting that we know was replaced by recognition that we do not know. No system, myth, or philosophy, let alone technical skill, can pierce that unknowing. Unknowing can be pierced only by our generous gift of ourselves to respond to the generous gift of God, to the erotic dynamism of the divine. This term refers to the ancient and modern idea that God pours himself out into and through the cosmos *con amor e con desio,* as Dante put it, "with love and desire." God's pure generosity of spirit and action evokes in us gratitude and desire to return to him, however little we can understand him.[89] This loving generosity, Carlson maintained, transcends both logical theology and Postmodernist negation. "Heaven" opens up as an icon of the divine, "where the subject of experience is undone by precisely the God, ineffable and incomprehensible, who gives all experience."[90]

It was generally accepted among the elite intelligentsia that "now we know better" than to believe in heaven. If one were to believe at all, it had to be something original with a clever new angle.[91] This personal construction of heaven led to the underlying deconstruction of heaven: if heaven is only what Ann thinks it is for her and Jim thinks it is for him, the concept loses meaning. But a number of serious writers among Catholics, Protestants, and even agnostics approached the subject more freshly and seriously. Liberal Catholic theologians such as Hans Küng and Karl Rahner tried in the 1960s and 1970s to bring theology closer to current philosophical and critical understanding. Küng argued, much like the Protestant Rudolf Bultmann, that Christianity did not teach resurrection as a return to this life and time or as the culmination of this life in space and time. Instead, he believed, resurrection is "an assumption into God's *incomprehensible and comprehensive absolutely final and absolutely first reality.*"[92] Simon Tugwell argued that everything exists eternally in the mind of God. What has been and what will be are in God, and in God the dead are always alive, a philosophical view with which much sympathy could be found from the time of Augustine onward. Still, it left the question of whether that included only humans or animals as well, and if animals, whether it included the fleas on the cat as well as the cat.

In 1979, the Vatican affirmed the Catholic teaching of the resurrection of the dead, the resurrection of the whole person, the survival of a spiritual element after death, and the happiness of the just in heaven with Christ. It confirmed "the continuation and subsistence, after death, of a spiritual element, endowed with consciousness and will, in such a way that the human 'I' subsists, though for the moment lacking its body. This spiritual element is conveniently called the soul." It also cautioned that "neither the Bible nor the theologians supply us with enough light to be able to describe properly the life that is to come after death."[93] Joseph Ratzinger (later Pope Benedict XVI), writing in 1988, perceived the Kingdom of God as Christ's breaking through human history at the First and Second Comings. The individual's salvation is whole and entire only when the salvation of the cosmos and of all those who love God has come to full fruition. For the redeemed are not simply adjacent to each other in heaven. Rather, in their being together as the one Christ, they *are* heaven. In that moment, the whole creation will become song.[94] The Catholic Catechism of 1994 (#1024) says, "This communion of life and love with the Trinity, with the Virgin Mary, the angels and all the blessed—is called 'Heaven.' Heaven is the ultimate end and fulfillment of the deepest human longings."

Some Christian writers, such as David Tracy and Andrew Greeley, revived what Tracy called "analogical imagination." Greeley pointed out that "religion was symbol and story long before it became theology and philosophy."[95] For example, metaphor expresses meaning "over and above what would be said by a bold literal assertion"; as Dante knew, language can "leap."[96] Metaphor serves a purpose that "standard discursive language [ordinary prose] will not and cannot serve."[97] "Metaphor is that strategy of discourse by which language divests itself of its function of direct description in order to reach the mythic level where its function of discovery is set free" to move into deeper reality.[98] Both metaphorical and scientific statements, both synthetical and analytical statements, are valid in that they have reference to "reality"—that is, to something beyond the structure of the words themselves. One kind of statement attempts to close down by precision, the other sort of statement tries to open up to a richness that eludes "our ordinary literal vocabulary"; both have standing in the quest for truth.[99]

Derrida argued that some metaphors that die can come alive again when we enter into the worldview that produces them. Although Christian metaphor and poetics had become stale by the 1960s and so crumbled easily in the 1970s, they only need a revival of the imagination. Our idea of heaven is a metaphor for heaven itself. Statements such as "heaven is just a metaphor" or "heaven is nothing but a metaphor" ignore the fact that every human idea is a metaphor and that some of those metaphors are pointed toward reality. None is more pointed to reality than heaven, the metaphor that draws all depth metaphors toward it and into it. Heaven is the metaphor of metaphors, where all confusion and all pretension are caught up in loving truth. Metaphor grows in richness and reference unless we are taught to block it out.

Neural networks do shut down during childhood as a result of disuse. For instance, almost everyone is born with an innate ability to pronounce the sounds of Chinese, English, Arabic, or any other language. The ability to discern and reproduce those sounds that the child does not hear begins decreasing before the end of the first year and continues to decline throughout adulthood.[100] As with the withering of linguistic neural connections, neural networks relating to metaphor and poetry may also be shut down early by physicalist and literalist education. It is possible that people unlearn spirituality and metaphor as children owing to lack of exposure to them. Ricoeur argued that "true metaphor is vertical, ascending, transcendent," and that there is no abyss that separates metaphor from meaning, as some philosophers maintained.[101] Heaven was not a difficulty: "Space-time metaphors for what is necessarily nonspatiotemporal do not raise any linguistic problem different in kind from those of any other metaphors."[102] Philip Wheelwright said that a true metaphor commands "depth assent [and the] fullest imaginative response."[103]

A way out of dogmatism whether religious or secular appeared at the beginning of the new century in the recognition that any certainty is unwarranted and that opening minds out is a better way to understanding than shutting them down. Our efforts to find truth are aimed at piercing the cloud of unknowing, but only the arrow of love can penetrate.[104] Only that arrow can move us ahead toward our goal.

CHAPTER 8

Here

We are here in the twenty-first century. The question is whether heaven is here with us. Heaven, despite centuries of attack and ridicule, survives and flourishes in the early twenty-first century, because its deep conceptual meaning remains true. Heaven is here and now, and the idea of heaven is here and now. Heaven is the ceaseless, dynamic, restful, harmonious opening up to God and his cosmos in love, gratitude, and generosity. Heaven will go away only if we deliberately choose to give it up and shut it away in a closed room; even then it does not go away for those who choose it by loving, yearning, responding, and embracing. Some contemporary thinkers reveal dogmatism, contempt, arrogance, cleverness, and intimidation; others, generosity and openness of mind and spirit. You judge which attitudes are more likely to be true.

The concept of heaven has changed over time, not in its core concept but in the images associated with it, many stemming from the Old Testament. The hymn "All honor, laud, and glory to You, Redeemer King" was frequently sung only half a century ago, but now the words "honor," "laud" (praise), "glory," "redeemer", and "king" have ceased to evoke intellectual or even emotional response among most people in Western civilization. (Also some people imagine that words such as "thee" and "thou" were invented to make religion seem more mysterious, whereas in fact they were everyday speech into the eighteenth century.) These images have referents that continue to exist, and some still find them stirring, but their appeal is certainly no longer universal. Rather than abandoning old metaphors, however, it is helpful to revitalize them.

Other old metaphors, also rooted in the Bible, have been more intermittently alive in the past two millennia but have recently been revived. God as loving Mother, for example, is an ancient but only sporadically used image that has powerfully and rightly been brought to the fore again. God is not gender-specific. He is both Father and Mother. It is good that feminists remind us of this. Indeed, Jesus was often thought of as "mother" without in any way compromising his personal gender.[1] With all the metaphors, the core meaning remains the same: open-hearted loving embrace with God, cosmos, other creatures, and other people.

This core meaning pervades many faiths, of course. Focusing on Christianity in this book has been fitting, because for several decades it has been fashionable in parts of Western society to devalue heaven while seeking spiritual treasures in far regions and ignoring the limitless beauty, power, and truth that is in our own hearth. Although in 1598 Jean Bodin cleverly remarked of religions that "each is refuted by all," the deeper truth is that each is confirmed, complemented, and deepened by all.[2] Most religions (though not all) add to the richness of understanding of the immortal by mortals. It is disingenuous to pretend that all religions are equally valid: does anyone seriously want to place Buddhism and Satanism on the same level? The relative validity of religions may be judged. The more valid exhibit internal consistency; coherent tradition; trueness to type; experience by large numbers over time and space; richness and variety; openness; admission of limitations; sense of mystery, the holy, the wholly Other; sense of the universe as a cosmos, an entity to be loved. The less valid exhibit self-righteousness; pride; repression; violence and cruelty; manipulation of others; exploitation of the planet; dogmatism; and unwarranted certainty.

This book has addressed some of the reasons and conditions that have shuttered up the consciousness of heaven in the minds of many moderns. Here is an opportunity to open up a window of reality. It is my wish not to shut any windows myself, certainly not to skepticism, for skepticism is our inoculation against the fundamental fallibility of our perceptions. But some windows have been slammed, shuttered, and barred, and that is true of the common skepticism that claims that our minds (cognitive faculties) are nothing but the brain—nothing but meat—and therefore their ideas are unreliable. If that idea is true, then the very idea that they are unreliable is itself unreliable. As Alvin Plantinga put it, "if I *argue* to skepticism, then of course I rely on the very cognitive faculties whose unreliability is the conclusion of my skeptical argument."[3] An even more darkly-shuttered window is dogmatic skepticism, which is not really skepticism at all but an axiomatic assumption that religious expression is meaningless because only the physical is real. But what is that assumption based on? If Christianity is true, we are capable of knowledge, because God has created our minds in such a way that we can know; but if physicalism is true, then we can have no confidence in our thought processes or even our consciousness, so we are unable to know.[4] The greatest achievement of humanity is the ordered mind, right reason, understanding tuned to the reality of the cosmos.

Is heaven real? Clearly the concept of it is real, one with both consistency and development over two millennia. Does it have reality beyond the human concept of it? All answers to that are contingent upon presuppositions or axioms. Mine are that God subsists both beyond and within the universe; that humans strive to attain truth; that love is deeper and greater than intellect; that we can be, by our own choice and God's grace, in the presence of God. "Believing in heaven" really means living a life of love. What we say is important; what we do is more important; what we are is most important. We each are granted the munificent opportunity to live in God with gratitude and generosity. As Jerry Walls put it, "Union with God is the central integrating pleasure of heaven and . . . all other things are enjoyed in such a way that God is recognized as their source and glorified thereby."[5] And that is happiness itself. God's "very nature is to be ecstatically happy."[6] "In the logic of eternal love, in exchanges with the ultimate giver of gifts, more is received than can ever be given."[7]

In a civilization as technocratic as ours, those who are open to the reality "deep down things"[8] act in a zone of creative tension. On the one hand, if they wish to communicate they must use the language of the broader society; on the other hand, they must, if they wish to be meaningful, remain faithful to their scriptural and traditional roots. A balance between the scientific and the spiritual is needed. When theologians rush to embrace a new scientific or social theory, they often are ungainly and lose their balance. But, when properly and openly discussed without malice or contempt, the tension between the scientific and the spiritual can become creative dynamism that opens and deepens both love and understanding. Science does not include theology and art, but theology and art include science. Though theologians need to be extremely cautious in addressing scientific arguments, they are perfectly entitled to address the metaphysical assumptions made by physicalist scientists and their followers.

Once people deeply recognize that not just trillions and trillions, but actually trillions times trillions times trillions times trillions of organisms exist, have existed, and will exist, people may come to think that the importance of any one of them is reduced. Do we hesitate to remove dental plaque? Crunch on corn? Slap mosquitoes? Butcher cattle? Ought we to value human life especially? If humans are merely a part of the biosphere, like other life, then it would seem that no organism has a privileged position over any other organism, and the human species has no more intrinsic right to dominance or even existence than any other. In this view, the only consideration that allows us more "right" is simply our power to assert our supremacy over other beings, a technological power that is of recent origins and is geologically highly unlikely to last for more than a few million years longer at most.

Something else follows: what holds true for the species holds true for the individual. We do not grant one housefly privilege over another, one cow over another, or even one dog or cat over another (except when we act from personal sentimental feelings). Why then should one human be privileged over another? Lack of privilege, however, could be construed in diametrically opposite ways. It might lead to lofty proclamations of the highest dignity being accorded to all, contrary to all our natural instincts: the oral plaque is as worthy of dignity as the flea, which is of equal dignity as the dog, because all are a part of the tree of life. Or it might lead to the conclusion that just as one ant or slime mold is of little consideration in the scheme of things, one man or woman is of equally little consideration. And that conclusion could imply that the extinction of a human life is of no more importance than the extinction of a flea, *and that consequently murder, torture, slavery, child molesting, and even genocide are of no great matter in the scheme of things.* If humans are nothing but part of the biosphere, the record of human history and human nature is that it is less likely that the proposition will be interpreted in liberal and philanthropic terms than that it will be interpreted as license for one group to exploit, debase, and even exterminate another. That is the most likely consequence of denying the inherent dignity of human life.

Heaven is certainly real but the question remains, what is the most meaningful way of thinking of it? What may one expect the concept of heaven to be a century hence? The answer is much less likely to be what a few historians and other critics say today than the concept as it was developed over centuries. Is that concept true? Whether one "believes in heaven" or "doesn't believe in heaven," the most meaningful and fullest way to understand it is through its tradition. It remains stunning that the cosmos exists, that life exists, and that consciousness exists. It is wondrous that humans, even if they may be unintended products of a pointless universe, should be able to penetrate intellectually and even visually nearly to the end of space and the beginning of time; it is even more remarkable that, despite the horrors that surround us, we continue knowing, loving, yearning. Whatever we humans are, we are part of the cosmos, and we wonder about it, and that means that the cosmos wonders about itself. That is astounding enough, one might think, to give pause to those who find the cosmos without mind or purpose.

That at this moment atheism thrives is not strange, since now the greater part of humankind is wedged apart from God in noisy and light-polluted cities. Direct experience of the cosmos is so rare that educated people can be found seriously arguing about the reasons why stars do not give light. They have apparently never experienced a clear moonless night in the mountains or desert or at sea. Still, although I personally find little spiritual nourishment in cities, I firmly concede that the metaphors of the City of God and the New

Jerusalem, along with the essential idea of the communion of saints, are the main current of the Christian idea of heaven.

That any sentient being can and does walk upon the earth with gratitude, seeing and scenting its sweet delights, is itself heaven. That the cosmos wonders at itself is deeply moving. Heaven is "A condition of complete simplicity / (Costing not less than everything)."[9] Heaven is demanding: it requires a state of no less than complete honesty with our pretensions and rationalizations burned clean. It is we—not God—who have entrapped so many in cities where starshine and sealight are blocked up. We made the darkness that smothers us from God.

> Where were you when the western winds blew cold
> and salt snow dusted the dry dunes
> seeding them with absence?
> You were like an unseen spirit
> with whom one converses in a dark church,
> its presence close as the soul
> yet remote and untouchable as starlight.
> A distant star whose white point was perceived
> only at the eye's far corner, yet always firm in its place,
> to focus invisible, therefore some time overlooked,
> but in the inner gaze where the eye's drawn home to God
> always bright with Him, forgotten never.
>
> Then, the sky broke suddenly,
> burst by the star's pure strength.
> Then, grace shot the gap,
> downpouring liquid light,
> catching me on the mountain
> holding me in its firm flood,
> containing me in love.
> Oh now before then ever you are
> where you were and are and will be.
> The dark church is bright with boughs, green with laughter,
> and at last I see, I see your light bright face.[10]

Heaven subsists. To believe in heaven is to believe in ideals beyond which humans have never reached. My previous book *A History of Heaven: The Singing Silence* explored the rich paradoxes of heaven.[11] Here, I will say only that heaven is liberation, freedom, fulfillment of the individual self in vast horizons, fulfillment of the social self through participation; and liberation of the divine self in the presence of God. Heaven is the human being perfectly fulfilled. Heaven is the fulfillment of what we most value: love, knowledge, integrity, creativity, openness, kindness, dynamic transformation, above all joy. It is our hope to fit with generosity and gratitude into the cosmos God creates. "Fare forward, voyagers,"[12] not down into narrowing darkness but opening up and out, rising.

> To you I come
> from the split seafloor's rent rind
> where the fire of the earth's life squeezes out
> from its mother's kind and violent heart
> in passages that move our veins' blood
> I come
> from the caves of the sea's dark depths
> where sightless fish make silent home
> to you I rise
> ascending from the deaf water's icy immotion
> through the dancing warm waters colored by coral
> breaking through the surface sun-scattered light
> I mount
> through the warm and constant winds
> through the thin emptiness beyond earth's eggshell
> outward opening past the solitary stars
> To find you
> at the heart's homecoming
> in the light that fires the suns
> in the dark and secret passages of the sea
> in the hidden channels of my body's blood
> Christ, my love. [13]

This book has explored the Christian tradition of heaven and the arguments against it, finding those arguments radically insufficient. The arguments are also radically insufficient against any traditional view of heaven, whether Buddhist, Hindu, Jewish, Muslim, or whatever. It is good that each tradition maintain the full richness of its concepts of heaven over time, so that each can draw upon the richness of each. We lose unlimited treasure by seeking inclusiveness through the lowest common denominator. "I will draw all people to myself" (John 12:32). The virtue of hope includes hope that there is more than we can understand, and the virtue of generosity includes being grateful to the seekers of truth whose views enrich our own. Who among us, when our friends ask for bread, would give them a stone—or a sponge? Taste and see: heaven is here if we only allow ourselves to open up to it.

Notes

CHAPTER 1

1. Jeffrey Burton Russell, *A History of Heaven: The Singing Silence* (Princeton, N.J.: Princeton University Press, 1997).
2. Peter Stanford, *Heaven: A Traveller's Guide to the Undiscovered Country* (London: HarperCollins, 2002), 351.
3. Jerry L. Walls, *Heaven: The Logic of Eternal Joy* (Oxford: Oxford University Press, 2002), 110.
4. Carol Zaleski and Philip Zaleski, *The Book of Heaven* (Oxford: Oxford University Press, 2000); Christopher Jay Johnson and Marsha G. McGee, *How Different Religions View Death and Afterlife*, 2nd ed. (Philadelphia: The Charles Press, 1998).
5. Alvin Plantinga, *Warranted Christian Belief* (Oxford: Oxford University Press, 2000), vii; Jaroslav Pelikan, *Credo: Historical and Theological Guide to Creeds and Confessions of Faith in the Christian Tradition* (New Haven: Yale University Press, 2003).
6. John Paul II, *Fides et Ratio* (1998), paragraph 85.
7. Tony Walter, *The Eclipse of Eternity: A Sociology of the Afterlife* (New York: St. Martin's Press, 1996), 173–79; Carol Zaleski, *Otherworld Journeys: Accounts of Near-Death Experience in Medieval and Modern Times* (New York: Oxford University Press, 1987).
8. Walls, *Heaven*, 33.
9. *Christian Century*, 121, no. 2 (2004): 14.
10. I am grateful to Professor Rodney Stark for the figures and their interpretation.
11. Russell, *History of Heaven*.
12. Jeffrey Burton Russell, "Glory in Time," *Soundings* 22 (1991): 52.
13. Richard Swinburne, *The Evolution of the Soul*, 2nd ed. (Oxford: Oxford University Press, 1997), 354; Russell, *History of Heaven*, 24–25, 44–45, 67; Simon Tugwell, *Human Immortality and the Redemption of Death* (London: Darton, 1990).

14. Vladimir Lossky, *The Mystical Theology of the Eastern Church* (London: James Clark, 1957), 65.

15. Examples in artworks: *The Garden of Paradise* by the Master of the Middle Rhine, ca. 1420, *Gothic Painting* (Geneva: Skira, 1954), 184: flowers, banquets, birds, fruit, meadow, book, zither, crown, walled garden, spring, winged angel—and a dead demon; Albrecht Dürer, *Adoration of the Holy Trinity* 1511: angels, blessed, martyrs above the earth with the three Persons of the Trinity. *Painting in the Sixteenth Century* (Geneva: Skira, 1956), 99.

16. Russell, *History of Heaven,* 13–15; 157–85.

17. Revelation 21:2 (New Revised Standard Version).

18. On concepts see Arthur O. Lovejoy, *The Great Chain of Being* (Cambridge, Mass: Harvard University Press, 1936); Hilary Putnam, *Representation and Reality* (Cambridge, Mass.: MIT Press, 1988), 19–41; Jeffrey Burton Russell, *The Devil: Perceptions of Evil From Antiquity to Primitive Christianity* (Ithaca: Cornell University Press, 1977), 40–54; Stephen Toulmin, *Human Understanding* (Princeton: Princeton University Press, 1972); Richard M. Weaver, *Ideas Have Consequences* (Chicago: University of Chicago Press, 1948).

19. Hilary Putnam, *Representation and Reality* (Cambridge, Mass.: MIT Press, 1988), 11. See also Paul Ricoeur, *The Rule of Metaphor* (Toronto: Toronto University Press, 1977), 257–59.

20. Putnam, *Representation and Reality,* 13.

21. Gibor B. Basri, "What Is a Planet?" *Mercury* (November/December 2003): 27–34.

22. Norman Kreitman, *The Roots of Metaphor* (Brookfield, Vt.: Ashgate, 1999), 120–21.

23. Ibid., 157.

24. Russell, *History of Heaven,* 6–9.

25. Shakespeare, *The Merchant of Venice,* V.i.54.

26. Kreitman, *Roots of Metaphor,* 169.

27. Russell, *History of Heaven,* 70–71.

28. Michael A. Arbib and Mary B. Hesse, *The Construction of Reality* (Cambridge: Cambridge University Press, 1986), 237.

CHAPTER 2

1. Philip C. Almond, *Heaven and Hell in Enlightenment England* (Cambridge: Cambridge University Press, 1994), 43.

2. Jeffrey Burton Russell, *Encyclopaedia Britannica* (2002), vol. 25, s.v. "Witchcraft," 92–98; Russell, *Satan: The Early Christian Tradition* (Cornell University Press, 1981); Russell, *Lucifer: The Devil in the Middle Ages* (Cornell University Press, 1984); Russell, *Mephistopheles: The Devil in the Modern World* (Cornell University Press, 1986); Rodney Stark, *For the Glory of God* (Princeton: Princeton University Press, 2003).

3. *Encyclopaedia Britannica,* 92–98.

4. Stark, *For the Glory of God,* 202 and 398, n7.

5. Colleen McDannell and Bernhard Lang, *Heaven: A History* (New Haven: Yale University Press, 1988), 145–80.

6. John Bunyan, *Christian Behaviour; The Holy City; The Resurrection of the Dead* (1678–1684), ed. J. Sears McGee (Oxford: Clarendon, 1987), 238.

7. Jean Delumeau, *Que reste-t-il du paradis?* (Paris: Fayard, 2000), 454–55.

8. Ibid., 356–57.

9. Sir Walter Raleigh, "The Passionate Man's Pilgrimage," *Oxford Book of Christian Verse* (Oxford: Clarendon, 1940), 60.

10. Delumeau, *Que reste-t-il du paradis?*, 382–95; W. G. L. Randles, *The Unmaking of the Medieval Christian Cosmos, 1500–1760* (Aldershot: Ashgate, 1999), 133–50, 181–82, 219–23.

11. Jeffrey Burton Russell, *A History of Heaven: The Singing Silence* (Princeton: Princeton University Press, 1997), 46–47; Jerry L. Walls, *Heaven: The Logic of Eternal Joy* (Oxford: Oxford University Press, 2002), 93–112.

12. Simon Tugwell, *Human Immortality and the Redemption of Death* (London: Darton, Longman, and Todd, 1990), 81, 160–76.

13. Tugwell, *Human Immortality*, 3, 73. Trent I. xii. 2 in Heinrich Denzinger, ed., *Enchiridion symbolorum* (Rome: Herder, 1960), 272–73.

14. R. W. K. Paterson, *Philosophy and the Belief in a Life after Death* (London: Macmillan, 1995), 74; Susanne Rupp, *From Grace to Glory: Himmelsvorstellungen in der englischen Theologie und Literatur des 17. Jahrhunderts* (Heidelberg: Universitätsverlag, 2001), 107–08.

15. *Oxford Book of Seventeenth-Century Verse* (Oxford: Clarendon Press, 1934), 129. Donne here makes "Saint Lucy's night" (December 13) the longest night of the year, although even by the Julian calendar in use at Donne's time it was not.

16. William Perkins, *A Golden Chaine: Or, The Description of Theologie* (London: John Legat, 1600), 141–42.

17. John Donne, *Oxford Book of Seventeenth-Century Verse*, 135.

18. Catherine Brown Tkacz, "Typology," in *Augustine through the Ages*, ed. Allan D. Fitzgerald (Grand Rapids, Mich.: Eerdmans, 1999), 855–57; C. Tkacz, *The Key to the Brescia Casket: Typology and the Early Christian Imagination* (Notre Dame, Ind.: University of Notre Dame Press, 2002); C. Tkacz, "*Aneboesen phone megale*: Susanna and the Synoptic Passion Narratives," *Gregorianum* 87 (2006).

19. Henry More, *The Immortality of the Soul* (London, 1659); *Sacred Theory of the World*; William Assheton, *A Vindication of the Immortality of the Soul and a Future State* (London, 1703); Almond, *Heaven and Hell*, 138–40.

20. John J. Collins, Bernard McGinn, and Stephen J. Stein, eds., *The Encyclopedia of Apocalypticism*, 3 vols. (New York: Continuum, 1998); Douglas Lumsden, *And Then the End Will Come* (New York: Garland, 2002).

21. Almond, *Heaven and Hell*, 121.

22. Rupp, *From Grace to Glory*, 195–257; quotation from 200: Thomas Traherne, *Centuries*.

23. Helen Gardner, ed., *John Donne: The Divine Poems* (Oxford: Clarendon, 1952), 114.

24. Almond, *Heaven and Hell*, 11, 38–47, 140.

25. Jonathan I. Israel, *Radical Enlightenment: Philosophy and the Making of Modernity 1650–1750* (Oxford: Oxford University Press, 2001), 406–35.
26. Donne, *Oxford Book of Seventeenth-Century Verse*, 105.
27. Walls, *Heaven*, 112.
28. On grace and justification, see Alister McGrath, *Iustitia Dei: A History of the Christian Doctrine of Justification* (Cambridge: Cambridge University Press, 1986).
29. Nathanael Culverwel, *Spiritual Opticks*, in *An Elegant and Learned Discourse of the Light of Nature, with Several Other Treatises* (Oxford: Thomas Williams, 1669), 181, 183.
30. Milton, "The Christian Doctrine," in *The Student's Milton*, ed. Frank Allen Patterson (New York: Appleton-Century-Crofts, 1930), 1020.
31. Israel, *Radical Enlightenment*, 50.
32. Ibid., 59–71.
33. *Pilgrim's Progress*, cited in Carol Zaleski and Philip Zaleski, *The Book of Heaven* (Oxford: Oxford University Press, 2001), 31–32. On Bunyan, see Alister McGrath, *A Brief History of Heaven* (Oxford: Blackwell, 2003), 29–30; Rupp, *From Grace to Glory*, 253–305.
34. Rupp, *From Grace to Glory*, 131.
35. Milton, *Paradise Lost*, 3:344–71, *Oxford Book of Seventeenth-Century Verse* (Oxford: Clarendon Press, 1934), 519–20.
36. *Oxford Book of Seventeenth-Century Verse*, 782.
37. Ibid., 131.
38. W. G. H. Randles, *The Unmaking of the Medieval Christian Cosmos, 1500–1760* (Aldershof: Ashgate, 1999).
39. Delumeau, *Que reste-t-il du paradis?*; Edward Grant, *The Foundations of Modern Science in the Middle Ages* (Cambridge: Cambridge University Press, 1996); Grant, *God and Reason in the Middle Ages* (Cambridge: Cambridge University Press, 2001); David C. Lindberg, *The Beginnings of Western Science* (Chicago: University of Chicago Press, 1992).
40. Carl Becker, *The Heavenly City of the Eighteenth-Century Philosophers* (New Haven: Yale University Press, 1932).
41. Francis Oakley, "The Absolute and Ordained Power of God in Sixteenth-Century and Seventeenth-Century Theology," *Journal of the History of Ideas* 59 (1998): 437–62.
42. Jeffrey Burton Russell, *Inventing the Flat Earth: Columbus and Modern Historians* (New York, 1991).
43. Michael Arbib and Mary B. Hesse, *The Construction of Reality* (Cambridge, Cambridge University Press, 1986), 149; Edwin Arthur Burtt, *The Metaphysical Foundation of Modern Physical Science* (London: Routledge and Kegan Paul, 1932), 67.
44. Leonard Marsak, "The Idea of Reason in Seventeenth-Century France," *Journal of World History* 11 (1968): 407–16.
45. Rick Kennedy, *A History of Reasonableness: Testimony and Authority in the Art of Thinking* (Rochester, N.Y: University of Rochester Press, 2004), 116; Robert A. Nisbet, *History of the Idea of Progress* (New York: Basic Books, 1980).

46. *The Barnhart Concise Dictionary of Etymology* (New York: HarperCollins, 1995), 268.

47. Carl Becker, *The Heavenly City of the Eighteenth-Century* Philosophers (New Haven: Yale University Press, 1932), 132–33.

48. Russell, *History of Heaven*, 178–85.

49. Delumeau, *Que reste-t-il du paradis?*, 413.

50. Ibid., 402–3.

51. David C. Lindberg and Ronald Numbers, eds., *God and Nature* (Berkeley: University of California Press, 1986).

52. Burtt, *Metaphysical Foundation*, 83, 101.

53. Ibid., 126–27.

54. Ibid., 107.

55. Leonora Rosenfield, *From Beast-Machine to Man-Machine* (New York: Oxford University Press, 1940).

56. Delumeau, *Que reste-t-il du paradis?*, 370–73.

57. Richard Swinburne, *The Evolution of the Soul*, 2nd ed. (Oxford: Clarendon Press, 1997), 180–96.

58. Brendan Maurice Dooley, "*Veritas Filia Temporis*: Experience and Belief in Early Modern Culture," *Journal of the History of Ideas* 60 (1999): 241–56.

59. John Locke, *The Reasonableness of Christianity As Delivered in the Scriptures*, ed. John C. Higgins-Biddle (Oxford: Clarendon, 1999), 11–16.

60. Kennedy, *History of Reasonableness*, 142–46.

61. Ibid., 252.

62. Alvin Plantinga, *Warranted Christian Belief* (Oxford: Oxford University Press, 2000), 81–82.

63. Burtt, *Metaphysical Foundation*, 26.

64. Thomas Kuhn, *The Copernican Revolution* (Cambridge, Mass.: Harvard University Press, 1985 [1957]), 262–63.

CHAPTER 3

1. Louis Dupré, *The Enlightenment and the Intellectual Foundations of Modern Culture* (New Haven, Conn.: Yale University Press, 2004). The phrase "*Die Entzauberung der Welt*" was coined later by Max Weber (1864–1920).

2. Jonathan I. Israel, *Radical Enlightenment: Philosophy and the Making of Modernity 1650–1750* (Oxford: Oxford University Press, 2001), 11.

3. Frank Manuel, *The Eighteenth Century Confronts the Gods* (Cambridge, Mass.: Harvard University Press, 1959), 5.

4. Alvin Plantinga, *God, Freedom, and Evil* (Grand Rapids: Eerdmans, 1974); Jeffrey Burton Russell, *The Devil* (Ithaca: Cornell University Press, 1978); *Satan* (Cornell University Press, 1981); *Lucifer* (Cornell University Press, 1984); *Mephistopheles* (Cornell University Press, 1986); *The Prince of Darkness* (Cornell University Press, 1988); also Roy F. Baumeister, *Evil: Inside Human Violence and Cruelty* (New York: Henry Holt and Co., 1997); James Waller, *Becoming Evil:*

How Ordinary People Commit Genocide and Mass Killing (Oxford: Oxford University Press, 2002); Joseph F. Kelly, *The Problem of Evil: The Western Tradition* (Collegeville, Minn.: Liturgical Press, 2002); Susan Neiman, *Evil: An Alternative History of Philosophy* (Princeton, N.J.: Princeton University Press, 2002); Lance Morrow, *Evil: An Investigation* (New York: Basic Books, 2003); Predrag Cicovacki, ed., *Destined for Evil* (Rochester, N.Y.: University of Rochester Press, 2005). Michael Shermer, *The Science of Good and Evil* (New York: Holt, 2004) has an antitheist agenda. A conference on evil (in New York April 30–May 1, 2005) was sponsored by The Metropolitan Center for Mental Health and The Metropolitan Institute for Training in Psychoanalytic Psychotherapy. An excellent summary of recent theodicies, along with a "defeater" for the idea that the existence of evil refutes the existence of God is Alvin Plantinga, *Warranted Christian Belief* (Oxford: Oxford University Press, 2000), 458–99. Recent genetic research indicates that some people are born with a greater tendency to destructiveness than others, *The Economist* (May 28, 2005): 82.

5. Peter Harrison, "Original Sin and the Problem of Knowledge in Early Modern Europe," *Journal of the History of Ideas* 63 (2002): 239–60.

6. Carl Becker, *The Heavenly City of the Eighteenth-Century Philosophers* (New Haven: Yale University Press, 1932), 102.

7. Klaus P. Fischer, "John Locke in the German Enlightenment," *Journal of the History of Ideas* 36 (1975): 440, 446.

8. David Hume, *An Enquiry concerning Human Understanding*, ed. Tom L. Beauchamp (Oxford: Oxford University Press, 2000), 102, 105. Hume originally wrote this essay in the 1730s and was planning to publish it in his *Treatise of Human Nature*, but he withdrew it from that treatise, later publishing it in the *Enquiry concerning Human Understanding* (1748). His *Dialogues concerning Natural Religion* were written in 1757 but published posthumously in 1779.

9. Hume, *Enquiry*, 106.

10. Hume, *Treatise of Human Nature*, ed. L. A. Selby-Bigge (Oxford: Clarendon, 1949), 279.

11. Manuel, *Eighteenth Century Confronts the Gods*, 169.

12. A. Seth Pringle-Pattison, *The Idea of God in the Light of Recent Philosophy* (New York: Oxford University Press, 1920), 8.

13. William A. Dembski, *The Design Revolution: Answering the Toughest Questions about Intelligent Design* (Downers Grove, Ill.: Intervarsity Press, 2004), 226–27.

14. Hume, *Dialogues*, 205.

15. Hume, *Enquiry*, 99. The essay "On Miracles" is section 10 of the *Enquiry*. The most accessible and convincing contemporary account of miracles is Randall Sullivan, *The Miracle Detective* (New York: Grove, 2004).

16. Flannery O'Connor, *Wise Blood*, in *O'Connor*, ed. Sally Fitzgerald (New York: The Library of America, 1987), 94.

17. Alvin Plantinga, *Warranted Christian Belief* (Oxford: Oxford University Press, 2000); Hilary Putnam, *Representation and Reality* (Cambridge, Mass: MIT Press, 1988).

18. Boston School of Theology, www.religiosityscalesproject.com

19. Hume, *Enquiry*, 97.
20. Rick Kennedy, *A History of Reasonableness: Testimony and Authority in the Art of Thinking* (Rochester, N.Y.: University of Rochester Press, 2004), 158–61.
21. Becker, *Heavenly City*, 157.
22. Manuel, *Eighteenth Century Confronts the Gods*, 228.
23. Denis Diderot, *Encyclopédie*, s.v. "Bible," "Ciel," "Paradis."
24. J. B. Bury, *The Idea of Progress* (London: Macmillan, 1920); Robert Nisbet, *History of the Idea of Progress* (New York: Basic Books, 1980); Christopher Lasch, *The True and Only Heaven: Progress and Its Critics* (New York: Norton, 1991).
25. Norman Cohn, *The Pursuit of the Millennium*, 2nd ed. (New York: Oxford University Press, 1970).
26. Manuel, *Eighteenth Century Confronts the Gods*, 141.
27. Robert Nisbet, *History of the Idea of Progress* (New York: Basic Books, 1980), 199.
28. Philip Morin Freneau, *A Poem on the Rising Glory of America* (Philadelphia: Cruikshank for Aitkin), 1772. Early American Imprints, first series, no. 12398.
29. Timothy Dwight, *Greenfield Hill: A Poem in Seven Parts* (New York: Childs and Swaine, 1794), 52, 159; see also *America: Or, a Poem on the Settlement of the British Colonies; Addressed to the Friends of Freedom, and their Country* (New Haven: Thomas and Samuel Green, 1780).
30. Colleen McDannell and Bernhard Lang, *Heaven: A History* (New Haven: Yale University Press, 1988), 204–7.
31. Israel, *Radical Enlightenment*, 320–21.
32. Joseph Addison, *Cato*, 5.1. (London: Tonson, 1713).
33. Henry Vaughan, "The World," *The Oxford Book of Christian Verse*, 232.
34. Vaughan, "They Are All Gone into the World of Light," ibid., 244.
35. John Richard Watson, ed., *An Annotated Anthology of Hymns* (Oxford: Oxford University Press, 2002); Watson, *The English Hymn: A Critical and Historical Survey* (New York: Oxford University Press, 1997); John Julian, *A Dictionary of Hymnology* (New York: Scribner's, 1892).
36. Isaac Watts, "God's Dominion and Decree," in Hoxie Neale Fairchild, *Religious Trends in English Poetry*, 6 vols. (New York: Columbia University Press, 1939–68), 1:124.
37. Watts, "Heaven and Hell," ibid. 1:125.
38. Watts, "The Song of Angels Above," ibid 1:127.
39. Watts, "Come, Lord Jesus," ibid. 1:133–34.
40. Watts, "A Prospect of Heaven Makes Death Easy," *Oxford Book of Eighteenth-Century Verse*, 53–54.
41. Elizabeth Singer Rowe, "Hymn," in Fairchild, *Religious Trends in English Poetry* 1.140.
42. *Oxford Book of Christian Verse*, 257.
43. Alister McGrath, *A Brief History of Heaven* (Oxford: Blackwell, 2003), 158–59. See Ronald Corp, *Spirituals of the Deep South* (London: Faber, 1993).
44. Jerry L. Walls, *Heaven: The Logic of Eternal Joy* (Oxford: Oxford University Press, 2002), 39.

45. Emanuel Swedenborg, *A Treatise concerning Heaven and Hell* (London: J. Phillips, 1778). McDannell and Lang, *Heaven: A History,* 181–227.

46. Thomas A. Kselman, *Death and the Afterlife in Modern France* (Princeton: Princeton University Press, 1993), 148–49.

47. McDannell and Lang, *Heaven: A History,* 188.

48. Carol Zaleski and Philip Zaleski, *The Book of Heaven* (Oxford: Oxford University Press, 2000), 272.

49. Immanuel Kant, *Foundations of the Metaphysics of Morals; What is Enlightenment* (Chicago: University of Chicago Press, 1950).

50. Fischer, "John Locke in the German Enlightenment," 439.

51. Plantinga, *Warranted Christian Belief,* 3–30. Plantinga points out that there are two large different schools of thought about what Kant meant by noumena and phenomena.

52. William Barrett, *Death of the Soul: From Descartes to the Computer* (Garden City, N.Y.: Anchor Doubleday, 1987), 82.

53. James Collins, *God in Modern Philosophy* (Chicago: Regnery, 1959), 191.

54. Immanuel Kant, *Critique of Practical Reason,* ed. Mary Gregor (Cambridge: Cambridge University Press, 1997).

55. Barrett, *Death of the Soul,* 101.

56. Ibid., 102–3.

57. Etienne Gilson, *Modern Philosophy: Descartes to Kant* (New York: Random House, 1963), 444.

58. Leonard Marsak suggested this phrase.

CHAPTER 4

1. Richard Dawkins, *The Blind Watchmaker* (New York: Norton, 1986).

2. Auguste Comte, *The Catechism of Positive Religion,* trans. Richard Congreve, 3rd ed. (London: Kegan, Paul, Trench, Trübner, 1891).

3. Jacques Barzun, *Darwin, Marx, Wagner: Critique of a Heritage* (Boston: Little Brown, 1947), 99.

4. Collins, *God,* 238–39.

5. Ludwig Feuerbach, *The Essence of Christianity,* trans. George Eliot. (New York: Harper, 1957), 315–17.

6. Walt Whitman, "Song of Myself," in Whitman, *Complete Poetry and Collected Prose* (New York: The Library of America, 1982), 188.

7. Friedrich Schleiermacher, *On Religion: Speeches to its Cultural Despisers,* trans. John Oman (New York: Harper and Row, 1958).

8. Ernest Renan, *L'avenir de la science,* in *Oeuvres complètes,* 12 vols. (Paris: Calmann-Lévy, 1949) 3: 991–92.

9. Georg Wilhelm Friedrich Hegel, *Lectures on the Philosophy of Religion,* ed. Peter C. Hodgson, 3 vols. (Berkeley: University of California Press, 1988) 3:208–9.

10. Ibid., 3:304.

11. Ralph Waldo Emerson, *The Journals and Miscellaneous Notebooks* (Cambridge, Mass.: Belknap, 1969); Catherine Albanese, *Corresponding Motion: Transcendental America and the New America* (Philadelphia: Temple University Press, 1977). Compare William Ellery Channing, "The Future Life," in *The Works of William E. Channing* (Boston: American Unitarian Association, 1880). I was surrounded by these influences when I was growing up in Berkeley: I went to Emerson Elementary School, and Channing Way was only a few streets from my house. Quote from Robert Bellah, *The Habits of the Heart* (Berkeley: University of California Press, 1985), 63.

12. Norman Cohn, *The Pursuit of the Millennium*, 2nd ed. (New York: Oxford University Press, 1970).

13. Karl Marx and Friedrich Engels, *On Religion*, trans. Reinhold Niebuhr (Chico, Calif.: Scholar's Press, 1966), 41–42. Original italics.

14. Ibid., 147–49.

15. "Consumerism" appeared first in 1944.

16. Immanuel Kant, *Critique of the Power of Judgment*, ed. Paul Guyer (Cambridge: Cambridge University Press, 2000), 308–9.

17. W. J. T. Mitchell, *The Last Dinosaur Book* (Chicago: University of Chicago Press, 1998); Keith Parsons, *The Great Dinosaur Controversy: A Guide to the Debates* (Santa Barbara: ABC-CLIO, 2003).

18. For example, Johann Georg Hamann (1730–88) and Johann Gottfried Herder (1744–1803).

19. Frank Manuel, *The Eighteenth Century Confronts the Gods* (Cambridge, Mass.: Harvard University Press, 1959), 283–86, 308.

20. William Blake, *The Poetical Works of William Blake* (Oxford: Oxford University Press, 1913), 241 368, 247–61, 133.

21. William Wordsworth, "Ode: Intimations of Immortality," *Oxford Book of English Verse* (Oxford: Clarendon, 1921), 609–16.

22. Ralph Waldo Emerson, *Journals*, July 1855 and May 1849.

23. Elizabeth Barrett Browning, *Aurora Leigh* (1857), book 7, line 820.

24. Fyodor Dostoevsky, *The Brothers Karamazov* (1879–80), bk. 2, chap. 6.

25. McDannell and Lang, *Heaven: A History* (New Haven: Yale University Press, 1988), especially 247–72; quotation from 265; Thomas A. Kselman, *Death and the Afterlife in Modern France* (Princeton: Princeton University Press, 1993), 143–53.

26. Kselman, *Death and the Afterlife*, 152.

27. Ibid., 158.

28. Ibid., 149–50.

29. Ibid., 137.

30. Susan Chitty, *The Beast and the Monk: A Life of Charles Kingsley* (London: Hodder and Stoughton, 1974); On Moody and Sankey, see J. H. S. Kent, *Holding the Fort: Studies in Victorian Revivalism* (London: Epworth Press, 1978).

31. McDannell and Lang, *Heaven: A History*, 286; Russell, *A History of Heaven: The Singing Silence* (Princeton: Princeton University Press, 1997), 88–148.

32. McDannell and Lang on Phelps, *Heaven: A History,* 228, 264–68; on the number of books, 228; on the Presbyterian sermon of 1877, 258; on Kingsley, 261–64; on family prayers in heaven, 272–73; on Progress in the other world, 276–87; on good works in heaven, 278–86; on Robert M. Patterson, 279.

33. Edward Fitzgerald, *The Rubaiyat of Omar Khayyam* (1859), *Oxford Book of Victorian Verse* (Oxford: Clarendon Press, 1912), 185.

CHAPTER 5

1. A. J. Conyers, *Eclipse of Heaven* (South Bend, Ind.: St. Augustine's Press, 1992); Tony Walter, *The Eclipse of Eternity: A Sociology of the Afterlife* (New York: St. Martin's Press, 1996); Martin Buber, *The Eclipse of God* (New York: Harper, 1952).

2. John C. Greene, *Darwin and the Modern World View* (Baton Rouge: Louisiana State University Press, 1961), 95–96.

3. Peter J. Bowler, *Evolution: The History of an Idea,* 2nd ed. (Berkeley: University of California Press, 1989), 9.

4. Gregory Claeys, "The 'Survival of the Fittest' and the Origins of Social Darwinism," *Journal of the History of Ideas* 61 (2000): 223–40; Gertrude Himmelfarb, *Darwin and the Darwinian Revolution* (Garden City, N.Y.: Doubleday, 1959), 216; Jacques Barzun, *Darwin, Marx, Wagner: Critique of a Heritage* (Boston: Little Brown, 1947), 61. On the phrase "survival of the fittest," see Herbert Spencer, *The Principles of Biology,* 2 vols. (London: William and Norgate, 1864–67) 1:444–45. The original date was established by Diane B. Paul, "The Selection of the 'Survival of the Fittest,'" *Journal of the History of Biology* 64 (2003): 411–22.

5. A popular children's book, *A Picturesque Tale of Progress* by Olive Beaupré Miller (Chicago: The Book House for Children, 1929), made an enormous impression on me and my friends. The endpapers show the gradual advance from a prehistoric cave to the culmination of Progress: the Empire State Building!

6. John C. Greene, *Science, Ideology, and World View* (Berkeley: University of California Press, 1981), 130–38.

7. Greene, *Darwin,* 78; Greene, *Science,* 134.

8. Greene, *Science,* 73.

9. Ibid., 71–87.

10. Himmelfarb, *Darwin and the Darwinian Revolution,* 255.

11. Richard Weikart, *From Darwin to Hitler: Evolutionary Ethics, Eugenics, and Racism in Germany* (New York: Palgrave Macmillan, 2004): the following paragraphs owe much to Weikart's work; Edwin Black, *War Against the Weak: Eugenics and America's Campaign to Create a Master Race* (New York: Four Walls Eight Windows, 2003); Ian Dowbiggin, *A Merciful End: The Euthanasia Movement in Modern America* (Oxford: Oxford University Press, 2003); N. D. A. Kemp, *"Merciful Release": The History of the British Euthanasia Movement* (Manchester: Manchester University Press, 2002); Christine Rosen, *Preaching Eugenics: Religious Leaders and the American Eugenics Movement* (Oxford: Oxford University Press, 2004). Rosen and Black are reviewed in Amy Lauren Hall, "The Eugenics Temptation: Good Breeding," *Christian Century,* November 2, 2004: 24–29.

12. Weikart, 10, 24, 75, 114, 135, 138, 146, 163, 222, 232; Martin Ottenheimer, *Forbidden Relatives: The American Myth of Cousin-Marriage* (Urbana, Ill.: University of Illinois Press: 1996), 19–60.

13. Sharon M. Leon, "'A Human Being, and Not a Mere Social Factor:' Catholic Strategies for Dealing with Sterilization Statutes in the 1920s," *Church History* 73 (2004): 383–411.

14. Hall, "The Eugenics Temptation: Good Breeding," 24.

15. Janet Browne, *Charles Darwin: Voyaging* (Princeton, N.J.: Princeton University Press, 1995), x; Browne: *Charles Darwin: The Power of Place* (Princeton, N.J.: Princeton University Press, 2002), 59. Browne's biography is definitive.

16. Browne, *Charles Darwin: The Power of Place*, 218.

17. Wallace, quoted in Greene, *Science*, 146.

18. Arthur O. Lovejoy, *The Great Chain of Being* (Cambridge, Mass: Harvard University Press, 1936).

19. Browne, *Charles Darwin: Voyaging*, 542–43.

20. Susan Budd, *Varieties of Unbelief: Atheists and Agnostics in English Society, 1850–1960* (London: Heinemann, 1977), 104–49.

21. Himmelfarb, *Darwin and the Darwinian Revolution*, 238–39.

22. Francis Darwin, ed., *The Life and Letters of Charles Darwin: Including an Autobiographical Chapter*, 3 vols. (London: John Murray, 1887) 2:312.

23. Browne, *Charles Darwin: The Power of Place*, 54.

24. Francis Darwin, ed., *Autobiography of Charles Darwin, with Two Appendices* (London: Watts & Co., 1929), 139–54, quotations from 139, 142–47.

25. Francis Darwin, ed., *The Life and Letters of Charles Darwin*, 2:7.

26. Greene, *Science*, 150.

27. Ibid., 102–3.

28. Charles Darwin, *The Descent of Man* (New York: Appleton, 1888), 136.

29. Browne, *Charles Darwin: Voyaging*, 437–38.

30. *Encyclopaedia Britannica* (2002), 8:559.

31. Peter J. Bowler, *Evolution: The History of an Idea*, passim.

32. Ronald C. Numbers, *Darwinism Comes to America* (Cambridge, Mass.: Harvard University Press, 1998), 23, lists common misperceptions about the history of Darwinism.

33. Darwin, *Descent*, 621.

34. Greene, *Science*, 102.

35. Ibid., 103.

36. Darwin, *Descent*, 129–48; 169–202; 594; 633; 622; 634; 623.

37. Francis Darwin, ed., *Autobiography of Charles Darwin*, 153–54.

38. Darwin, *Descent*, 627.

39. Barzun, *Darwin, Marx, Wagner*, 71.

40. Browne, *Charles Darwin: The Power of Place*, 247–49, 329, 383; David Klinghoffer, "The Branding of a Heretic," *Wall Street Journal*, January 28, 2005.

41. Bowler, *Evolution*, 218–21, 237, 243–44.

42. Ibid., 325.

43. Browne, *Charles Darwin: The Power of Place*, 297.

44. Greene, *Darwin,* 78.
45. Bowler, *Evolution,* 221.
46. Paul Lawrence Farber, *The Temptations of Evolutionary Ethics* (Berkeley: University of California Press, 1994), 63–69, 77.
47. Nineteenth-century writers: John W. Draper, *History of the Conflict between Religion and Science* (New York: Appleton , 1874); William Whewell, *History of the Inductive Sciences from the Earliest to the Present Time* (New York: Appleton, 1890); Andrew Dickson White, *A History of the Warfare of Science with Theology in Christendom* (New York: Appleton, 1896). For critiques, see Jeffrey Burton Russell, *Inventing the Flat Earth: Columbus and Modern Historians* (New York: Praeger, 1991); David N. Livingstone, "Re-placing Darwinism and Christianity," in David C. Lindberg and Ronald L. Numbers, ed., *When Science and Christianity Meet* (Chicago: University of Chicago Press, 2003), 183–202.
48. Susan Budd, *Varieties of Unbelief: Atheists and Agnostics in English Society, 1850-1960* (London: Heinemann, 1977), 124–49.
49. Barzun, *Darwin, Marx, Wagner,* 351–52.
50. *Teaching about Evolution and the Nature of Science* (Washington, D.C.: National Academy of Sciences Press, 1998), 58.
51. Numbers, *The Creationists* (Berkeley: University of California Press, 1992), 300.
52. Jeffrey Burton Russell, *Inventing the Flat Earth* (New York: Praeger, 1991).
53. Bowler, *Evolution,* 318.
54. Jeffrey Burton Russell, *The Devil* (Ithaca: Cornell University Press, 1977); *Satan* (Cornell, 1981); *Lucifer* (Cornell University Press, 1984); *Mephistopheles* (Cornell University Press, 1986); *The Prince of Darkness* (Cornell University Press, 1988). These books approach the subject of evil through the history of concepts. The last in the series deals most specifically on ways to reconcile God's goodness and power with the existence of evil.
55. Heinrich Denzinger, *Enchiridion symbolorum,* 31st ed. (Freiburg-im-Breisgau: Herder, 1960), 482–90.
56. Himmelfarb, *Darwin and the Darwinian Revolution,* 375–76; Numbers, *Darwinism Comes,* 2.
57. Christoph Schönborn, "Finding Design in Nature," Op-Ed, *New York Times,* July 7, 2005.
58. Gerard Manley Hopkins, "The Caged Skylark," *Poems of Gerard Manley Hopkins,* ed. Robert Bridges (Oxford: Oxford University Press, 1948), 75.
59. Ronald C. Numbers, *Darwinism Comes,* 5, 12; Numbers, *The Creationists,* 72–101, 300, 323–35.
60. McDannell and Lang, *Heaven: A History* (New Haven: Yale University Press, 1988), 313–22; Philip Barlow, *Mormons and the Bible: The Place of Latter-day Saints in American Religion* (New York: Oxford University Press, 1991).
61. Elizabeth Stuart Phelps, *The Gates Ajar* (Boston: Fields, Osgood, and Co., 1868); cited at length in Carol Zaleski and Philip Zaleski, *The Book of Heaven* (Oxford: Oxford University Press, 2000), 135–47 and discussed by McDannell and Lang, *Heaven: A History,* 265–67.
62. Ibid.

63. McDannell and Lang note numerous other untraditional nineteenth-century views, for example (392 n40) Eliza Bisbee Duffey, *Heaven Revised: A Narrative of Personal Experiences after the Change Called Death*, 10th ed. (Manchester: "The Two Worlds," 1898).

64. Matthew Arnold, "Dover Beach," *Oxford Book of Victorian Verse*, 369.

65. Mark Twain, "An Extract from Captain Stormfield's Visit to Heaven," in Twain, *The Complete Short Stories of Mark Twain*, ed. Charles Neider (Garden City, N.Y.: Doubleday, 1985), 583–84.

66. Mark Twain, *Letters from the Earth* (New York: Perennial Classics, 2004), 2.

67. Mark Twain, *No. 44, The Mysterious Stranger* (Berkeley: University of California Press, 1982), 187.

68. Alfred Lord Tennyson, *In memoriam*, xxi, *The Poetic and Dramatic Works of Alfred Lord Tennyson* (Boston and New York: Houghton, Mifflin, 1899).

69. Ibid., lvi, 233.

70. Ibid., cxxxi, 259.

71. Tennyson, "St. Agnes' Eve," *Oxford Book of Victorian Verse*, 204; "Crossing the Bar," *Oxford Book of Victorian Verse,* 227.

72. Gerard Manley Hopkins, "God's Grandeur," *Poems of Gerard Manley Hopkins*, ed. Robert Bridges and W. H. Gardner (New York: Oxford University Press, 1948), 70.

73. On Mill, see R. W. K. Paterson, *Philosophy and the Belief in a Life after Death* (London: Macmillan, 1995), 112–14; William James, *The Will to Believe* (New York: Longmans, Green, 1897); *Human Immortality: Two Supposed Objections to the Doctrine* (Boston: Houghton Mifflin, 1898); *The Varieties of Religious Experience* (New York: Longmans, Green, 1903); *Psychology* (New York: Henry Holt, 1908).

74. Friedrich Nietzsche, *Beyond Good and Evil* (New York: Boni and Liveright, 1917); *Der Wille zur Macht* (*The Will to Power*, Edinburgh: T. N. Foulis, 1910). Leni Riefenstahl's famous propaganda film for Hitler bears the title *Der Triumph des Willens*.

75. Michael Lackey, "Killing God, Liberating the 'Subject': Nietzsche and Post-God Freedom, *Journal of the History of Ideas* 60 (1999): 737–54.

76. Russell, *Mephistopheles*, 224–25.

77. Friedrich Nietzsche, *Thus Spake Zarathustra* (1883–85); *Beyond Good and Evil* (1886); *The Will to Power* (1901). See William Barrett, *Irrational Man: A Study in Existential Philosophy* (Garden City, N.Y.: Doubleday Anchor, 1958), 158–83; "We have no language that allows us to speak of God." Thomas Carlson, *Indiscretion: Finitude and the Naming of God* (Chicago: University of Chicago Press, 1999), 23.

CHAPTER 6

1. Bruno Bettelheim, *Freud and Man's Soul* (New York: Knopf, 1974); Ana Maria Rizzuto, *Why Did Freud Reject God? A Psychodynamic Interpretation* (New Haven: Yale University Press, 1998), 162.

2. Charles Brenner, *An Elementary Textbook of Psychoanalysis* (Garden City, N.Y.: Doubleday, 1957), 118.

3. Alvin Plantinga, *Warranted Christian Belief* (Oxford: Oxford University Press, 2000), 142.

4. Ibid., 140. Later Freudian analysts put "fairy tales" in a different category from "folk tales" and both in categories different from "religions."

5. The standard, but seriously flawed, English translation of Freud is James Strachey, ed., *The Standard Edition of the Complete Psychological Works of Sigmund Freud* (London: Hogarth, 1961), vol. 21. Freud's *Moses and Monotheism* (1939) is considered, even by Freudians, to be strange. Citations from Donald Capps, ed., *Freud and Freudians on Religion* (New Haven: Yale University Press, 2001), 17–24, 51–71. See also Bettelheim, *Freud and Man's Soul*; Kirk A. Bingaman, *Freud and Faith: Living in Tension* (Albany: State University of New York Press, 2003); James Forsyth, *Freud, Jung, and Christianity* (Ottawa: Ottawa University Press, 1989); Diane Jonte-Pace, ed., *Teaching Freud* (Oxford: Oxford University Press, 2003); W. W. Meissner, *Psychoanalysis and Religious Experience* (New Haven: Yale University Press, 1984); William Lloyd Newell, *The Secular Magi: Marx, Freud, and Nietzsche on Religion* (New York: Pilgrim, 1986); Michael Palmer, *Freud and Jung on Religion* (London: Routledge, 1997).

6. Rizzuto, *Why Did Freud Reject God?*, 159.

7. Bettelheim, *Freud and Man's Soul*, vii–xii, 51–60, 70–78.

8. Ibid., 64.

9. Andrew Newberg, Eugene d'Aquili, and Vince Rause, *Why God Won't Go Away: Brain Science and the Biology of Belief* (New York: Ballantine, 2001). The question is hotly debated, as in *The Economist* (December 18, 2004): 127.

10. C. G. Jung, *The Spiritual Problem of Modern Man* (London: K. Paul, Trench, Trübner, and Co., 1928); *Modern Man in Search of a Soul* (London: K. Paul, Trench, Trübner, and Co., 1933); *Psychology and Religion* (New Haven, Conn.: Yale University Press, 1960); *Man and his Symbols* (London: Aldus, 1961).

11. Stephen Carter, *The Culture of Disbelief* (New York: Basic Books, 1993).

12. *The Penguin Dictionary of Philosophy*, ed. Thomas Mautner (revised edition: Harmondsworth: Penguin, 2000), 441.

13. Ibid., 441.

14. Philip Wheelwright, *The Burning Fountain* (Bloomington, Ind.: Indiana University Press, 1968), 67.

15. John Watson, *Behaviorism* (New York: Norton, 1925).

16. Emile Durkheim, *The Elementary Forms of the Religious Life* (New York: Oxford University Press, 2001); Gaston Richard, "Dogmatic Atheism in the Sociology of Religion," (1923) in W. S. F. Pickering, ed., *Durkheim on Religion* (Atlanta: Scholars Press, 1994), 228–76.

17. Anthony F. C. Wallace, *Religion: An Anthropological View* (New York: Random House, 1966), 264–65.

18. Stark, *For the Glory of God* (Princeton, N.J.: Princeton University Press, 2003), 369.

19. Ibid., 368.

20. Albert Einstein, *Ideas and Opinions* (New York: Crown, 1954), 46.
21. William Barrett, *The Illusion of Technique* (Garden City, N.Y.: Anchor/Doubleday, 1978), 91.
22. Ian Barbour, *Religion and Science: Historical and Contemporary Issues* (San Francisco: HarperSanFrancisco, 1997), 78.
23. Bertrand Russell and Alfred North Whitehead, *Principia mathematica* (1910).
24. Bertrand Russell, *Why I Am Not a Christian* (New York: Simon and Schuster, 1957 [1918]), 107, 115–16; B. Russell, *Religion and Science* (New York: Oxford University Press, 1935).
25. B. Russell, *Religion and Science*, 81. *Religion and Science* drew upon the polemical book by the iconic president of Cornell University, Andrew Dickson White, *A History of the Warfare of Science with Theology in Christendom*, 2 vols. (New York, 1896).
26. B. Russell, *Religion and Science*, 136.
27. A. J. Ayer, *Language, Truth, and Logic* (New York: Dover, 1946).
28. Ludwig Wittgenstein, *Lectures and Conversations on Aesthetics, Psychology, and Religious Belief* (Berkeley: University of California Press, 1967).
29. Michael A. Arbib and Mary B. Hesse, *The Construction of Reality* (Cambridge: Cambridge University Press, 1994), 351.
30. Saussure's famous work was not a book but the posthumously published notes to his *Cours de linguistique général*.
31. Paul Ricoeur, *The Rule of Metaphor* (Toronto: University of Toronto Press, 1977), 220.
32. Philippe Ariès, *The Hour of Our Death* (Oxford: Oxford University Press, 1991).
33. Ibid., 90–91.
34. Martin Heidegger, *Being and Time* (San Francisco: HarperSanFrancisco, 1962); Karl Jaspers, *Man in the Modern Age* (London: Routledge and Kegan Paul, 1951); Jean-Paul Sartre, *Being and Nothingness* (New York: Philosophical Library, 1956); Albert Camus, *The Plague* (New York: Knopf, 1948).
35. Thomas Carlson, *Indiscretion: Finitude and the Naming of God* (Chicago: University of Chicago Press, 1999), 117–19.
36. Jerry L. Walls, *Heaven: The Logic of Eternal Joy* (Oxford: Oxford University Press, 2002), 179–81.
37. Johann Wolfgang von Goethe, *Faust*, lines 1338–84, 1851–67, 3711, 625–56, 6954–62, 11350–369, 11544–550, 11596–603.
38. Edmund Husserl, *The Idea of Phenomenology* (1907, trans. Lee Hardy, Dordrecht: Kluwer, 1999); Husserl, *Ideas: General Introduction to Pure Phenomenology* (1913, trans. W. R. Boyce Gibson, London: Allen and Unwin, 1958).
39. Alfred North Whitehead, *Process and Reality* (New York: Macmillan, 1929), 350, xiii, 342.
40. Charles Hartshorne, *The Divine Relativity* (New Haven: Yale University Press, 1948).
41. Arbib and Hesse, *Construction of Reality*, 216.
42. Carol Zaleski and Philip Zaleski, *The Book of Heaven* (Oxford: Oxford University Press, 2000), 237.

43. Oscar Cullmann, *Christ in Time* (Philadelphia: Westminster Press, 1950); *Salvation in History* (New York: Harper and Row, 1967).

44. Jean Delumeau, *Que reste-t-il du paradis?* (Paris: Fayard, 2000), 442.

45. Martin Buber, *Two Types of Faith* (New York: Macmillan, 1951).

46. Delumeau, *Que reste-t-il du paradis?* 443.

47. McDannell and Lang, *Heaven: A History* (New Haven: Yale University Press, 1988), 326.

48. Carlson, *Indiscretion.*

49. Martin Buber, *I and Thou* (Edinburgh: T. and T. Clark, 1937).

50. Rainer Maria von Rilke, "Herbst," *Oxford Book of German Verse*, 2nd ed. (Oxford: Oxford University Press, 1927), 555, my translation.

51. Delumeau, *Que reste-t-il du paradis?*, 442–43.

52. Karl Barth, *Church Dogmatics* (Edinburgh: T. and T. Clark, 1936–1960), vol. 3, part 3, 418–76; quotations in order from 426, 424, 426, 447.

53. Walter Rauschenbusch, *Christianity and the Social Crisis* (New York: Macmillan, 1907).

54. Kenneth Woodward, "*The Passion*'s Passionate Despisers," *First Things* 144 (June/July 2004): 13–16.

55. Plantinga, *Warranted Christian Belief*, 395–98, 414–18.

56. Ibid., 390–95.

57. McDannell and Lang, *Heaven: A History*, 331–32, from their translation of unpublished manuscript correspondence by Bultmann.

58. Plantinga, *Warranted Christian Belief*, 402.

59. Catherine Brown Tkacz, *The Key to the Brescia Casket* (Notre Dame, Ind.: University of Notre Dame Press, 2002); C. Tkacz, "Singing Women's Words as Sacramental Mimesis," *Recherches de théologie et philosophie médiévales* 70 (2003): 275–328; C. Tkacz, "Women as Types of Christ," *Gregorianum,* 85 (2004): 278–311; C. Tkacz, "*Aneboesen phone megale,*" *Gregorianum* 87 (2006), in press.

60. Heinrich Denzinger, ed., *Enchiridion symbolorum* (Rome: Herder, 1960), 686–88.

61. George Marsden, *Fundamentalism and American Culture* (Oxford: Oxford University Press, 1980).

62. Philip Jenkins, *The New Anti-Catholicism: The Last Acceptable Prejudice* (Oxford: Oxford University Press, 2003).

63. George Marsden, *The Soul of the American University: From Protestant Establishment to Established Nonbelief* (New York: Oxford University Press, 1994), 6. See also Michael L. Buddle and John Wright, *Conflicting Allegiances: The Church-Based University in a Liberal Democratic Society* (Grand Rapids, Mich.: Brazos, 2004).

64. Marsden, *Soul of the American University*, 6; Stephen Carter, *Culture of Disbelief.*

65. Marsden, *Soul of the American University*, 6.

66. George Orwell, *1984* (New York, 1949); "The Politics of the English Language," Richard H. Rovere, ed., *The Orwell Reader: Fiction, Essays, and Reportage* (New York: Harvest, 1956), 355–66.

67. Flannery O'Connor, "Revelation," in *O'Connor,* Sally Fitzgerald, ed. (New York: The Library of America, 1988), 633–54.

68. William Barrett, *Irrational Man* (Garden City, N.Y.: Doubleday, 1958), 251.
69. Zaleski and Zaleski, *Book of Heaven*, 87–88.

CHAPTER 7

1. Gabriel Vahanian, *The Death of God*, 2nd ed. (New York: Braziller, 1961), 164. Rodney Stark argued in *The One True God* (Princeton: Princeton University Press, 2001) that the more a religion demands of its adherents the more it will retain them and increase their numbers.
2. Dorothy Rowe, *The Construction of Life and Death*, 2nd ed. (London: Fontana, 1989).
3. Robert Bellah, *The Habits of the Heart: Individualism and Commitment in American Life* (Berkeley: University of California Press, 1985), 47–48, 64–65, 272.
4. Tony Walter, *The Eclipse of Eternity: A Sociology of the Afterlife* (New York: St. Martin's Press, 1996), 27–45.
5. Good accounts of heaven in news magazines include Mark Ralls, "Reclaiming Heaven," *The Christian Century* 121, no. 25 (December 14, 2004; responses in 122, no. 3 (February 8, 2005); David van Biema, *Time* (March 24, 1997); Kenneth Woodward, *Newsweek* (November 27, 1989).
6. Walter, *Eclipse of Eternity*, 181–84.
7. Hilary Putnam, *Representation and Reality* (Cambridge, Mass.: MIT Press, 1988), 120.
8. Edward O. Wilson, *Consilience* (New York: Knopf, 1998), 261.
9. Douglas Futuyma, *Evolution* (Sunderland, Mass.: Sinauer, 1986), 2.
10. Richard Lewontin, "Billions and Billions of Demons," *New York Review of Books* 9 (January 1997).
11. Richard Dawkins, *River out of Eden* (New York: Basic Books, 1995), 96; Dawkins, *The Blind Watchmaker* (New York: Norton, 1986); Dawkins, *Unweaving the Rainbow: Science, Delusion, and the Appetite for Wonder* (Boston: Houghton Mifflin, 1998).
12. Daniel Dennett, *Darwin's Dangerous Idea* (New York: Simon and Schuster, 1995), 515.
13. E. O. Wilson, *On Human Nature* (Cambridge, Mass.: Harvard University Press, 1978), 192.
14. Wendell Berry, *Life is a Miracle* (Washington: Counterpoint, 2000), 50.
15. E. O. Wilson, *Consilience*, 97, 119–20.
16. Neil Postman, *Technopoly* (New York: Knopf, 1992).
17. Barrett, *The Illusion of Technique: A Search for Meaning in a Technological Civilization* (Garden City, N.Y.: Anchor Doubleday, 1978), 210.
18. Dean H Hamer, *The God Gene: How Faith is Hardwired into Our Genes* (New York: Doubleday, 2004).
19. Daniel Dennett, *Darwin's Dangerous Idea* (New York: Simon and Schuster, 1995), 155.
20. Ibid., 468.

21. Ibid., 520.
22. Neil deGrasse Tyson and Donald Goldsmith, *Origins: Fourteen Billion Years of Cosmic Evolution* (New York: Norton, 2004), 44–45.
23. Michael J. Behe, *Darwin's Black Box: The Biochemical Challenge to Evolution* (New York: Free Press, 1996); William A. Dembski, *The Design Revolution: Answering the Toughest Questions about Intelligent Design* (Downers Grove, Ill., Intervarsity Press: 2004); Pierre-Paul Grasse, *Evolution of Living Organisms* (New York: Academic Press, 1977); Phillip E. Johnson, *The Wedge of Truth: Splitting the Foundations of Naturalism* (Downers Grove, Ill.: Intervarsity Press, 2000); Niall Shanks, *God, the Devil, and Darwin* (Oxford: Oxford University Press, 2004), argues in opposition to Intelligent Design. See *Los Angeles Times*, November 5, 2005.
24. Phillip Johnson, *Darwin on Trial* (Washington, D.C.: Regnery, 1991); Johnson, *Wedge of Truth*; Michael Behe, *Darwin's Black Box: The Biochemical Challenge to Evolution* (New York: Free Press, 2000).
25. Biology educator Art Battson, letter to author, January 29, 2005.
26. Dembski, *Design Revolution*, 45.
27. Antony Flew, *God and Philosophy*, 2nd ed. (Amherst, N.Y.: Prometheus, 2005); Gary R. Habermas, "My Pilgrimage from Atheism to Theism: An Exclusive Interview with Former British Atheist Professor Antony Flew," *Philosophia Christi* (Winter 2005).
28. "Intelligent Design Rears Its Head," *The Economist*, July 30, 2005, 30–31.
29. Michael A. Arbib and Mary B. Hesse, *The Construction of Reality* (Cambridge: Cambridge University Press, 1986), 160.
30. Jerry L. Walls, *Heaven: The Logic of Eternal Joy* (Oxford: Oxford University Press, 2002), 199.
31. John C. Greene, *Science, Ideology, and World View* (Berkeley: University of California Press, 1981), 186–89; Stephen M. Barr, *Modern Physics and Ancient Faith* (Notre Dame, Ind.: University of Notre Dame Press, 2003); Richard Olson, *Science Deified and Science Defied: The Historical Significance of Western Culture* (Berkeley: University of California Press, 1982).
32. Owen Barfield, *Saving the Appearances* (New York: Harcourt, 1965), 163.
33. John D. Barrow and Frank J. Tipler, *The Anthropic Cosmological Principle* (Oxford: Oxford University Press, 1986); Barrow, *The Artful Universe* (Oxford: Oxford University Press, 1995); Barrow, *Impossibility: The Limits of Science and the Science of Limits* (Oxford, Oxford University Press, 1998); F. Bertola and U. Curri, eds., *The Anthropic Principle* (Cambridge: Cambridge University Press, 1993); Nick Bostrom, *Anthropic Bias* (New York: Routledge, 2002); Michael J. Denton, *Nature's Destiny* (New York: Free Press, 1998); John Polkinghorne, *The God of Hope and the End of the World* (New Haven: Yale University Press, 2002); Shanks, *God, the Devil, and Darwin*, 206–7; Peter Ward and David Brownlee, *Rare Earth* (New York: Copernicus, 2000). On Carter, see Bryan Bunch, ed. *The History of Science and Technology* (Boston: Houghton Mifflin, 2004), 640.
34. John Polkinghorne, *Belief in God in an Age of Science* (New Haven: Yale University Press, 1998), 7.
35. Art Battson, letter to author, January 29, 2005.

36. Brian Greene, *The Fabric of the Cosmos* (New York: Vintage, 2005), 254–68.
37. Steven J. Dick, *Plurality of Worlds: The Origins of the Extraterrestrial Life Debate from Democritus to Kant* (New York: Cambridge University Press, 1982), 78.
38. Robert Naeye, "The Drake Equation," *Mercury* (November/December 2003): 20.
39. Mario Livio, ed., *Astrophysics of Life* (Cambridge: Cambridge University Press, 2005).
40. Greene, *Fabric of the Cosmos*; Joseph Silk, *On the Shores of the Unknown: A Short History of the Universe* (Cambridge: Cambridge University Press, 2005).
41. Postman, *Technopoly*, 52–87; quotations from 58, 61, 63, 70.
42. B. F. Skinner, *Beyond Freedom and Dignity* (New York: Bantam, 1971); Skinner, *Walden Two* (New York: Macmillan, 1948).
43. Skinner, personal interview with author, 1962.
44. Daniel Dennett, *Consciousness Explained* (Boston: Little Brown, 1991), 433.
45. Joseph A. Amato, *Victims and Values: A History and a Theory of Suffering* (Westport, Conn.: Praeger, 1990).
46. Dennett, *Darwin's Dangerous Idea*, 504–5.
47. Tony Walter, *The Eclipse of Eternity: A Sociology of the Afterlife* (New York: St. Martin's Press, 1996), 170–71.
48. Jonathan Shaw, "Stem-Cell Science," *Harvard Magazine* 106.6 (July/August 2004): 39, quoting Professor Losick. On "ethics" v. morality: David B. Wilkins, "Good Work: On Professional Norms and the Treacherous Temptation of 'Moral Freedom,'" *Harvard Magazine* 106.5 (May/June 2004): 21–28.
49. Postman, *Technopoly*, 69; Plantinga, *Warranted Christian Belief* (Oxford: Oxford University Press, 2000), 422–27; Gerald James Holton, "The Rise of Postmodernism and the 'End of Science,'" *Journal of the History of Ideas* 61 (2000): 327–42.
50. Thomas Carlson, *Indiscretion: Finitude and the Naming of God* (Chicago: University of Chicago Press, 1999), 225.
51. William Barrett, *Death of the Soul: From Descartes to the Computer* (Garden City, N.Y.: Anchor Doubleday, 1987), 128.
52. Dennett, *Consciousness Explained*, 200–226.
53. Alan Sokal, *Fashionable Nonsense: Postmodern Intellectuals' Abuse of Science* (New York: Picador USA, 1998).
54. Plantinga, *Warranted Christian Belief*, 437.
55. Walter, *Eclipse of Eternity*, 192; Stephen Carter, *The Culture of Disbelief* (New York: Basic Books, 1993).
56. Greene, *Science*, 172–75.
57. Postman, *Technopoly*, 111.
58. Compare for example page 137 of the original edition of L. Frank Baum's *The Patchwork Girl of Oz* with that of 1995; pages 294–95 of the original edition of *Rinkitink in Oz* with that of 1998; and chap. 6 of the original edition of P. L. Travers' *Mary Poppins* (New York: Harcourt, Brace, and Co., 1934) with the revised version (London: Collins, 1982).
59. Chris Impey, "Truth and Beauty in Cosmology: Does the Universe Have an Aesthetic?" *Mercury* 33, no. 1 (Jan./Feb. 2004): 30–40.

60. C. S. Lewis, *The Weight of Glory* (San Francisco: HarperSanFrancisco, 2001 [1949]). A powerful allegory of heaven appears in Lewis, *The Last Battle* (New York: Macmillan: 1956).

61. Hal Lindsey, *The Late Great Planet Earth* (Grand Rapids: Eerdmans, 1970); Amy Johnson Frykholm, *Rapture Culture: Left Behind in Evangelical America* (New York: Oxford University Press, 2004).

62. Brooks Alexander, *Witchcraft Goes Mainstream* (Eugene, Ore.: Harvest House, 2004); James A. Herrick, *The Making of the New Spirituality: The Eclipse of the Western Religious Tradition* (Downers Grove, Ill.: Intervarsity Press, 2003); Robert Wuthnow, *After Heaven: Spirituality in America since the 1950s* (Berkeley: University of California Press, 1998).

63. Alexander, *Witchcraft Goes Mainstream,* 37, 43.

64. Jana Riess, *What Would Buffy Do? The Vampire Slayer as Spiritual Guide* (San Francisco: Jossey-Bass, 2004).

65. The movie *What the Bleep Do We Know,* 2004.

66. Herrick, *Making of the New Spirituality,* 15–19, 23–24.

67. Philip Jenkins, *The New Anti-Catholicism: The Last Acceptable Prejudice* (New York: Oxford University Press, 2003).

68. Stephen M. Barr, *Modern Physics and Ancient Faith* (Notre Dame, Ind.: University of Notre Dame Press, 2003); Willem Drees, *Religion, Science and Naturalism* (Cambridge: Cambridge University Press, 1996); Stephen Jay Gould, *Dinosaur in a Haystack: Selections in Natural History* (New York: Crown, 1995); R. W. K. Paterson, *Philosophy and the Belief in a Life after Death* (New York: St. Martin's Press, 1995); Polkinghorne, *Belief in God.*

69. Michael Tkacz, "A Designer Universe: Chance, Design, and Cosmic Order" (speech, Gonzaga University, Spokane, Wash., 2004); Frank Manuel, *The Eighteenth Century Confronts the Gods* (Cambridge, Mass., Harvard University Press, 1959), 85, 84, 257.

70. Drees, *Religion, Science and Naturalism,* 8, 12.

71. Arbib and Hesse, *Construction of Reality,* 198.

72. John Polkinghorne, *Belief in God,* 111.

73. Arbib and Hesse, *Construction of Reality,* 223.

74. Manuel, *Eighteenth Century,* 309; B. Alan Wallace, *The Taboo of Subjectivity* (Oxford: Oxford University Press, 2000); Polkinghorne, *Faith, Science and Understanding* (New Haven: Yale University Press, 2000), 119. On religious evidence in law, see Jack B. Weinstein, John H. Mansfield, Norman Abrams, and Margaret A. Berger, *Evidence,* 9th ed. (Westbury, N.Y.: The Foundation Press, 1997), 35–60, 77–78, 238, 287–92.

75. Putnam, *Representation and Reality,* 11, 120.

76. Views of heaven in various religions are presented in Christopher Jay Johnson and Marsha G. McGee, *How Different Religions View Death and the Afterlife,* 2nd ed. (Philadelphia: The Charles Press, 1998), and in Carol Zaleski and Philip Zaleski, *The Book of Heaven* (Oxford: Oxford University Press, 2000).

77. Mary Daly, *Beyond God the Father* (Boston: Beacon, 1973); Rosemary R. Ruether, *Sexism and God-Talk* (Boston: Beacon, 1983); on "Wicca," see *Encyclopaedia Britannica* (2002), s.v. "Witchcraft."

78. Grace Jantzen, *Becoming Divine: Towards a Feminist Philosophy of Religion* (Bloomington, Ind.: Indiana University Press, 1999); Pamela Anderson, *Feminist Philosophy of Religions* (Oxford: Blackwell, 1998). Jantzen, while vehemently rejecting a dichotomy between truth and falsehood as unnecessarily "binary," declared "masculinist" religions to be "wrong"; in fact, she described Christians as "necrophiles" (3).

79. Charles Hartshorne, *Omnipotence and Other Theological Mistakes* (Albany: State University of New York Press, 1984); Alfred North Whitehead, *Process and Reality* (New York: Macmillan, 1929), 350, xiii, 342.

80. Polkinghorne, *Belief in God,* 69–75; Polkinghorne, *Faith, Science, and Understanding,* 151–52.

81. Michael Keller, *Creative Tension: Essays on Science and Religion* (Philadelphia: Templeton Foundation Press, 2003), 76.

82. Gabriel Vahanian, *The Death of God: The Culture of Our Post-Christian Era* (New York: Braziller, 1961), 139.

83. Gordon Kaufman, *Systematic Theology: A Historicist Perspective* (New York: Scribner, 1968), 455–74

84. Rodney Stark, *One True God* (Princeton: Princeton University Press, 2001); Stark, *For the Glory of God* (Princeton: Princeton University Press, 2003).

85. "The Gift of Salvation," *First Things* 79 (January 1998): 21.

86. *Christian Century* 121, no. 24 (November 30, 2004) is largely devoted to the "Emergent Church."

87. Thomas Altizer and William Hamilton, *Radical Theology and the Death of God* (Indianapolis, Ind.: Bobbs-Merrill, 1966).

88. Jean-Luc Marion, *God without Being,* trans. Thomas Carlson (Chicago: University of Chicago Press, 1991); Carlson, *Indiscretion*; Raimundo Panikkar, *The Cosmotheandric Experience: Emerging Religious Consciousness* (Maryknoll, N.Y.: Orbis, 1993).

89. Carlson, *Indiscretion,* 159, 160, 193, 194.

90. Ibid., 261.

91. For a satire of this view, see A. J. Conyers, *Eclipse of Heaven* (South Bend, Ind.: St. Augustine's Press, 1992), 26–28.

92. Hans Küng, *Eternal Life?* (Garden City, N.Y.: Doubleday, 1984), 113. See also Karl Rahner, *On the Theology of Death,* 2nd ed. (New York: Herder and Herder, 1965); Simon Tugwell, *Human Immortality and the Redemption of Death* (London: Darton, Longman, and Todd, 1990).

93. "Letter on Certain Questions Concerning Eschatology," *Acta Apostolicae Sedis* 71 (1979): 939–43, *Osservatore Romano,* 591, May 17, 1979; Tugwell, *Human Immortality,* 175–77.

94. Joseph Ratzinger, *Eschatology: Death and Eternal Life* (Washington, D.C.: Catholic University of America Press, 1988), 238; Ratzinger, *The Spirit of the Liturgy* (San Francisco: St. Ignatius Press, 2000), 53–56, 209–16. See also Peter van Inwagen, "The Possibility of Resurrection," *International Journal for Philosophy of Religion* 9 (1978): 114–21; George Mavrodes, "The Life Everlasting and the Bodily Continuation of Identity," *Nous* 11 (1977): 27–39; Antonie van den Bild, "*Non posse peccare*: On the Inability to Sin in Eternal Life," *Religious Studies* 25 (1989): 521–35.

95. David Tracy, *The Analogical Imagination* (New York: Crossroad, 1981), xii; Andrew Greeley, *The Catholic Imagination* (Berkeley: University of California Press, 2000), 37; Jeffrey B. Russell, *A History of Heaven* (Princeton: Princeton University Press, 1997).
96. Roger M. White, *The Structure of Metaphor* (Oxford: Blackwell, 1996), 203.
97. Norman Kreitman, *The Roots of Metaphor* (Brookfield, Vt.: Ashgate, 1999), 169.
98. Paul Ricoeur, *The Rule of Metaphor* (Toronto: University of Toronto Press, 1977), 247.
99. A. E. Denham, *Metaphor and Moral Experience* (Oxford: Clarendon, 2000), 230.
100. "Secrets of the Teen Brain," *Time*, May 10, 2004, 56–65.
101. Ricoeur, *Rule of Metaphor*, 287, 294.
102. Arbib and Hesse, *Construction of Reality*, 237.
103. Philip Wheelwright, *The Burning Fountain*, 2nd ed. (Bloomington, Ind., Indiana University Press, 1962), 205.
104. Jennifer Russell, *The Threshing Floor* (Mahwah, N.J.: Paulist Press, 1987).

CHAPTER 8

1. Isa. 49:15; Matt. 23:37; Luke 13:34. For commentary see Prudence Allen, *The Concept of Women*, vol. 2, *The Early Humanist Reformation, 1250–1500* (Grand Rapids, Mich.: Eerdmans, 2002); Caroline Walker Bynum, *Jesus as Mother: Studies in the Spirituality of the High Middle Ages* (Berkeley: University of California Press, 1982); Patricia Ranft, *A Woman's Way: The Forgotten History of Women Spiritual Directors* (New York: Palgrave, 2000).
2. Alvin Plantinga, *Warranted Christian Belief* (Oxford: Oxford University Press, 2000), 438.
3. Ibid., 219, n29.
4. Ibid., 350–51.
5. Jerry L. Walls, *Heaven: The Logic of Eternal Joy* (Oxford: Oxford University Press, 2002), 195.
6. Ibid., 197.
7. Ibid., 190.
8. Gerard Manley Hopkins, "God's Grandeur," *Poems of Gerard Manley Hopkins*, ed. Robert Bridges and W. H. Gardner, 3rd ed. (New York: Oxford University Press, 1948), 70.
9. T. S. Eliot, "Little Gidding," Eliot, *The Complete Poems and Plays 1909–1950* (New York: Harcourt, World and Brace, 1952), 145.
10. "Rising." Anonymous, twentieth century.
11. Jeffrey Burton Russell, *A History of Heaven: The Singing Silence* (Princeton: Princeton University Press, 1997), 186–89.
12. T. S. Eliot, "The Dry Salvages," Eliot, *The Complete Poems and Plays 1909–1950*, 135.
13. "Coldly West," Anonymous, twentieth century.

Bibliography

This bibliography includes the work of modern writers; for most pre-twentieth century authors, see the index and endnotes.

Albom, Mitch. *The Five People You Meet in Heaven*. New York: Hyperion, 2003.

Almond, Philip C. *Heaven and Hell in Enlightenment England*. Cambridge: Cambridge University Press, 1994.

Ankersmit, F. R. *History and Tropology: The Rise and Fall of Metaphor*. Berkeley: University of California Press, 1994.

Arbib, Michael A., and Mary B. Hesse. *The Construction of Reality*. Cambridge: Cambridge University Press, 1986.

Ariès, Philippe. *The Hour of Our Death*. New York: Knopf, 1981.

———. *Western Attitudes toward Death: From the Middle Ages to the Present*. Baltimore: Johns Hopkins University Press, 1974.

Armstrong, John. *The Paradise Myth*. New York: Oxford University Press, 1969.

Aron, Raymond. *Main Currents in Sociological Thought*. 2 vols. New York: Basic Books, 1965–67.

Badham, Paul. *Christian Beliefs about Life after Death*. London: Macmillan, 1976.

———, and Linda Badham. *Death and Immortality in the Religions of the World*. New York: Paragon House, 1987.

Baker, Don. *Heaven*. Portland, Ore.: Multnomah Press, 1983.

Barfield, Owen. *Saving the Appearances: A Study in Idolatry*. New York: Harcourt, 1965.

Barr, Stephen M. *Modern Physics and Ancient Faith*. Notre Dame, Ind.: University of Notre Dame Press, 2003.

Barrett, William. *Death of the Soul: From Descartes to the Computer*. Garden City, N.Y.: Anchor Doubleday, 1986.

———. *The Illusion of Technique: A Search for Meaning in a Technological Civilization*. Garden City, N.Y.: Anchor Doubleday, 1978.

————. *Irrational Man: A Study in Existential Philosophy*. Garden City, N.Y.: Doubleday, 1958.

Barrow, John D., and Frank Tipler. *The Anthropic Cosmological Principle*. Oxford: Oxford University Press, 1986.

Barth, Karl. *Church Dogmatics*. 4 vols. in 13. New York: Scribner's, 1936–39.

Barzun, Jacques. *Darwin, Marx, Wagner: Critique of a Heritage*. Boston: Little, Brown, 1947.

Becker, Carl. *The Heavenly City of the Eighteenth-Century Philosophers*. New Haven: Yale University Press, 1932.

Becker, Carl B. *Breaking the Circle: Death and the Afterlife in Buddhism*. Carbondale: Southern Illinois University Press, 1993.

Bellah, Robert. *The Habits of the Heart: Individualism and Commitment in American Life*. Berkeley: University of California Press, 1985.

Berman, Morris. *The Re-enchantment of the World*. Ithaca: Cornell University Press, 1981.

Bernstein, Alan. *The Formation of Hell*. Ithaca: Cornell University Press, 1993.

Berry, Wendell. *Life Is a Miracle: An Essay against Modern Superstition*. Washington, D.C.: Counterpoint, 2000.

Bettelheim, Bruno. *Freud and Man's Soul*. New York: Knopf, 1983.

Bowler, Peter J. *Evolution: The History of an Idea*. 2nd ed. Berkeley: University of California Press, 1989.

Bremmer, Jan N. *The Rise and Fall of the Afterlife: The 1995 Read-Tuckwell Lectures at the University of Bristol*. London: Routledge, 2002.

Brenner, Charles. *An Elementary Textbook of Psychoanalysis*. Garden City, N.Y.: Doubleday, 1957.

Brooke, John Hedley. *Science and Religion: Some Historical Perspectives*. Cambridge: Cambridge University Press, 1991.

————, and Geoffrey Cantor. *Reconstructing Nature: The Engagement of Science and Religion*. Oxford: Oxford University Press, 1998.

Browne, Janet. *Charles Darwin: Voyaging*. Princeton, N.J.: Princeton University Press, 1995.

————, *Charles Darwin: The Power of Place*. Princeton, N. J.: Princeton University Press, 2002.

Burtt, Edwin Arthur. *The Metaphysical Foundation of Modern Physical Science*. London: Routledge and Kegan Paul, 1932.

Butterfield, Herbert. *The Origins of Modern Science, 1300–1800*. 2nd ed. New York: Free Press, 1965.

Bynum, Caroline. *The Resurrection of the Body in Western Christianity, 200–1336*. New York: Columbia University Press, 1995.

Carlson, Thomas. *Indiscretion: Finitude and the Naming of God*. Chicago: University of Chicago Press, 1999.

Carnley, Peter. *The Structure of Resurrection Belief*. Oxford: Clarendon Press, 1987.

Cassirer, Ernst. *Language and Myth*. New York: Harper, 1946.

————. *The Philosophy of the Enlightenment*. Princeton: Princeton University Press, 1951.

Cavendish, Richard. *Visions of Heaven and Hell.* London: Orbis, 1977.

Cohn-Sherbok, Dan. "Death and Immortality in the Jewish Tradition." *Theology* 90 (1987): 263–73.

Collins, James. *God in Modern Philosophy.* Chicago: Regnery, 1959.

Colvin, Howard. *Architecture and the After-life.* New Haven: Yale University Press, 1991.

Conyers, A. J. *The Eclipse of Heaven: The Loss of Transcendence and Its Effect on Modern Life.* South Bend, Ind.: St. Augustine's Press, 1999.

Coward, Harold. *Life after Death in World Religions.* Maryknoll, N.Y.: Orbis, 1997.

———, and Toby Foshay, eds. *Derrida and Negative Theology.* Albany: State University of New York Press, 1992.

Cullmann, Oscar. *Immortality of the Soul or Resurrection of the Dead?* London: Epworth, 1958.

Danielson, Dennis R. "The Great Copernican Cliché." *American Journal of Physics Teachers* 69, no. 10 (October 2001).

Danto, Arthur. *The Philosophy of History.* Cambridge: Cambridge University Press, 1965.

Darwin, Charles. *The Descent of Man: And Selection in Relation to Sex.* 2nd ed. New York: Appleton, 1915.

Davidson, Clifford, ed. *The Iconography of Heaven.* Kalamazoo, Mich.: Medieval Institute Press, 1994.

Davies, J. G. *He Ascended into Heaven: The History of a Doctrine.* London: Butterworth, 1958.

Davis, Stephen T. *Death and Afterlife.* New York: St. Martin's Press, 1989.

Dawkins, Richard. *The Blind Watchmaker.* New York: Norton, 1986.

———. *River out of Eden: A Darwinian View of Life.* New York: Basic Books, 1995.

Delumeau, Jean. *Une Histoire du paradis.* 2 vols. Paris: Fayard, 1992.

———. *Que reste-t-il du paradis?* Paris: Fayard, 2000.

Denham, A. E. *Metaphor and Moral Experience.* Oxford: Clarendon, 2000.

Dennett, Daniel. *Consciousness Explained.* Boston: Little, Brown, 1991.

———. *Darwin's Dangerous Idea: Evolution and the Meaning of Life.* New York: Simon and Schuster, 1995.

DeStefano, Anthony. *A Travel Guide to Heaven.* New York: Doubleday, 2003.

Drees, Willem. *Religion, Science, and Naturalism.* New York: Cambridge University Press, 1996.

Dupré, Louis. "The Christian Experience of Mystical Union." *Journal of Religion* 69 (1989): 1–13.

Durkheim, Emile. *The Elementary Forms of the Religious Life.* New York: Oxford University Press, 2001.

Eliade, Mircea. *Patterns of Comparative Religion.* New York: Sheed and Ward, 1958.

Emerson, Jan, and Hugh Feiss, eds. *Imagining Heaven in the Middle Ages.* New York: Garland, 2000.

Farber, Paul Lawrence. *The Temptations of Evolutionary Ethics.* Berkeley: University of California Press, 1994.

Feuerbach, Ludwig. *The Essence of Christianity.* Translated by George Eliot. New York: Harper, 1959.

Finucane, Ronald C. *Appearances of the Dead: A Cultural History of Ghosts.* Buffalo, N.Y.: Prometheus Books, 1984.

Forsyth, James. *Freud, Jung, and Christianity.* Ottawa: University of Ottawa Press, 1989.

Foucault, Michel. *Religion and Culture.* New York: Routledge, 1999.

Freud, Sigmund. *Basic Writings.* New York: Modern Library, 1938.

Fuller, Robert C. *Spiritual, But Not Religious: Understanding Unchurched America.* Oxford: Oxford University Press, 2001.

Funkenstein, Amos. *Theology and the Scientific Imagination.* Princeton: Princeton University Press, 1986.

Gaine, Simon Francis. *Will There Be Free Will in Heaven: Freedom, Impeccability, and Beatitude.* London: T. and T. Clark, 2003.

Galison, Peter, and David J. Stump, eds. *The Disunity of Science: Boundaries, Contexts, and Power.* Stanford: Stanford University Press, 1996.

Gatch, Milton McC. *Death, Meaning and Mortality in Christian Thought and Contemporary Culture.* New York: Seabury, 1969.

Gay, Peter. *The Enlightenment: An Interpretation.* 2 vols. New York: Knopf, 1966–69.

Giamatti, A. Bartlett. *The Earthly Paradise and the Renaissance Epic.* Princeton: Princeton University Press, 1966.

Gilson, Etienne. *Modern Philosophy: Descartes to Kant.* New York: Random House, 1963.

Gould, Stephen Jay. *Dinosaur in a Haystack: Reflections in Natural History.* New York: Crown, 1995.

———. *The Hedgehog, the Fox, and the Magister's Pox.* New York: Harmony Books, 2003.

———. *Rocks of Ages: Science and Religion in the Fullness of Life.* New York: Ballantine, 1999.

Grant, Edward. *The Foundations of Modern Science in the Middle Ages: Their Religious, Institutional, and Intellectual Contexts.* Cambridge: Cambridge University Press, 1996.

———. *God and Reason in the Middle Ages.* Cambridge: Cambridge University Press, 2001.

Greeley, Andrew. *The Catholic Mind: The Behavior and Beliefs of American Catholics.* New York: Scribner's, 1990.

———. *Death and Beyond.* Chicago: Thomas More Press, 1976.

———. *Religion as Poetry.* New Brunswick, N.J.: Transaction, 1995.

Greene, Brian: *The Elegant Universe: Superstrings, Hidden Dimensions, and the Quest for Ultimate Theory.* New York: Norton, 1999.

Greene, John C. *Darwin and the Modern World View.* Baton Rouge, La.: Louisiana State University Press, 1961.

———. *The Death of Adam: Evolution and Its Impact on Western Thought.* 2nd ed. Ames, Iowa: Iowa State University Press, 1996.

———. *Science, Ideology, and World View.* Berkeley: University of California Press, 1981.

Hamer, Dean H. *The God Gene: How Faith is Hardwired into Our Genes.* New York: Doubleday, 2004.

Heidegger, Martin. *Being and Time.* New York: Harper and Row, 1962.

Hick, John D. *Death and Eternal Life*. London: Collins, 1976.

Himmelfarb, Gertrude. *Darwin and the Darwinian Revolution*. Garden City, N.Y.: Doubleday Anchor, 1959.

Hobart, Michael. *Science and Religion in the Thought of Nicolas Malebranche*. Chapel Hill, N.C.: University of North Carolina Press, 1982.

Hoekema, Anthony. "Heaven: Not Just an Eternal Day Off." *Christianity Today* 29, no. 13 (1985): 18–19.

Horgan, John. *The End of Science*. Reading, Mass.: Addison-Wesley, 1996.

Hossain, Mary. "Women and Paradise." *Journal of European Studies* 19 (1989): 293–310.

Hübsch, Hadayatullah. *Paradies und Hölle: Jenseitsvorstellungen im Islam*. Düsseldorf: Patmos, 2003.

Hughes, Robert. *Heaven and Hell in Western Art*. London: Weidenfeld and Nicolson, 1968.

Hyman, Stanley Edgar. *The Tangled Bank: Darwin, Marx, Frazer, and Freud as Imaginative Writers*. New York: Atheneum, 1962.

Irvine, William D. "Confronting Relativism." *Academic Questions* 14 (2000–2001)

Israel, Jonathan I. *Radical Enlightenment: Philosophy and the Making of Modernity 1650–1750*. Oxford: Oxford University Press, 2001.

Johnson, Christopher Jay, and Marsha G. McGee, eds. *How Different Religions View Death and the Afterlife*. 2nd ed. Philadelphia: The Charles Press, 1998.

Jones, Roger. *Physics as Metaphor*. Minneapolis: University of Minnesota Press, 1982.

Jung, Carl G. *Man and his Symbols*. London: Aldus, 1961.

———. *Psychology and Religion*. New Haven: Yale University Press, 1938.

Kantzer, Kenneth J. "Heaven and Hell: Who Will Go There and Why?" *Christianity Today* 35, no. 6 (1991): 29–39.

Kennedy, Rick. *A History of Reasonableness: Testimony and Authority in the Art of Thinking*. Rochester, N.Y.: University of Rochester Press, 2004.

Kerkofs, Jan. "Good Heavens." *Concilium* 123 (1979): 1–12.

Kreeft, Peter. *Everything You Ever Wanted to Know about Heaven . . . But Never Dreamed of Asking*. San Francisco: Harper and Row, 1982.

Kreitman, Norman. *The Roots of Metaphor: A Multidisciplinary Study in Aesthetics*. Brookfield, Vt.: Ashgate, 1999.

Kselman, Thomas A. *Death and the Afterlife in Modern France*. Princeton: Princeton University Press, 1993.

Kuhn, Thomas. *The Structure of Scientific Revolutions*. 2nd ed. Chicago: University of Chicago Press, 1970.

Küng, Hans. *Eternal Life? Life after Death as a Medical, Philosophical, and Theological Problem*. Garden City, N.Y.: Doubleday, 1984.

Landesman, Charles. "Confronting Relativism." *Academic Questions* 14 (2000–2001).

Lasch, Christopher. *The True and Only Heaven: Progress and Its Critics*. New York: Norton, 1991.

LeGoff, Jacques. *The Birth of Purgatory*. Chicago: Chicago University Press, 1984.

Lewis, C[live] S[taples]. *The Four Loves*. New York: Harcourt, Brace, Jovanovich, 1991.

———. *The Great Divorce*. New York: Macmillan, 1946.

———. *Miracles.* New York: Macmillan, 1947

———. *The Weight of Glory and Other Addresses.* 1949. Reprint, San Francisco: HarperSanFrancisco, 2001.

Lindberg, David C. *The Beginnings of Western Science: The European Scientific Tradition in Philosophical, Religious, and Institutional Context.* Chicago: University of Chicago Press, 1992.

———, and Ronald Numbers, eds. *God and Nature.* Berkeley: University of California Press, 1986.

———. *When Science and Christianity Meet.* Chicago: University of Chicago Press, 2003.

Lossky, Vladimir. *The Vision of God.* 3rd ed. New York, 1983.

Lovejoy, Arthur O. *The Great Chain of Being: A Study of the History of an Idea.* Cambridge, Mass.: Harvard University Press, 1937.

Lukacz, John. *At the End of an Age.* New Haven: Yale University Press, 2002.

MacGregor, Geddes. *Images of Afterlife: Beliefs from Antiquity to Modern Times.* New York: Paradigm House, 1992.

Manuel, Frank Edward. *The Eighteenth Century Confronts the Gods.* Cambridge, Mass.: Harvard University Press, 1959.

Marion, Jean-Luc. *God Without Being: Hors-texte.* Translated by Thomas Carlson. Chicago: University of Chicago Press, 1991.

Marsak, Leonard, ed. *The Enlightenment.* New York: Wiley, 1972.

Marsden, George M. *The Soul of the American University: From Protestant Establishment to Established Nonbelief.* New York: Oxford University Press, 1994.

Marshall, Peter. *Beliefs and the Dead in Reformation England.* Oxford: Oxford University Press, 2002.

Mavrodes, George. "The Life Everlasting and the Bodily Criterion of Identity." *Nous* 11 (1977): 27–39.

McDannell, Colleen, and Bernhard Lang. *Heaven: A History.* New Haven: Yale University Press, 1988.

McGrath, Alister. *A Brief History of Heaven.* Oxford: Blackwell, 2003.

———. *Iustitia Dei: A History of the Christian Doctrine of Justification.* Cambridge: Cambridge University Press, 1986.

Miles, Jack. *God: A Biography.* New York: Knopf, 1995.

Miller, Kenneth L. *Finding Darwin's God: A Scientist's Search for Common Ground between God and Evolution.* New York: HarperCollins, 1999.

Milne, Bruce. *The Message of Heaven and Hell: Grace and Destiny.* Downers Grove, Ill: Intervarsity Press, 2002.

Neusner, Jacob, ed. *Death and the Afterlife.* Cleveland, Ohio: Pilgrim Press, 2000.

Newberg, Andrew, Eugene D'Aquili, and Vince Rause. *Why God Won't Go Away: Brain Science and the Biology of Belief.* New York: Ballantine, 2001.

Nisbet, Robert. *History of the Idea of Progress.* New York: Basic Books, 1980.

Numbers, Ronald L. *The Creationists: The Evolution of Scientific Creationism.* Berkeley: University of California Press, 1992.

———. *Darwinism Comes to America.* Cambridge, Mass.: Harvard University Press, 1998.

Obayashi, Hiroshi. *Death and Afterlife*. New York: Hyperion, 1992.

Olson, Richard. *Science Deified and Science Defied: The Historical Significance of Science in Western Culture*. Berkeley: University of California Press, 1982.

Palmer, Robert. R. *Catholics and Unbelievers in Eighteenth-Century France*. Princeton: Princeton University Press, 1939.

Panikkar, Raimundo. *Myth, Faith, and Hermeneutics*. New York: Paulist, 1979.

Paterson, R. W. K. *Philosophy and Belief in a Life after Death*. New York: St. Martin's Press, 1995.

Peacocke, Arthur R. *Theology for a Scientific Age: Being and Becoming—Natural, Divine, and Human*. Minneapolis: Fortress, 1993.

Pelikan, Jaroslav. *The Christian Tradition*. 5 vols. Chicago: University of Chicago Press, 1971–89.

Pellauer, Mary. "Is There a Gender Gap in Heaven?" *Christianity and Crisis* 47 (1987): 60–61.

Perrin, Robert G. *Herbert Spencer: A Primary and Secondary Bibliography*. New York: Garland, 1993.

Peters, Ted, Robert John Russell, and Michael Welker, eds., *Resurrection: Theological and Scientific Assessments*. Grand Rapids, Mich.: Eerdmans, 2002.

Phillips, D. Z. *Death and Immortality*. London: Macmillan, 1970.

Pickering, W. S. F., ed. *Durkheim on Religion*. Atlanta, Ga.: Scholars Press, 1994.

Pieper, Josef. *Death and Immortality*. New York: Herder and Herder, 1969.

Plantinga, Alvin C. *Warranted Christian Belief*. Oxford: Oxford University Press, 2000.

Pölzl, Birgit, ed. *Himmel: mit Originalbeiträgen von Zsofia Balla*. Vienna: Korrespondenzen: 2003.

Polkinghorne, John. *Belief in God in an Age of Science*. New Haven: Yale University Press, 1998.

———. *Faith, Science, and Understanding*. New Haven: Yale University Press, 2000.

Pringle-Pattison, A. Seth. *The Idea of God in the Light of Recent Philosophy*. New York: Oxford University Press, 1920.

———. *The Idea of Immortality*. Oxford: Clarendon, 1922.

Putnam, Hilary. *Representation and Reality*. Cambridge, Mass.: MIT Press, 1988.

Radman, Zdravko. *From a Metaphorical Point of View: A Multidisciplinary Approach to the Cognitive Content of Metaphor*. Berlin: De Gruyter, 1995.

Rahner, Karl. *On the Theology of Death*. 2nd ed. New York: Herder and Herder, 1965.

Randles, W. G. L. *The Unmaking of the Medieval Christian Cosmos, 1500–1760: From Solid Heavens to Boundless Aether*. Aldershot: Ashgate, 1999.

Ratzinger, Joseph (Pope Benedict XVI). *Eschatology: Death and Eternal Life*. Washington, D.C.: Catholic University of America Press, 1988.

———. *The Spirit of the Liturgy*. San Francisco: Ignatius Press, 2000.

Ricoeur, Paul. *The Rule of Metaphor*. Translated by Robert Czerny. Toronto: University of Toronto Press, 1977.

Rosenfield, Leonora. *From Beast-Machine to Man-Machine*. New York: Oxford University Press, 1940.

Ruether, Rosemary Radford. *Sexism and God-Talk: Toward a Feminist Theology*. Boston: Beacon, 1983.

Rupp, Susanne. *"From Grace to Glory": Himmelsvorstellungen in der englischen Theologie und Literatur des 17. Jahrhunderts.* Heidelberg: Universitätsverlag, 2001.

Russell, Bertrand. *Religion and Science.* London: Oxford University Press, 1949.

Russell, Jeffrey Burton. *A History of Heaven: The Singing Silence.* Princeton: Princeton University Press, 1997.

———. *Mephistopheles: The Devil in the Modern World.* Ithaca: Cornell University Press, 1986.

———. *The Prince of Darkness.* Ithaca: Cornell University Press, 1988.

Sartre, Jean-Paul. *Being and Nothingness: An Essay on Phenomenological Ontology.* New York: Citadel, 1956.

Segal, Alan F. *Life after Death: A History of the Afterlife in Western Religion.* New York: Doubleday, 2004.

Sells, Michael A. *Mystical Languages of Unsaying.* Chicago: University of Chicago Press, 1994.

Simon, Ulrich. *Heaven in the Christian Tradition.* London: Rockliff, 1958.

Skinner, B. F. *Beyond Freedom and Dignity.* New York: Bantam, 1972.

Smart, Ninian. *The Phenomenon of Religion.* London: Macmillan, 1973.

Sokal, Alan. *Fashionable Nonsense: Postmodern Intellectuals' Abuse of Science.* New York: PicadorUSA: 1998.

Stanford, Peter. *Heaven: A Traveller's Guide to the Undiscovered Country.* London: HarperCollins, 2002.

Stark, Rodney. *For the Glory of God.* Princeton: Princeton University Press, 2003.

———. *One True God.* Princeton: Princeton University Press, 2001.

———. *The Rise of Christianity: A Sociologist Reconsiders History.* Princeton: Princeton University Press, 1996.

Sullivan, Randall. *The Miracle Detective.* New York: Grove, 2004.

Swinburne, Richard. *The Evolution of the Soul.* 2nd ed. New York: Oxford University Press, 1997.

———. *Revelation: From Metaphor to Analogy.* Oxford: Clarendon, 1992.

Taylor, Richard P. *Death and the Afterlife: A Cultural Encyclopedia.* Santa Barbara, Calif.: ABC Clio Press, 2000.

Tillich, Paul. *Morality and Beyond.* New York: Harper and Row, 1963.

Tipler, Frank J. *The Physics of Immortality.* New York: Anchor, 1995.

Tracy, David. *The Analogical Imagination.* New York: Crossroad, 1981.

Toulmin, Stephen. *Human Understanding: The Collective Use and Evolution of Concepts.* Princeton: Princeton University Press, 1972.

Tugwell, Simon. *Human Immortality and the Redemption of Death.* London: Darton, Longman and Todd, 1990.

Turner, Denys. *The Darkness of God: Negativity in Christian Mysticism.* Cambridge: Cambridge University Press, 1995.

Turner, Victor. "The Center Out There: Pilgrim and Goal." *History of Religion* 12, no. 3 (1973): 191–230.

Vahanian, Gabriel. *The Death of God: The Culture of Our Post-Christian Era.* New York: Braziller, 1961.

Van den Beld, Antonie. "*Non posse peccare*: On the Inability to Sin in Eternal Life." *Religious Studies* 25 (1989): 521–35.

Van Inwagen, Peter. "The Possibility of Resurrection." *International Journal for Philosophy of Religion* 9 (1978): 114–21.

Van Scott, Miriam. *Encyclopedia of Heaven*. New York: St. Martin's Press, 1999.

Walker, Richard. *From Darwin to Hitler: Evolutionary Ethics, Eugenics, and Racism in Germany*. New York: Palgrave Macmillan, 2004.

Wallace, B. Alan. *The Taboo of Subjectivity: Toward a New Science of Consciousness*. Oxford: Oxford University Press, 2000.

Walls, Jerry L. *Heaven: The Logic of Eternal Joy*. Oxford: Oxford University Press, 2002.

Walter, Tony. *The Eclipse of Eternity: A Sociology of the Afterlife*. New York: St. Martin's Press, 1996.

Weinberg, Stephen. "Can Science Explain Everything? Anything?" *New York Review of Books*, May 31, 2001.

Wertheim, Margaret. *The Pearly Gates of Cyberspace: A History of Space from Dante to the Internet*. New York: Norton, 1999.

Wheeler, Michael. *Death and the Future Life in Victorian Literature and Theology*. Cambridge: Cambridge University Press, 1994.

Wheelwright, Philip. *The Burning Fountain*. 2nd ed. Bloomington, Ind.: Indiana University Press, 1968.

———. *Metaphor and Reality*. Bloomington: Indiana University Press, 1962.

White, Roger M. *The Structure of Metaphor: The Way the Language of Metaphor Works*. Oxford: Blackwell, 1996.

Wilson, Edward O. *Consilience*. New York: Knopf, 1998.

Woodward, Kenneth. *Making Saints: How the Catholic Church Determines Who Becomes a Saint, Who Doesn't, and Why*. New York: Simon and Schuster, 1990.

Wright, J. Edward. *The Early History of Heaven*. Oxford: Oxford University Press, 2000.

Zaleski, Carol. "In Defense of Immortality." *First Things* 105 (September 2000): 36–42.

———. *Near-Death Experience and Christian Hope: The Life of the World to Come*. New York: Oxford University Press, 1996.

———. *Otherworld Journeys: Accounts of Near-Death Experiences in Medieval and Modern Times*. Oxford: Oxford University Press, 1987.

———, and Philip Zaleski. *The Book of Heaven*. Oxford: Oxford University Press, 2001.

Index